Having been mined the ore / supposing it contains tin / is separated out through cleaning / over a fire or a loam-pit / especially if it be coarsely beaten = so that it remains in lumps / the said ore yet contains poisonous impurities / thus it would yield no pure tin / if it were straightway smolten. It must be once more roasted / in the common tin-stone furnace / to rid it fully of the impurities / it must be cleaned again / so as to be fit for smelting / though in the roasting it gives off poisonous smoke / the latter is in no wise inferior to the former sort / despite emitting more noxious fumes.

Balthasar Rössler, *Hell-polierter Berg-Bau-Spiegel*, Dresden, 1700.

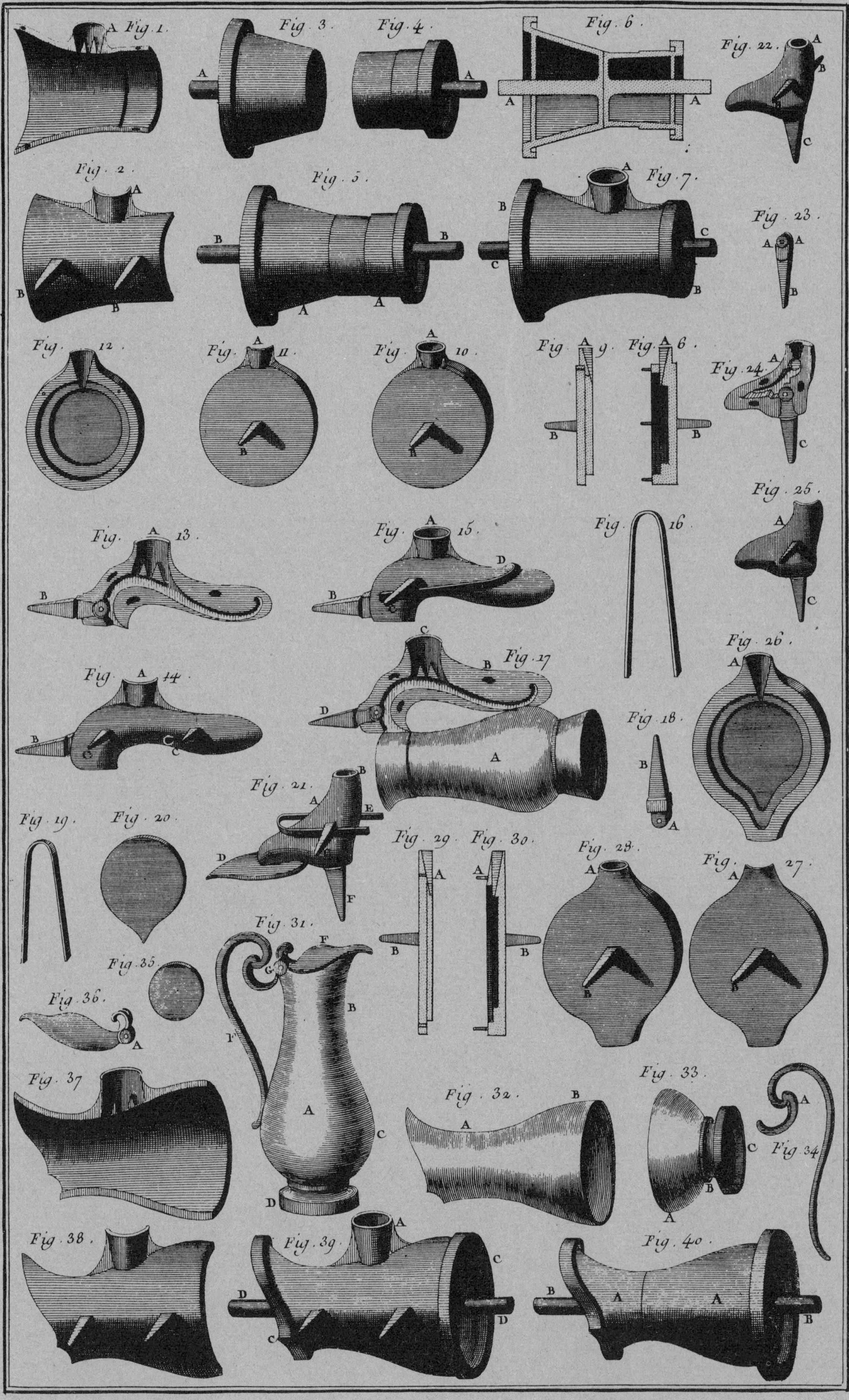

The entire work of the pewter- and jug-caster consists mainly of four parts, firstly the melting, then the moulds, thirdly in the casting and fourthly in the turning.
It is necessary that they be provided with a great variety of moulds, almost to a surfeit because their work, as we will soon relate, consists of almost innumerable pieces, of which none is made free-hand, but all are moulded and cast.
To achieve this, the pewterer must take care to pour at the right moment, lest, if the pewter be too hot, the vessel which has been cast runs out pell-mell blue and reddish, or if it is too cold, does not pour well and is full of holes.

Christoph Weigel, *Abbildung der Gemein-Nützlichen Haupt-Stände von denen Regenten und ihren so in Friedens- als in Kriegs-Zeiten zugeordneten Bedienten an biss auf alle Künstler und Handwercker.* Regensburg, 1698.

Dieter Nadolski
Old Household Pewterware

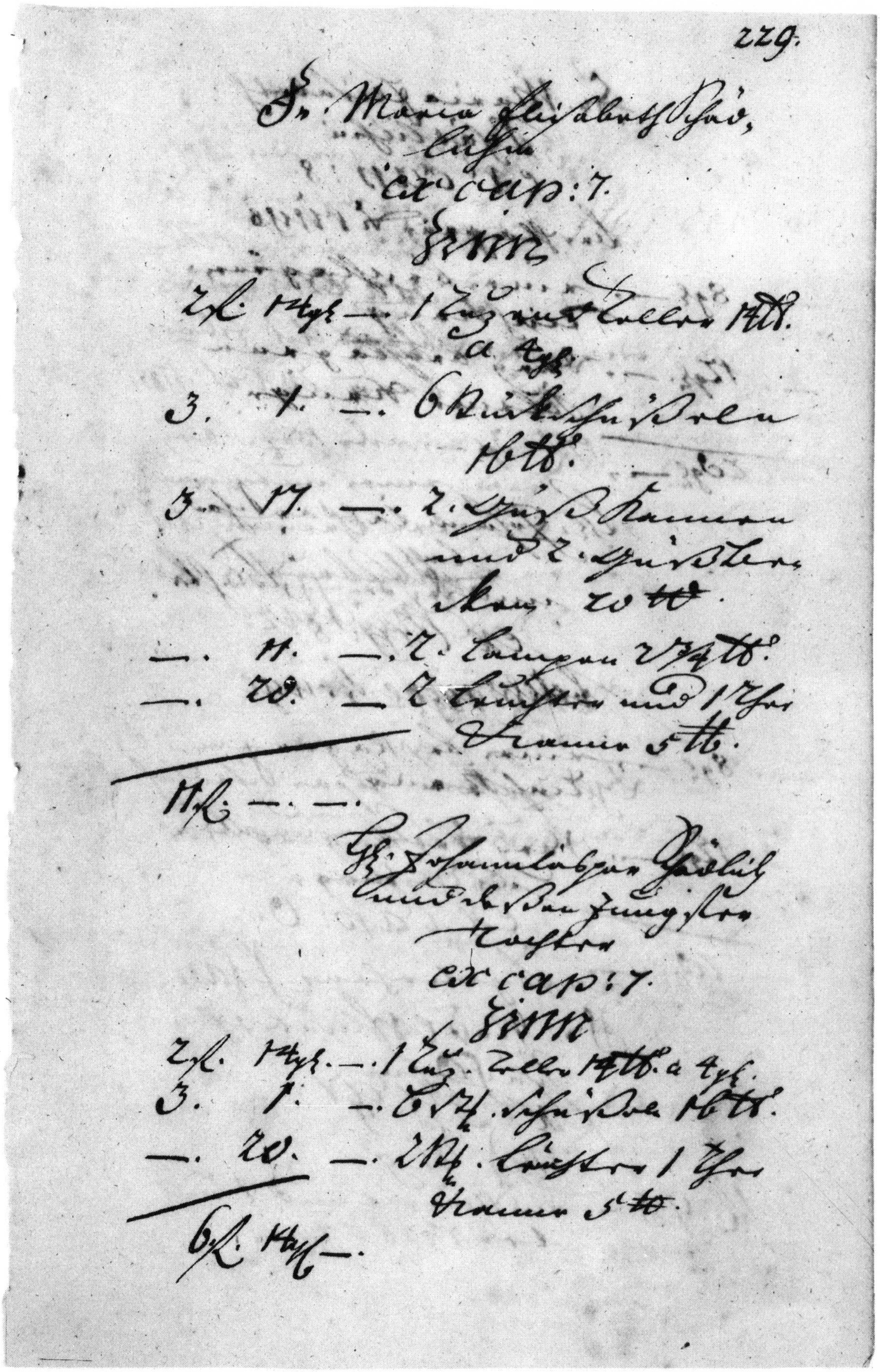

Inventory of pewter possessions, 18th century

DIETER NADOLSKI

OLD HOUSEHOLD PEWTER-WARE

its Appearance and
Function in the Course
of 6 Centuries

With 401 illustrations
and 695 pewter marks
from many countries

Photos: Ulrich Piekara
Drawings
of the pewter marks:
Karl-Heinz Barnekow

HM
Holmes & Meier
Publishers
New York / London

Translated from the German by
M. O. A. Stanton

The Author would like to thank
the following for their share in the
creation of this book:
Dr. Dagmar Stará, Prague
Dr. Hanns-Ullrich Haedeke, Solingen
Piroska Weiner, Budapest
who provided useful suggestions;
Professor Gert Wunderlich, Leipzig,
who designed the book
as well as many museums and collectors,
the publishers and the printers.

First published in English translation 1987 by
Holmes and Meier Publishers, Inc.
30 Irving Place, New York, N.Y. 10003

Great Britain:
Holmes and Meier Publishers, Ltd.
Pindar Road, Hoddesdon
Hertfordshire EN11 OHF

First published in the German Democratic Republic as
Altes Gebrauchszinn

Library of Congress Cataloging-in-Publication Data

Nadolski, Dieter.
Old household pewterware.

Translation of: Altes Gebrauchszinn.
Bibliography: p.
Includes index.
1. Pewter. 2. Pewter—Marks. I. Piekara, Ulrich.
II. Barnekow, Karl-Heinz. III. Title.
NK8404.N313 1987 739'.533 86-7701
ISBN 0-8419-1088-X

Printed in the German Democratic Republic

About this book

From the late Renaissance, the richly nuanced French language has counted two expressions to describe pewterers' products: namely *poterie d'étain* (pottery in pewter) and *orfèvrerie d'étain* (goldsmiths' work in pewter). This highlights the fact that apart from potters' goods of pewter, which the trade had long produced, something separate had emerged, namely goldsmiths' work in pewter. About 300 years later, one of the most influential collectors and scholars of pewter, the German Hans Demiani, coined the term *Edelzinn* (noble pewter) for the products of the artist-craftsmen whose works were primarily intended for display. The names of artisan pewterers of worldwide renown are associated with "noble pewter". Among the foremost were Rollin Greffet, Lyons (d. 1568), Nicolaus Horchaimer, Nuremberg (d. 1583), Mathias Bachmann, Memmingen (d. ca. 1593), François Briot (Montbéliard) (d. ca. 1616), Hans Lichtenhahn, Schneeberg (Saxony) (d. 1619), Caspar Enderlein, Nuremberg (d. 1633) and Isaac Faust, Strasbourg (d. 1669). These and other specialists among pewterers produced works of high artistic quality which rightly find their admirers to the present day. The acquisition of "noble pewter", goldsmiths' work in pewter or display pewter (exhibition and ornamental pewter) was logically included among the striven-after goals of every museum of decorative art established in the past and numbered among their first public exhibits. This development, however, also gave rise to the possibility of pewterers being regarded too much as artist-craftsmen and too little as simply craftsmen. Even if in Renaissance times a distinction emerged between the production of functional pewter on the one hand and prestige or display pewter on the other, most pewterers remained what they in fact were, craftsmen who, partly under pressure of circumstances, increasingly produced their goods primarily for use in people's everyday-life. Even though all social levels at any particular time were unable to afford pewterware, this naturally did not alter the type of work which they produced, that is those products orientated to practical use. This book is devoted to those of the pewterers' wares made for daily use.

At the present time, interest in old pewter as a collectors' subject has seen rapid growth. Even simple craftsman-made goods have already been collected and treasured for a considerable time but until now a work corresponding to this development and its associated queries has been lacking. We hope to close this gap with our book.

After an introductory survey of the pewterers' trade, the goods they produced are discussed according to the purpose which they fulfilled in house and home, at work, when travelling—in short, in the life of the people. Only pewter toys have been disregarded because they clearly require the framework of a separate book. In former times, exactly as today, whilst there was a predominating function for any given article, there were nevertheless many other uses. This must be borne in mind as one consults individual chapters. Having once begun the organization of the book to follow functional standpoints, it was very attractive, in contrast to almost all other books about pewter which have hitherto been published, to proceed within the various chapters themselves not by following chronology or characteristics of shape but here also to make each separate functional purpose the principle governing their arrangement. This clearly reveals the gaps which today exist in our knowledge of everyday-life in past times and in particular about the use of pewter.

Although the study of encyclopaedic works—principally of the 18th century—contributed very much more to our book than had been expected and much was brought to light by regional popular writings, a great deal remains fragmentary. Certainly, however, the accumulated details have made possible a picture which the Reader can usefully survey. The extracts quoted from a round hundred historical documents as well as the photographic reproductions from the archives of the pewterers' trade do a great deal to illuminate the role of pewter in the life of working people and the diligent toil of its producers.

Among the many attractions incidental to an interest in pewter at the present day is the possibility of determining the provenance and age of a piece by the marks struck upon it. This is the reason why over a period a good dozen specialized and extensive books on the subject of marks have appeared, but which often cannot be of assistance because many marks are still unknown or—if they have been elucidated—have only been published in writings of limited circulation. In this book relevant marks from all over the world have been brought together, above all, however, many are now published for the first time. The greater part of the pewterware which is illustrated has never before been published in photographs. That this has now been achieved is thanks to the assistance of many museums and private collectors.

The usual practice of giving the master's name for each item illustrated has not been followed because all too often a false impression is thereby given that a particular piece was actually made to conform with a methodology in art-craftsmanship; its regional character, on the other hand, is more informative, which in certain instances is indicated in a caption to the illustration or in the text.

We trust that our book will assist towards an understanding of the products of pewterers' craftsmanship as a contribution to the history of the everyday-life of working people.

D. N.

The Pewterers' Trade

The beginnings of commercial pewter-founding will indeed remain forever in historical obscurity yet those periods which pass for the culminating points in the expansion of the craft—the 16th to the 18th centuries—stand out all the more clearly. Here the paths from apprenticeship to master can be followed exactly but often those paths have so many deviations that one can only generalize about them with many reservations. This is similarly true about the practices of marking—the multiplicity of regulations, local variations and frequent departures from the rules are virtually indescribable. The same, in fact, also applies to the tribulations of pewterers' every-day-life, which cover an extraordinarily wide field and of which only a few impressions can be given here.

If in the search for early traces of pewterers' handwork, one comes across an item of utilitarian pewter at a point in time remote from the period of highest production, this can contribute the false conclusion that the possession of everyday pewter was "in later times" (e.g. during the 17th or 18th centuries) no longer something remarkable. One must, however, keep in mind that for centuries bitter poverty prevailed for a great part of the working population which never allowed the purchase of a piece of pewter in their lifetimes.

The early traces

The use of pewter wares in any quantity began in the 15th and continued increasingly in the 16th century. At that period two essential pre-conditions came about, namely considerably increased extraction of ore, made possible by technological improvements together with the development of merchanting enterprises who undertook the commercial distribution of the metal. Before this, probably for some two thousand years B.C., it was the caravans originating from Central Asia or ships returning from Indian islands which transported tin simply like any other trade commodity. In the territories southeast of the Caspian Sea and the Sea of Aral as well as in Malacca, Kuatan and Bangka (Indonesia), also in the south of England men had clearly learned at an early date to extract the plentiful tin ore deposits. If the ore—tin stone—lay combined with other stone, then its extraction was very wearisome. It is therefore conceivable that the tin stone which had already been exposed by the process of natural weathering, the stream tin was the first to be sought out and worked. As a result of suitable experience better extraction of the ore—even from tin stone—was later achieved by mechanical and chemical means. Even from early times the ore was smelted on the spot and the tin cast into slabs, bars or ingots ready for transport.

Even with the discovery in the 12th century of a further source from the kassiterit deposits in the Erzgebirge the most commonly used material for the production of wares for everyday life were still wood, which had predominated since the Bronze Age, followed by clay. About three centuries later, however, an increase in the quantity of pewter articles adopted for daily use is clearly recognizable. Until then indirect traces, i. e. from surviving writings are rare and actually extant pieces far rarer still. It is thanks to the poetry of Titus Maccius Plautus (died A. D. 184) and the chance survival of a part of his works that we have knowledge of pewter food vessels among the Romans. A relatively large number of pieces from about this time have been brought to light in England by the excavations of the Camerton Excavation Club. It is significant that these comprise almost only utilitarian wares and it may well also be instructive that the discovery of this particularly rich survival took place precisely in England where there were far the most productive tin mines of the old world.

Peculiarly enough, written references to tin for whatever purpose are rarer in the early Middle Ages than in Antiquity. The Anglo-Saxon King Edward the Confessor was nevertheless said to have possessed more than three hundred pewter plates, bowls and cups—i. e. domestic ware. Because there was no uniformity in tableware at any time during the Middle Ages and silver took precedence in royal circles not only in England, one can fairly assume that the pewter was mainly used by Edward's followers. In about 1100 a richly informative work was produced on painting, glass-painting and metal working which its author Theophilus modestly described as *Schedula diversarum artium* (papers on sundry arts). It is possible that the pseudonym conceals the Benedictine Monk Rogerus von Helmarshausen of whom there is evidence that he himself produced work of outstanding merit. Certainly Theophilus (to whom was ascribed the title Presbyter—the elder, in the sense of the more experienced) describes the casting of pewter dishes and spoons so informatively and knowledgeably that his own practical experience must be adduced. From the 13th century written sources in many European countries partly provide very detailed information about the existence of pewter wares. A bill from the Dutch town of Dordrecht, in which pewter articles are mentioned, dates from the year 1284. In 1362 the Hamburg master Thidericus Kannengheter equipped the cogs with pewter

Tin

German Zinn, Zien, Zihn, Latin stannum, Jupiter, because it was believed that tin received its influence from that planet, therefore its medicinal powers were dedicated to the liver by the ancients. It was named diabolus metallorum and in Syrian and Chaldean, bragmana, that is regnum Jovis, Jupiter's Kingdom, whence the word Brickmann and ultimately Brittman, came into being, because the majority of tin was found in England.

J. H. Zedler, *Grosses vollständiges Universallexikon aller Wissenschaften und Künste* (Comprehensive universal lexicon of all sciences and arts), Leipzig and Halle, 1749.

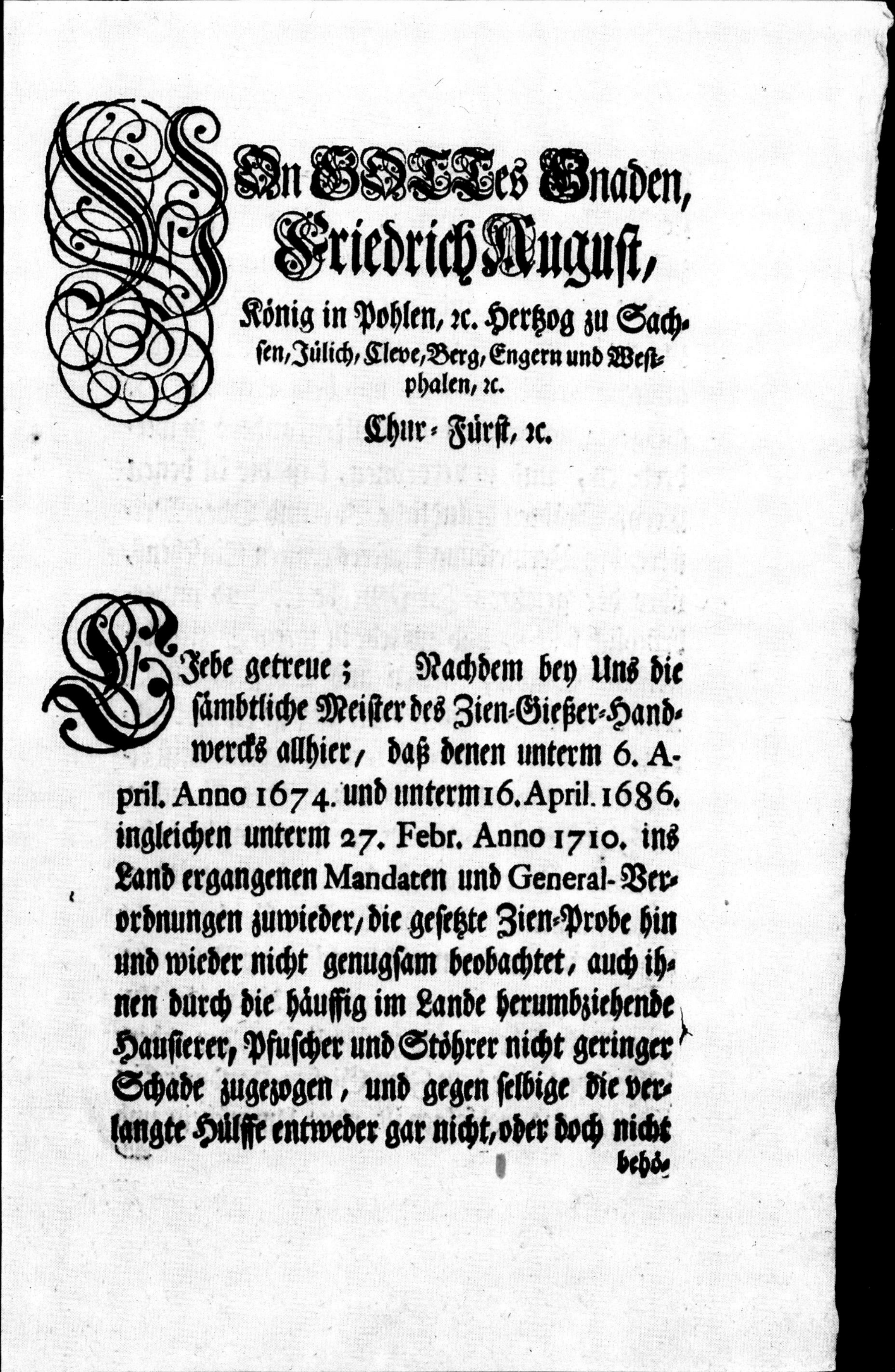
Von GOTTes Gnaden,
Friedrich August,
König in Pohlen, &c. Hertzog zu Sachsen, Jülich, Cleve, Berg, Engern und Westphalen, &c.
Chur-Fürst, &c.

Liebe getreue; Nachdem bey Uns die sämbtliche Meister des Zien-Gießer-Handwercks allhier, daß denen unterm 6. April. Anno 1674. und unterm 16. April. 1686. ingleichen unterm 27. Febr. Anno 1710. ins Land ergangenen Mandaten und General-Verordnungen zuwieder, die gesetzte Zien-Probe hin und wieder nicht genugsam beobachtet, auch ihnen durch die häuffig im Lande herumbziehende Hausierer, Pfuscher und Stöhrer nicht geringer Schade zugezogen, und gegen selbige die verlangte Hülffe entweder gar nicht, oder doch nicht

behö-

1 Ordinance of the Elector Frederick August of Saxony for the protection of pewterers from hawkers, bodgers and itinerant quacks; 1726.
In private ownership

2

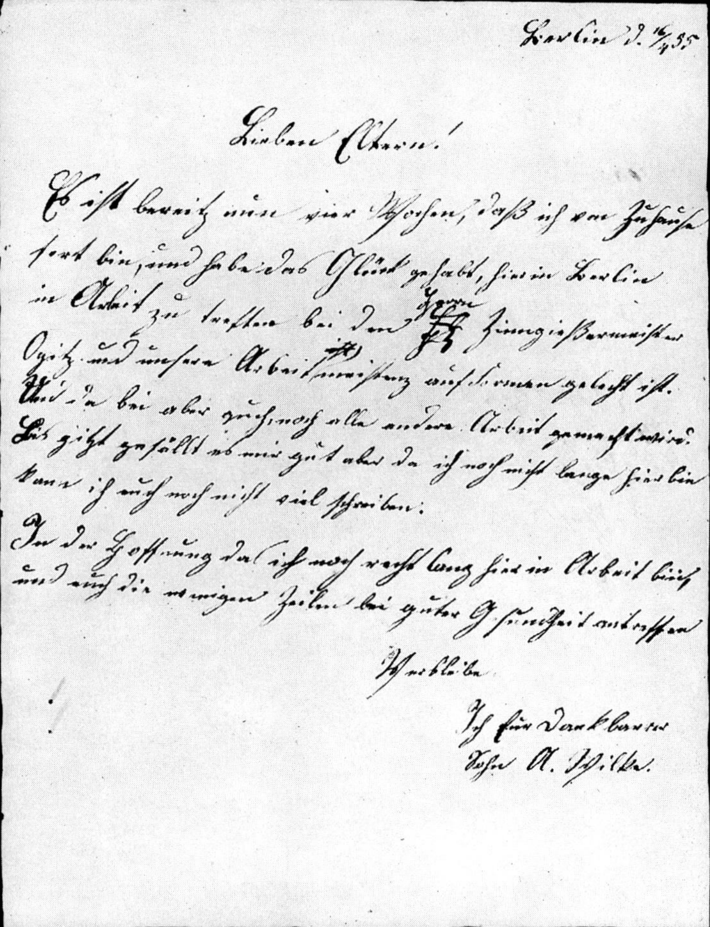

3

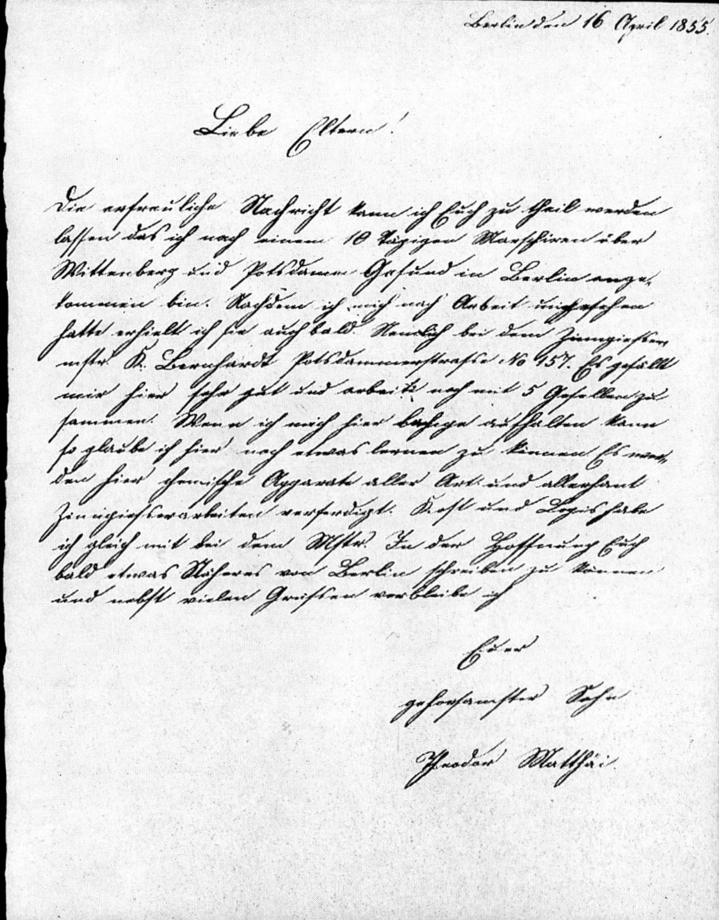

4

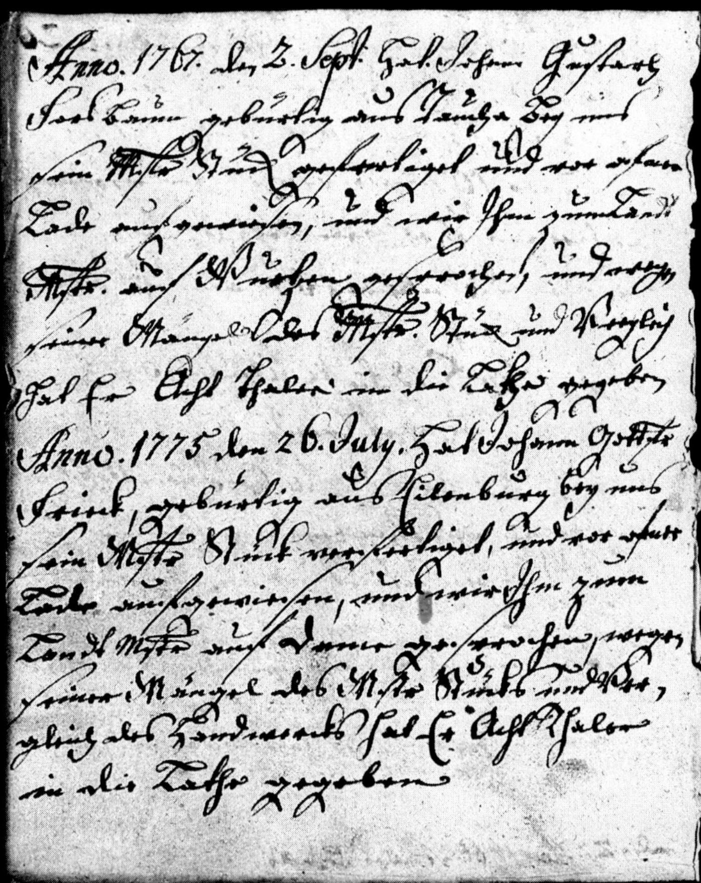

2/3 Letters from two journeymen to their parents in Halle/Saale to tell them that after a ten-day journey on foot through Wittenberg and Potsdam, they had been lucky enough to find work in Berlin with the masters Leonhardt and Opitz; 1855.
In private ownership

4 Note in a guild register concerning the mastership examination of a pewterer in 1775 with the ruling that due to a deficient masterpiece, eight thalers were to be paid into the Chest.
In private ownership

Regulation of 1623 for
ewterers relating to compo-
ition of material and price
tructure.
n private ownership

Vor ein Pfund Ehren umbzugiessen/ 2. in 3. Groschen.
Von ein Ventill/darnach es groß/ 1. fl. 1. fl. 6. Groschen.
Vor ein Bierhahn darnach er groß/ 4. 5. 6. in 7. Groschen.

Im Ertzgebürgischen Kreiß.

Ein Pfund Messing/an Leuchtern und Hähnen 8. Groschen.
Ein Pfund an Mörseln und andern groben Stücken 4. 5. Groschen.
Ein Pfund an grossen Hengeleuchtern/ 8. Groschen.
Ein Pfund Rincken oder Schnallen zu Riemen-Arbeit / groß und klein/ 5. Groschen.
Da sie aber poliret seyn / wegen der Arbeit etwas theurer ; Das ander giebt der Handkauff.

Kandel- oder Ziengiesser.

Durch alle Kreise.

Sollen auff 10. Pfund mehr nicht als 1. Pfund / und also auff einen Centner 10. Pfund Bley Zusatz nehmen

Vor ein Pfund neuer krummer Arbeit/an Handfassen/Kannen/Flaschen/Leuchter und dergleichen 6. Groschen.
Davon umbzugiessen 18. Pfennige.
An schlechter Arbeit/ von Schüsseln/Tellern/ Confect-Schalen 5. Groschen.
Davon umbzugiessen 1. Groschen.
Und wird ihnen auff 10. Pfund wegen Abgangs im Feuer 1. Pfund erlassen ; Sie sollen auch auff alle und iede Arbeit der Obrigkeit Wapen / und ihr Zeichen schlagen.

Eisenkauff.

Im Ertzgebürgischen Kreiß.

Eine Wage Cronen- oder Polnisch Eisen/ 1. Gülden 6. Groschen.
Eine Wage zwier geschmeltzt Eisen iedes nach der Güte 22. 24. und 26. Groschen.
Eine Wage Schien-Eisen 1. fl. 5. Groschen.
Eine Wage Stab Eisen/ ist dem zweygeschmeltzten gleich.
Eine Wage Renn und eingeschmeltzt Eisen/ 16. 18. Groschen.
Und sollen doch die jenigen Eisen/ so alter Ordnung nach/ vor die Bergwerge/ in einem geringern Preiß gegeben werden/ hiemit nicht gemeynet seyn / sondern bey demselben nochmals allenthalben wie vorhin / sein Bleibens haben.
Weil man auch des Eisens im Lande in grosser Menge bedürfftig/ so soll ohne sonderbahre Zulassung/ keines ausser Landes verkaufft werden.

Schlösser und Kleinschmiede.

Im Chur-Kreiß.

Von einer eingefasten Stubenthür / nach dem Häuptschlüssel 2. Gülden 6. Groschen.
Von einer eingefasten Kammerthür/ nach dem Häuptschlüssel 2. fl.
Von einer gemeinen Stubenthür 1. Gülden 15. Groschen.
Von einer gemeinen Kammerthür 1. Gülden 3. Groschen.
Von einer Haußthür vierdtehalben Gülden biß in 4. fl.
Von einem Fensterrahmen verzient 1. fl. 10. Groschen 6. Pfennige.
Unverzient schwartz 1. fl. auch 24. Groschen.
Vor ein eintzeln Stuben-Schloß 24. Groschen.

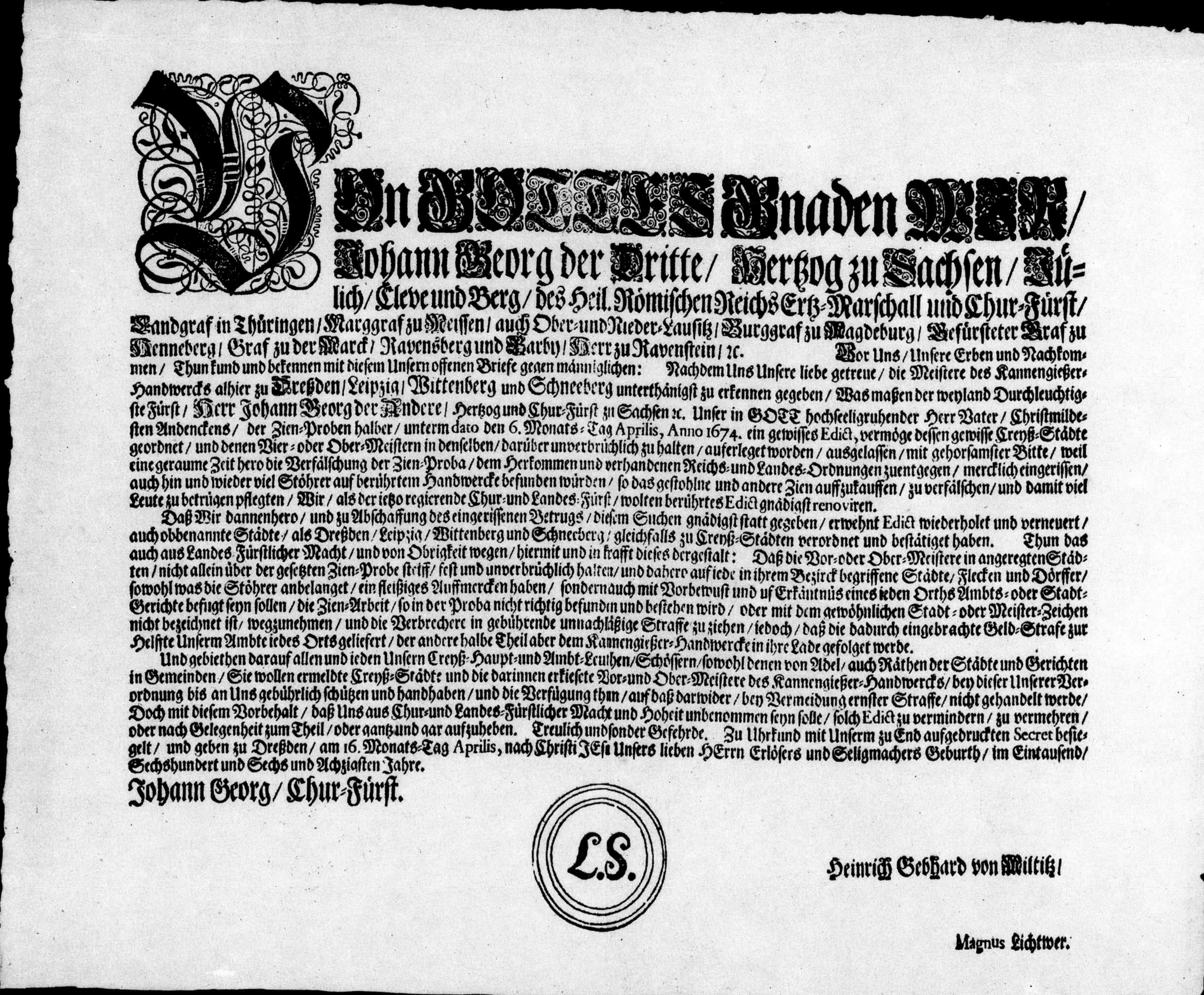

Von GOTTES Gnaden WIR / Johann Georg der Dritte / Hertzog zu Sachsen / Jülich / Cleve und Berg / des Heil. Römischen Reichs Ertz-Marschall und Chur-Fürst / Landgraf in Thüringen / Marggraf zu Meissen / auch Ober- und Nieder-Lausitz / Burggraf zu Magdeburg / Gefürsteter Graf zu Henneberg / Graf zu der Marck / Ravensberg und Barby / Herr zu Ravenstein / rc. Vor Uns / Unsere Erben und Nachkommen / Thun kund und bekennen mit diesem Unsern offenen Briefe gegen männiglichen: Nachdem Uns Unsere liebe getreue / die Meistere des Kannengießer-Handwercks alhier zu Dreßden / Leipzig / Wittenberg und Schneeberg unterthänigst zu erkennen gegeben / Was maßen der weyland Durchleuchtigste Fürst / Herr Johann Georg der Andere / Hertzog und Chur-Fürst zu Sachsen rc. Unser in GOTT hochseeligruhender Herr Vater / Christmildesten Andenckens / der Zien-Proben halber / unterm dato den 6. Monats-Tag Aprilis, Anno 1674. ein gewisses Edict, vermöge dessen gewisse Creyß-Städte geordnet / und denen Vier- oder Ober-Meistern in denselben / darüber unverbrüchlich zu halten / auferleget worden / ausgelassen / mit gehorsamster Bitte / weil eine geraume Zeit hero die Verfälschung der Zien-Proba / dem Herkommen und verhandenen Reichs- und Landes-Ordnungen zuentgegen / mercklich eingerissen / auch hin und wieder viel Stöhrer auf berührtem Handwercke befunden würden / so das gestohlne und andere Zien auffzukauffen / zu verfälschen / und damit viel Leute zu betrügen pflegten / Wir / als der ietzo regierende Chur- und Landes-Fürst / wolten berührtes Edict gnädigst renoviren.

Daß Wir dannenhero / und zu Abschaffung des eingerissenen Betrugs / diesem Suchen gnädigst statt gegeben / erwehnt Edict wiederholet und verneuert / auch obbenannte Städte / als Dreßden / Leipzig / Wittenberg und Schneeberg / gleichfalls zu Creyß-Städten verordnet und bestätiget haben. Thun das auch aus Landes-Fürstlicher Macht / und von Obrigkeit wegen / hiermit und in krafft dieses dergestalt: Daß die Vor- oder Ober-Meistere in angeregten Städten / nicht allein über der gesetzten Zien-Probe steiff / fest und unverbrüchlich halten / und dahero auf iede in ihrem Bezirck begriffene Städte / Flecken und Dörffer / sowohl was die Stöhrer anbelanget / ein fleißiges Auffmercken haben / sondern auch mit Vorbewust und uf Erkäntnüs eines ieden Orths Ambts- oder Stadt-Gerichte befugt seyn sollen / die Zien-Arbeit / so in der Proba nicht richtig befunden und bestehen wird / oder mit dem gewöhnlichen Stadt- oder Meister-Zeichen nicht bezeichnet ist / wegzunehmen / und die Verbrechere in gebührende unnachläßige Straffe zu ziehen / iedoch / daß die dadurch eingebrachte Geld-Strafe zur Helffte Unserm Ambte iedes Orts geliefert / der andere halbe Theil aber dem Kannengießer-Handwercke in ihre Lade gefolget werde.

Und gebiethen darauf allen und ieden Unsern Creyß-Haupt- und Ambt-Leuthen / Schössern / sowohl denen von Adel / auch Räthen der Städte und Gerichten in Gemeinden / Sie wollen ermeldte Creyß-Städte und die darinnen erkiesete Vor- und Ober-Meistere des Kannengießer-Handwercks / bey dieser Unserer Verordnung bis an Uns gebührlich schützen und handhaben / und die Verfügung thun / auf daß darwider / bey Vermeidung ernster Straffe / nicht gehandelt werde / Doch mit diesem Vorbehalt / daß Uns aus Chur- und Landes-Fürstlicher Macht und Hoheit unbenommen seyn solle / solch Edict zu vermindern / zu vermehren / oder nach Gelegenheit zum Theil / oder gantz und gar aufzuheben. Treulich und sonder Gefehrde. Zu Uhrkund mit Unserm zu End aufgedruckten Secret besiegelt / und geben zu Dreßden / am 16. Monats-Tag Aprilis, nach Christi JEsu Unsers lieben HErrn Erlösers und Seligmachers Geburth / im Eintausend / Sechshundert und Sechs und Achtzigsten Jahre.

Johann Georg / Chur-Fürst.

L.S.

Heinrich Gebhard von Miltitz /

Magnus Lichtwer.

6 Open letter from Johann Georg III to pewterers to strengthen the law for the testing of pewter proclaimed in Saxony in 1674; 1686.
In private ownership

7 Owner's mark in the form of a house-mark on the handle of a tankard; 16th century.
In private ownership

8 Relief mark in the interior base of a Swiss flagon; dated 1780.
In private ownership

9 Punch of foliage design for applied decoration; length 11 cm ($4^3/_8''$), c. 1800.
Heimatmuseum Mühlhausen/Thuringia

10 Concave pfennig soldered to the underside of a tankard cover; 2nd half of the 16th century.
In private ownership

7
8

9
10

LAURENT MORAND MARCHAND A LYON

Demeurant ruë Grenette, à la Fontaine Royalle, Essayeur Contrôlleur, Visiteur, & Marqueur des Ouvrages d'Etain dans ladite Ville & dans les Provinces du Lyonnois Forêts & Beaujolois, tenant la Foire de Beaucaire vend toutes sortes d'Etain fin, sonnant, cristallin, & rafiné d'Angleterre Scavoir Bassnis, Aiguieres, Plats, Assiette, Ovales, Basines, Ecuelles, Salieres Chandelier, Sucriers, Poivriers, Saladiers, Vinaigriers, Huiliers, Cuilliers, Fourchettes, Couteaux, Gardes Nappes, Pot à l'eau, Pot à Thé Pot au Ris, Pot à Boüillon, Cruches, Fontaines, Cuvettes, Flacons, Bouteilles, Pintes, Chopines, demi-Setiers, Pompes, Carrefons, Gobelets, Cuilliers a Pot, Ecumoires, Porte-dine, Bain Marie, Coquemards, Basins pour le lit & la Chaise, Seringues, Boëttes a Theriaques, Palettes, Crachoirs, Bassins a Barbe, Benitiers, Croix, Chandeliers d'Eglises, Burettes, Lavabo, Cremieres Ecritoires, Moules de Chandelles, Boutons pour les Regimens, Montres solaires, la veritable potée d'Etain pour polir les glaces de Miroirs & Ouvrages d'Argent, Cuivre & d'Acier, les veritables Tasses d'Antimoine, & toutes sortes d'ouvrages d'Argentine du Perou il change la vieille Vaisselle contre la neuve, ET LA VIEILLE LUI ETANT ADRESSÉE ET CONSIGNÉE EN SON NOM Sera exempte de payer les droits de Douanne, afin d'eviter que ces Coureurs qui la Refondent dans les Villes ou il n'y a nul Reglement pour la Maitrise dudit Art, comme pareillement dans les Bourgs, Villages et Châteaux, ne l'alterent, en faisant un melange de toutes Sortes de Mauvaises Matieres, ne travaillant pas au Titre de la Ville de Lyon, ce qui en diminue le prix, la qualité & l'usage.

11 Placard of the pewterer Laurent Morand Marchand from Lyons, used for advertising his products; *c.* 1700. Musée Historique, Lyons

12 A pewterer's order for materials, asking for the lowest possible price; 1864. Municipal archives, Eilenburg (Saxony)

13 Account for expenditure on repairs in a parsonage, showing that a pewterer fastened the screws and flowers on the arm of a brass candelabrum; *c.* 1695. In private ownership

14 A pewterer's receipt for two thalers received from the Leipzig guild; 1803. In private ownership

Following page:

15 A town mark and two master's touches on the underside of a plate; *c.* 1820. It is clear that the master's touch was struck in two positions to form an enclosed triangle round the centre of the plate. In private ownership

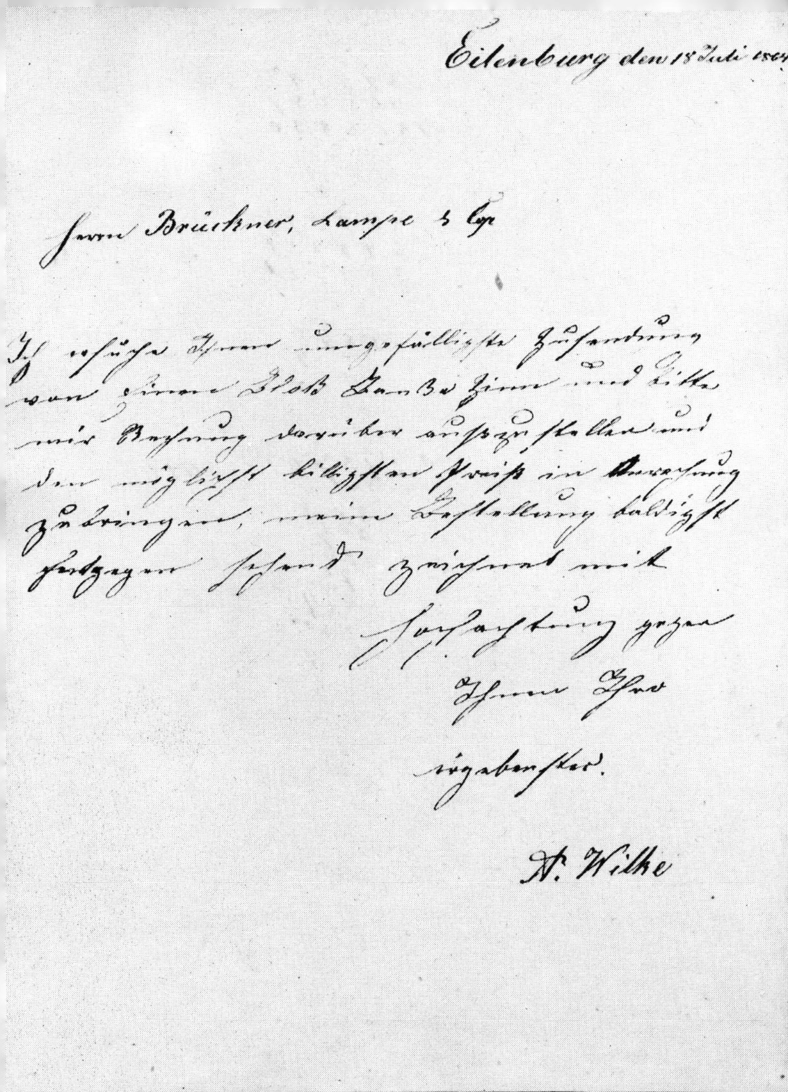

Eilenburg den 18 Juli 1804.

Herrn Brückner, ...

Ich ersuche Ihnen ungefälligste Zusendung von einem Stück ... Zinn und bitte mir Rechnung darüber auszustellen und den möglichst billigsten Preiß in Anrechnung zu bringen, meine Bestellung baldigst fertigen ... zeichnet mit Hochachtung gegen Ihnen Ihr ergebenster.

N. Wilke

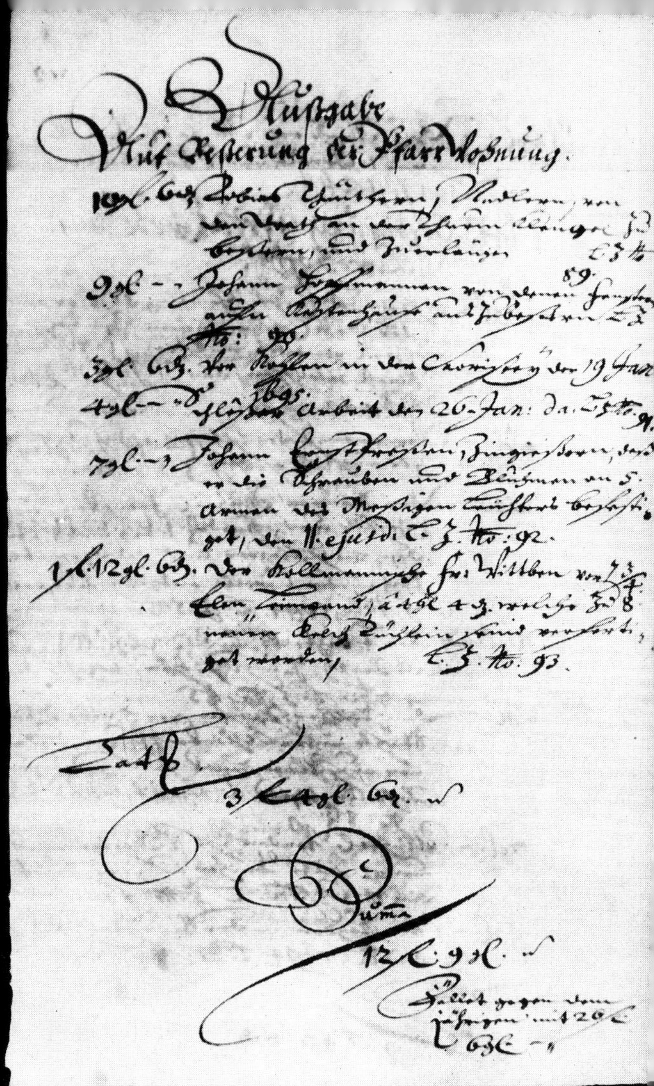

Ausgabe
Auf Besserung der Pfarr Wohnung.

Summa

14

Ich endes unterschriebener bekenne hier durch daß ich von dem Ehrsamen Handwerk der Zinngießer aus Leipzig zwey thaler in 20 X baar und richtig empfangen habe worüber ich quittire,

Sign Ehrenfriedersdorf bey Annaberg den 9 Februari 1803

Siegmund Hecht Zinngießer

1708
1708

goods for the war against King Valdemar of Denmark. In Austria, Switzerland and Germany, ownership of domestic pewter is disclosed in wills. An analysis of the wills of citizens of Lübeck for the years 1270 to 1370 reveals that simple pewter tableware was introduced into this region towards the end of the 13th century. Towards the middle of the 14th century well-to-do inhabitants of Lübeck even had complete table settings of pewter. Documents relating to the ownership of pewter by middle-class families in Denmark at this period have survived from the towns of Roskilde, Lund and Ribe, most of the items mentioned being jugs.

In the 13th century French Court officials contributed to the speedier introduction of pewter into municipalities by claiming a widespread customary right. At that time a large number of specially commissioned employees in the service of the Royal House were concerned with control of the quality of wine. Wine tasting was made from silver cups and a piece of bread to clear the palate was handed on a matching plate. Following the increasing appropriation of the silverware by the Court officials as souvenirs, mayors and councils came to introduce and encourage pewterware which was less costly. The fact that in France as in other countries almost nothing from that period has survived is certainly due primarily to the ease with which pieces which had become unsightly could have their appearance restored by melting down and re-casting.

In Italy and the Iberian peninsula pewter was scarce at every period not only for domestic but also for display or sacred purposes. Prolific clay diggings in Italy led to an abundant production of majolica ware from the 14th century onwards which was incomparably cheaper than pewter work. At a very early date the majority of Italian pewterers were therefore already going to German-speaking countries, to France and to the Netherlands. Pewterers are entirely unknown in Spain; in Portugal a few worked in Lisbon and Opporto. It can nevertheless be accepted that the low cost of pottery goods in Italy and other countries was not the only reason for an insignificant pewter industry. In the countries north of the Alps until well into the 17th century pottery was still one of the most important branches in the production of domestic ware and the manufacture of faience ware also provided strong competition for pewter. It nevertheless found a place in town and country homes whereas in southern lands this was virtually never the case. The material qualities of pottery, which lends itself outstandingly well to painting in bright colours are certainly more in keeping with the temperament of these peoples than the subdued warmth of pewter. Finally, economic circumstances may also have influenced the distribution of domestic pewterware since even if at many periods and in many places it became plentifully available in households it always remained valuable. Its acquisition and use were only possible with a certain affluence. Now and again at the present time tankards, jugs, candelabra, bowls and plates are found which once were buried or sunk in wells in time of war so that they did not become the booty of plundering troops. The most famous German prose-poet of the 17th century, Hans Jakob Christoffel von Grimmelshausen, in his work which includes autobiographical passages—*Der abenteuerliche Simplicissimus* (The Adventures of Simplicissimus)—writes of marauding horsemen who during their pillaging excursions during the Thirty Years' War hammered copper and pewter vessels to destruction and then packed up the bent and ruined pieces to carry away. Only a minimal reduction in the value of the goods was brought about by their being broken up; the looters were concerned with the value of the metal as such, which sometimes accounted for more than 85 per cent of the purchase price of an article. The authorities moreover also requisitioned at the highest level, as in about 1610 the Balkan Prince Gabriel Bathory who caused quantities of pewter to be carried off from Braşov for the founding of bronze cannon. An example of the noteworthy property which could already be found at this period in the households of many citizens emerges from the Council Register of Teplitz (now Teplice) relating to the estate of the council member Johann Dietrich which was taken over:

Bowls	3	Half-pint can	1
Plates	9	Salt-tub	1
Salvers	3	Beaker	1
Jug	1	Small pottery jug, pewter-mounted	1
Flasks	2		
Candlestick, pewter-mounted	1	Painted small jug, mounted	1

At home people put their possessions packed in barrels and chests into the cellar . . ., pewter and books into the well.

Chronicle from Scheibenberg/Erzgebirge of the year 1633.

This of course related to an estate comprising the possessions of a privileged citizen; in rural areas where by far the greater part of the populace lived and in simple citizens' homes pewter was a rarity. That privileged persons all along used pewterware in their everyday-life is illustrated by the equipment of the Swedish ship "Vasa" which sank in 1628 and was raised after 333 years: whereas exclusively wooden tableware was provided for the crew, pewterware was to be found in the officers' quarters.

After the end of the Thirty Years' War, pewter gained ground as household equipment and indeed not only in the countries directly smitten by that great conflict. Interest in pewterware suddenly expanded in England. The quality of English pewterers' wares and their materials impelled even the Czarist Russian Court to obtain plates, bowls and jugs from there for general use. Until then pewter had in fact been found in the kitchen amongst the French nobility but was disdained for the table. Because then under a decree of Louis XIV the nobility were obliged to donate to the king the tableware used for eating and drinking when he was lodged in their palaces, in gratitude for the honour, pewterers were able to look forward to increasing demand for their products from the nobility, and were much encouraged. The second half of the 17th century brought with it a great impetus to the pewterers' trade in the Netherlands, Belgium, Hungary and all German-speaking countries. In Scandinavia wood nevertheless remained even then the principal material—if pewter was introduced into a home, it was primarily as a sign of affluence. Even items which were made only for practical use were mainly positioned on shelves or on the wall for show.

In the meantime pewterers had also arrived in America. In about 1640 they were to be found in Philadelphia, Newport, Boston and a few decades later, in New York. But it is only from the following century that significant traces survive which was in fact the most promising for this branch of craftsmanship.

For quite a long time eating and drinking ware consisted exclusively of pewter but after 1850 it nevertheless largely disappeared even more quickly than in European countries. In fact, also in Europe the cheaper porcelain and pottery drove the more costly, clumsier and dull-seeming pewter out of citizens' houses as a result of which it was brought into rural households where it was particularly valued and cherished. There are regional variations from country to country in this respect and within countries themselves. Thus pewter is comparatively scarce in Austrian farmers' homes but in Switzerland, on the contrary, unbreakable pewter houseware was included in the equipment of rural households at a very early date. In Germany the first half of the 19th century brought a renewed blossoming of the pewterers' craft in various regions and the flowering has sometimes lasted into our own century. The reasons for the longevity of utilitarian pewter in this field are country people's holding fast to that which has been handed down of old, their consciousness of tradition and the indisputable practical value of much pewterware.

It is, in fact, not untruthful to say that owing to a change in fashion among the upper classes the use of pewter begins to become less frequent as time goes by. However, its use is becoming correspondingly more plentiful among the citizens and peasants, for whom potters' goods are too poor and who look for pewterers' wares instead.

Letter from the pewterer Joseph Heinrich Setzer, Heilbronn, 1791.

From apprentice to master

If the question is to be answered, how the pewterers' craft might be learned, it is necessary to say something about the organizational pivot and fulcrum of this procedure—the guilds, corporations, associations, companies and unions. All these terms stand for unions of craftsmen which came into being in Europe at a very early date and lasted in some countries until well into the 19th century. It is true that in England signs of dissolution became apparent about the year 1700 whilst in France the revolution of 1789/93 brought with it the extermination of the guilds. At no time and nowhere in America were guilds to be found. Whereas there the methods of training in the crafts essentially developed sporadically and following customary practices, the associations of craftsmen in the Old World were preoccupied with corresponding controls. According to the importance of the matter to be determined, it could be resolved by the united masters of the guild, under the chairmanship of the Alderman or Senior Master or it had to be put before the authorities by the guild for confirmation. Apprentice- and mastership in pewterworking in almost all European countries was on the basis of established guild articles.

Such articles were obtained by the pot casters of Nuremberg, united since 1285, in Vienna an appropriate regulation from 1416 can be cited, the ordinances of the Salzburg pewterers date from 1487, those of Stockholm from 1545. There is documentary proof of pewterers' guilds from 1419 in York and from 1456 in Bristol; organizations of pewterers together with their regulations in Scotland are known from the same century.

Masters who did not belong to any association were found even in countries with a very strongly developed guild system. There were usually two grounds against them—that the number of pewterers was too small for the creation of an association of their own or that the masters put no value on membership of a guild. Guildlessness for the first of these reasons was relatively common in Germany in Westphalia, for example. In most cases it was usual to try to unite one guild with other types of trade if there were not sufficient masters of one's own calling. Therefore in Riga only four and in exceptional cases even only three masters were required. Related trades were naturally preferred as associates. In German Schwäbisch-Gmünd pewterers belonged to the guild of "workers with fire" to whom belonged gold- and silversmiths, gun-makers, sword cutlers, clock-makers, nail-makers, farriers, coppersmiths, axe-forgers as well as tinmen and locksmiths. One learns with surprise that the smiths of Gmünd also included masons in their ranks. Pewterers at no time had their own guild there; in Brünn (now Brno) they were also always grouped together with other craftsmen, often with the glassworkers. In the Swiss town of Neuenburg they were united with the masons, smiths and carpenters into the "Corporation des maçons, favres et chapuis". Because the guild was the only organization to afford some protection from a variety of arbitrary acts men were not too particular at certain times as to those with whom they became united. In Switzerland where the smiths' guild was the usual resort of the pewterers, unions were also formed with the foresters (in Biel) or the agricultural workers (in Zofingen). In Bohemian Leipa (now Česká Lípa) it was the cloth workers.

While questions are being asked round, every person must sit still until it is his turn and then firmly pronounce his opinion; if, however, one or the other irritates the rest with unnecessary chatter, he shall pay a fine of three groschen.

Guild regulation of the Glogau (Glogow) pewterers, 1711.

What impelled many masters to place no value on membership of a guild, namely to become guild-masters? Mainly it was when they had the advantage of being employed by a town council or even by a highly-placed Court official and therefore had a semi-assured income. In return they were not allowed to employ apprentices or journeymen and were also forbidden a hanging sign outside their workshop. Free masters of this kind are known from Bremen from 1591; where in the 17th century were about 30 accredited masters and three directly subject to the Council who were not members of the guild. In Riga free masters had the honour of being permitted to describe themselves as "Pewterers to the Ducal Court". They frequently looked upon themselves as something so special that they tried to remove from the streets of the smiths. Sections of streets like this were created even from the early Middle Ages to achieve a measure of protection for neighbouring residents from fire danger and noise (particularly the smiths). But also the reek emanating from the greased moulds when molten pewter was poured into them made segregation desirable. In about 1650 even something akin to a pewterers' quarter came into being in Moscow with workshops and sales booths.

Of quite a different type were those guildless pewterers who were described as quacks. These were those craftsmen who were precluded from being initiated into a guild principally for reasons of their origin. These consisted of either native masters who had moved or craftsmen who had wandered in from other countries. In each case they were regarded as competitors and treated accordingly. Central European countries were widely frequented by Italian pewterers who for centuries came principally from the areas north of Milan, especially from the small community of Forno. Switzerland appears to have attracted Italian pewterers principally from the Calancatal, the neighbouring valley to the Misox, in Italian Bunden. Soon these guildless craftsmen who wandered from place to place and who derived sparse subsistence from casual work were contemptuously called *calancers* by the
1 inhabitants. In 1726 the Elector Frederick Augustus of Saxony issued a sharp mandate to combat the "many hawkers, bodgers and quacks travelling round the country"; in Article 19 of the statutes of Parisian pewterers in 1613 sale of pewter by pedlars, patchers and others was strictly forbidden. Nevertheless in many cases foreigners succeeded in becoming resident and admitted to the guild and sometimes even to arrive at modest prosperity.

Following this we hereby convey to our subordinates and public officers, as well as to all judicial and lower authorities, our determined will and pleasure that the aforementioned hawkers, bodgers and quacks, in addition to those known as Italians, which latter carry with them their turning lathes, moulds and other tools, are no longer in any wise to be tolerated nor to be given work and where any of them appear, immediately to put them under arrest, to destroy the tools of their trade and moreover, as you may think fit, to impose a severe punishment upon them.

Mandate of Frederick Augustus, Elector of Saxony, 1726.

In each case an aspiring apprentice had to find a guild master and to convince him of his honourable birth. If his father practised a dishonourable trade, for better or worse he had to expect a refusal. In many countries dishonourable trades included barbers, millers and shepherds. Executioners also followed a calling which entailed dishonourable birth for their children. Apprenticeship began with the "initiation" in front of the assembled guild and—as sign of an official procedure—the opened Chest. The initiation was recorded in the guild register with details of the master, the new apprentice and the term provided for his apprenticeship. Remarks like "ran away" are not uncommon, occasionally when young apprentices aged nine or ten already came to experience the hardships of the pewter trade. Added to this, many masters were quick to hand with a cruel thrashing and the master's wife was not far behind in this respect when a young apprentice did not carry out the invariably numerous household tasks well and quickly enough. Police ordinances were occasionally needed to protect apprentices from excessively arbitrary treatment, as for example in Kiel in 1795. The period of apprenticeship was variable and generally became shorter towards the 19th century. Masters' sons were always advantaged and in many places were released, i.e. raised to the status of guild journeyman, in half the usual time.

"Release" was once again performed before the opened Chest. Other than in England, France and America it was now the duty of the newly fledged pewterworker to go on a tour to perfect himself in his craft. Exceptions to this obligation are very rare, as for instance in Chur in Switzerland. Here the town council feared a coarsening of morals as a result of the tour and during the period of the Thirty Years' War forbade the circuit. The wan-
2/3 dering journeymen were invariably unmarried and their parents in their homeland were diligently kept informed by letter, where they were working, boarding and lodging. Whilst abroad, money was saved assiduously so as one day to be able to solicit the honour of mastership. A two-year exile was usually necessary to allow a first petition for mastership. Petition here means a ceremonial application. The journeyman was then ceremoniously presented to the guild by the senior master. First of all, however, the petition fee, in German the *mutgroschen*, a substantial sum of money, had to be paid. The sons of masters and also those journeymen who had married a master's widow were able to make their second and third petitions as soon as the following two quarters, with the *mutgroschen* to be forthcoming each time. Because a widow was allowed to continue running a workshop and to employ journeymen, but mastership or the training of apprentices was forbidden to her, remarriages within the craft were frequent. If the journeyman was neither master's son nor the fortunate spouse of a late master's widow, he would mostly have to wait another two or three years for his next petition. Then, at last creation of his masterpiece could be begun.

Upon the expiry of these four years of learning, no-one shall be permitted to undertake a masterpiece, it shall then be that according to long-standing trade custom he shall have travelled a further two years in the trade, after which if such a journeyman wishes to submit a masterpiece, he shall pay five reichthalers to us and likewise five reichsthalers to the trade.

Concession for the Pewterers' Guild issued in Paderborn in 1712.

There were also considerable differences for the making of a masterpiece according to the antecedents and status of a journeyman. For instance, under an ordinance of 1499 to regulate the pewter trade in Breslau (Wrocław) the sons of masters were entirely exempted and it was not until 1560 that it became an obligation for them also. Then, however, as in most other towns, they had to produce only a "miniature masterpiece". In 1589 Georg Mair of Augsburg was allowed to settle there as a master without a masterpiece although he was ordered to marry within six weeks. Since, however, he had in the meantime gained a large order for a marriage in the influential Fugger family, the master was readily able to propose that his own marriage date be postponed until completion of the order. Craftsmen who had gained admission by marriage were advantageously treated similarly to the sons of masters or pewterers in the service of great houses. Whilst a workshop was allotted to outsiders for the production of their masterpiece, these others were able to make use of a workshop of their own choice and to be assisted by the youngest apprentice. Rules of this kind naturally did not apply everywhere in detail but it was generally regarded as important not to make access to mastership difficult to those from their own ranks. Candidates under the supervision of two newly admitted masters were usually allowed 14 days in which to complete their (normally specified) tasks. In many towns (e.g. Kaschau

Working hours for journeymen pewterers and apprentices:
For journeymen without board, from 6 in the morning until 12 noon and from 1 in the afternoon until 7 in the evening; for journeymen on piece-work the same; for journeymen on wages and board and for apprentices, from 6 in the morning until 7 in the evening.

Regulation of the Department of Trade and Business Establishment, Berlin, 1854.

—now Košice) it was nevertheless permitted to take up to 8 weeks for the making of a masterpiece. Daily working hours were likewise regulated. It was usually possible to work 15 hours a day, as a rule from 4 a.m. until 7 o'clock in the evening. Beer had to be provided for the supervising masters; after presentation of the piece a celebratory repast for the guild together with a further payment would be due. Moreover, many guilds appear to have taken their love of tippling into account when they acknowledged masterpieces
4 with merely a remark in the records that due to poor quality a stipulated and not inconsiderable sum must be donated to the guild for its welfare. In many places such customs held good for decades. Many a young master therefore began working for himself with a considerable burden of debt.

To the masters' dinner there shall be brought and served a stew of beef, a fish dish, roasts of beef, veal and pork together with a leg of mutton, then a green or smoked ham together with a cake, for drink an eighth of beer and two pots of wine.

Pewterers' regulation, Altenburg, 1661.

The first days of work on the masterpiece were devoted to the preparation of drawings and moulds. Now and again the use of moulds which were already available was permitted but this was the exception. Even in the 19th century, when a considerable slackening of the once stringent regulations had become general, the professional status of the pewterers of the Vaud in Switzerland was disputed because they used old moulds for casting and apparently were not conversant with the making of new ones. Sand, clay, slate, sandstone and plaster were the earliest materials for the manufacture of moulds; later came the more durable but also more expensive metal moulds. During the peak period of the craft moulds had to be made for three or four different pieces; in the 19th century mostly only two. For centuries a jug and a dish were the typical wares which had to be cast. A regulation in the statute of the Parisian pewterers of 1613 is extremely unusual because it made the type of masterpiece to be produced dependent on the specialization aspired to. Thus the pewterer who intended in future to produce only hollow ware, the *potier rond*, had to cast a pot whose body had to be in a single piece. A future *maître de forge* (hammerman) was required to produce deep and flat hammered dishes (condensed by hammer blows). Finally the *menuisier* who wished to make only small and delicate work later on, had to create an ink-stand for his masterpiece.

In most of the large towns pewterers use moulds of brass, at least for the current fashions...
In contrast, such costly tools would produce a poor return in small towns and for this reason masters resident there use stone moulds for the majority of large articles...
Plaster moulds are used only for goods which are not often sold and are made as an expedient or if something has to be cast in a hurry.

J. S. Haller, *Werkstätten der heutigen Künste oder die neue Kunsthistorie* (Workshops of today's arts or the new history of art), Brandenburg and Leipzig, 1761.

Once the completed pieces had been approved as up to standard, the necessary money paid and the striven-after dignity duly documented, the new master had to provide himself with a marking punch in all haste so that to comply with the regulations, he could identify the products of his workshop as manufactures for which he was answerable.

Marking

The pewterer procured a blank marking punch from a smith and passed it on to the engraver with a commission to sink the reverse of a design in one end which was from then on impressed on his pewterware as his master's touch or mark. Often his own skill and tools enabled him to make the complete punch himself. Although infrequently, now and again the same marking punch was used through two or three generations. If his father's workshop had the reputation of producing sound work then the son was very glad to exploit the good repute conveyed by the touch. In normal cases it was the ambition of every master to introduce a touch of his own as had always been customary. Marked pewterware and its related regulations are known from well into the past, from about 1258 and 1303 in France, 1355 in the Netherlands. That such regulations were necessary was firstly for economic reasons.

It was soon learned that tin intended for the production of goods of all kinds was easier to work if it was not cast in a pure state but mixed with a quantity of lead. Because lead is considerably cheaper than tin and wares leaving the workshop were only partly sold on appearance but rather by 5 weight there was a constant endeavour to include in the alloy as much lead as was ever possible to make a greater profit. Demand from craftsmen themselves for binding regulations for material quality increased in proportion as the number of pewterers in a given territory grew larger. The authorities responded to these demands particularly once the health damaging properties of pewter containing too much lead was exposed. In spite of considerable regional differences in the regulations an average for all countries was a 10:1 ratio of tin to lead. Items which were not intended for eating and drinking, jug-handles, etc., were for a time permitted to contain considerably more lead; extremes are the *mankgut* in Stralsund (3:1) and the "rotten pewter" *(faulzinn)* in Lucerne (2:1).

No pewterer is to sell any pewterware which weighs more than half-a-pound, other than by weight and not at all by eye, subject to a penalty of three gulden each time one such transgresses, to be paid without any outstanding.

Regulation of the Principalities and guilds of the Margravates of Baden and Hachberg, etc., 1715.

When the material quality to be maintained had been prescribed an instrument became necessary by which observance of the regulations could be verified. From the end of the 14th until approximately the end of the 16th century view-masters were appointed for this purpose in many towns, who—like for example the "wardens" in the Netherlands—were sworn-in with great ceremonial display in front of the town council stringently to exercise control. The view-masters were not necessarily solely pewterers. In St. Gallen for example this function was undertaken by a barber, a surgeon, a goldsmith and a glassworker amongst others. Every item of pewterware which was awaiting sale had to be stamped with the town mark in the workshop by them. The considerable increase in the number of pewterers and their products from decade to decade at this time and the consequent ever increasing cost of the viewers meant that more rational methods had to be sought. As a start many towns tried to put the onus on pewterers to bring their goods themselves for viewing. This had been compulsory in Esslingen from 1589 and shortly afterwards pewterers were already complaining bitterly about the harm this caused. On the one hand potential customers often found the pewterer absent from his workshop and on the other, much time was wasted and training of apprentices suffered. Could they not, they asked, also do as was done in other towns in Wurttemberg, each master to mark his wares himself?

Preceding page:

16 Pewterware on a dinner-table of the 15th century. Painting by the Master of the altar-piece of St. Bartholomew; Cologne, 1480–1495. Musées royaux des Beaux Arts de Belgique, Brussels

17 Tankard of *stitzen* shape, South Germany; height 28 cm (11″), *c.* 1580. In the interior of the tankard is a rosette-like medallion, with which the bottom was "sealed"; a concave pfennig is soldered into the cover. In private ownership

18 Tea-pot; height 16 cm ($6^1/_4$″), dated 1801. In private ownership

T P 1801

19 Wide-based flagon; height 39 cm ($15^3/_8$″), *c.* 1680. In private ownership

20 Slender-necked faience jugs with pewter mounts; height 32 cm ($12^5/_8$″), *c.* 1730. In private ownership

21 Flattened flask on a tapestry "La Promenade"; 1st quarter of the 16th century.
Musée de Cluny, Paris

22 Measuring jug gauged for one *nösel* of brandy (0.496 litre); height 23 cm (9"), *c.* 1730.
In private ownership

21

23 Screwed flask with exuberant engraving; height 24.5 cm ($9\frac{5}{8}$"), dated 1776. In private ownership

It had in fact in the meantime widely proved advantageous to give pewterers the right to mark their own products under their own hand. The authorities then only required a register showing which master used which mark when there was room for spot-checks at any time and if, on the other hand, there were complaints the transgressor was readily traceable. The senior master of the guild was usually made responsible for ensuring that the regulations were observed and was frequently reminded of this duty by "open
6 letters". This procedure to a certain extent assumed properly functioning associations of craftsmen. Although, for example, stringent regulations for marking were issued by the Municipality of Paris during the reign of Louis XIII, the dissolution of the guilds which was ordered by Louis XVI in 1776 and brought about by the Revolution, led to considerable abuses.

It is disputed whether the same mark for all pewterers in a given town emerged first or whether initially each master had only to have his own specific touch on the pewterware from his workshop. There is considerable evidence that at first the master's touch was sufficient and that it only became necessary to add the town mark after trade had reached an extent that pewterware was leaving the town and finding customers elsewhere. On the other hand unmarked jugs survive from the late Middle Ages with concave small coins of particular towns soldered into them, which may always have served
10, 15 as a town mark. The short life-span of any and every single mark on its own is nevertheless certain; pewter was already impressed with town and master's marks or with a combination of the two at an early date. Sometimes state marks were added, for instance about 1694 in the Mark of Brandenburg under an edict of Frederick III which took the form of a sceptre or an eagle. A year later mark-viewers were moreover re-introduced there for a short period who generated considerable revenue from their inspectorate function and thus helped to alleviate the monetary problems of the ruling house.

Town and master's marks have remained a frequently consulted source of information up to the present day. It is, of course, no longer possible when necessary to consult the touchplates of the marks of the masters working in their district which were maintained by guilds or councils but instead extensive registers of marks have meanwhile been prepared in a good dozen countries. They include works by Bossard (Switzerland), Boucaud and Tardy (France), Bruzelli (Sweden), Cotterell and Peal (Great Britain), Dubbe and Verster (Netherlands), Hintze (Germany—now GDR and FRG—German-speaking regions), Laughlin (USA), Löfgren and Martenson (Finland), Tischer (Bohemia—now CSSR), Uldall (Denmark), Weiner (Hungary) and van Zeller (Portugal). Although many thousands of pewter marks are identified in these works (see also the bibliography), very far from all masters' and town marks can be elucidated. Many will never be solved to tell of the origin of a piece, others will be revealed by systematic research. In ad-

For viewing, each master shall forcefully strike his mark on the pewter which he has made next to the town mark on every piece, whether large or small, however delicate the work may be.

Pewterers' regulation, Bautzen, 1616.

dition to the marks taken from various works listed in the bibliography a large number which have hitherto been unknown are published in this book.

Principally in the 19th century pewter came into the market which bore neither town nor master's marks as had been the custom in the past, but which were only stamped with a quality mark which contained the master's initials or even his full name in conjunction with a crowned rose or an angel. From as early as 1650 a mark of particularly good quality material (such as was superior to the average required) in the form of a crowned rose was to be seen in Nuremberg. In northern Germany and the Netherlands it emerged a good 100 years later and has survived, as also in France, to most recent times. In the districts round the tin-ore-rich German Erzgebirge rose marks are less common and from the beginning of the 18th century were increasingly superceded by the angel mark which was becoming more widespread. There and in Thuringia the letters CL (clar = clear and lauter = pure) were also used to indicate particularly pure lead-free material. High purity was also indicated by the legend "Englisch Zinn", "Blockzinn" or "London", usually within an angel mark. Many pieces bearing both rose and angel marks came from workshops in Holland and Lower Germany. It is possible that by this the master indicated an intermediate quality; documentary evidence of this appears no longer to be available.

In addition to the angel and to a lesser extent the rose marks most frequently encountered in Central Europe, England and America as a sign of good quality material, guilds, town councils and often also individual pewterers, elaborated a sometimes confusing abundance of variations. Even before the development of special marks of quality differing proportions of lead were impressed in the absence of or in addition to a master's, town and state marks. In the Netherlands and northern Germany a quartet of marks was struck which was reminiscent of silver marks. It would be easy to conclude that this would suggest to a potential purchaser that the goods contained a proportion of silver. The term *tinverlakkers* (tin painting) which emerged at this period also always indicates shoddy workmanship by its double meaning. In its true sense the term refers to those who painted pewter either to please a customer or to save cleaning at home. *Verlakken* in colloquial speech also means to defraud and in fact many a coat of red or black paint hides material of inferior quality.

Three men were burnt because they sold lead and tin in Spandau as silver / two men were condemned to be broken on the wheel / because of thieving in churches.

Sentences in Berlin/Cölln, 1431.

As early as 1403 an ordinance of the Council of Bremen stipulated that "fine goods" must be distinguished by a "whole" (i.e. closed grip) key and "half goods" with an open grip key. In Bremen a key and initials was used as combined town and master's mark. In 1770 a pewterer in the town of Soest (Westphalia) had a punch engraved with the inscription "Engels Gepolert Hart Zin" (Engel's pole-fluxed hard pewter) to draw attention to the fact that his pewter was carefully purified by "poling" (stirring with green wood). About the same time a Swiss master discovered a particularly publicity-ef-

fective quality mark in the form of an oval punch with the inscription "Wie das Gelt, so die War" ("goods as good as the money"). Indeed it seems that Swiss pewterers possessed above-average skill not only in forming vessels of a popularly pleasing shape but also in adapting official regulations in an original manner. For example, pewterers' marking obligations were some-
8 times fulfilled by a large seal in relief bearing all the stipulated marks, on the interior bottom of jugs and tankards and serving as decoration.

Pewterers were confronted with a continual problem by old pewterware brought for re-melting. Because functional articles were damaged by knife-cuts, overheating in the oven, falling or being dropped, amongst other things, or fashion demanding new shapes, considerable work was often at stake.

As desirable as it might be to have ample work in hand, equally great was always the fear that the goods might be stolen and the master prosecuted as a deceiver. Under pressure of increasing thefts of pewter a statute of 1529 in France obligated every owner to provide his pewter possessions with a monogram or other indication of ownership. Were a family able to afford a large provenance of pewter, then it would have a special punch engraved for
7 the purpose with its coat-of-arms or proprietary symbol so that an owner's mark could be struck. This not only made the recovery of stolen goods easier but also provided the pewterer who was re-melting with some certainty that he was dealing with honest people and legitimate goods. At about the same period in Schaffhausen a master had to exhibit any pewter intended for re-melting for two weeks. There always remained, however, the question, what was the quality of the pewter brought for re-melting? If it had originated from his own workshop, then there was no need to worry because a master naturally knew what material he had then been using and how far it conformed with any alterations in quality stipulations for new pieces. Unknown ware was tested by biting it; it grated on the teeth more or less according to quality. But confronted with a strict view or senior master this was too uncertain and the discolouration or turning blue of a boiling of red beet-root if the material contained excess lead was also too imprecise an indication. The practice of leaving re-melted pewter unmarked or specially marked "Alte Probe" (old proof) or "Vermischtes Zinn" (mixed pewter) therefore developed under constraint. A pewterer was thus relieved of responsibility for the quality of the material of re-melted pieces but many opportunities for fraud were also created. Therefore in many places re-melting was entirely forbidden to pewterers and masters were obliged under oath—as in some parts of Germany and Bohemia—to re-work old pewter in such a way that it was fit to view, i.e. so that the lead content conformed with the stipulated degree of quality. This came about at a point in time when the social need of most pewterers was exceedingly great and they therefore had to submit to every demand and task for the sake of their very existence.

If anyone wishes to have his old pewter which is mixed with lead re-cast, he is free to have this done; but the same must be marked by the senior master with the aforementioned existing stamp "old proof".

Guild letter of the pewter- and jug-founders in the Mark Brandenburg, 1735.

Day-to-day tribulations of the craftsmen

Documents relating to the pewterers' craft in all countries frequently disclose the needy existence of many masters; "Ruined, his wife a beggar-woman", "admitted to hospital, impoverished and with three wretched children", "died entirely destitute"—the remarks of the chroniclers read in this and similar vein. Naturally there were also pewterers who achieved prosperity and therefore esteem and honour, as for example Johann Georg Klingling of Frankfurt-on-Main, who rose to become a wholesale producer and whose stock at his death in 1749 comprised the following: 629 tea-pots, 427 pairs of candelabra, 613 salad-dishes, 331 coffee-pots, 286 chargers, 197 washing-bowls, 415 salts, beakers, spoons and tobacco-boxes.

From today's vantage point it is readily explicable that during a time of antagonistic social classes craftsmen became impoverished and a few accrued considerable possessions by clever exploitation of the disagreements which existed. The accelerated development of factory production in the 19th century enormously aggravated the situation of handicrafts; this could be sustained neither by more intensive work nor by longer hours—sometimes even in combination. In many places in Germany the failure of small crafts businesses increased tenfold from 1830 to 1847. Shopkeepers became significant competition to small enterprises of craftsmen, particularly in rural areas and small towns. As early as 1775 a chronicler complained that in the last hundred years the number of shopkeepers had trebled and of the craftsmen "something under half had been lost". There was virtually nothing which the shopkeeper would not handle, covertly or openly. The increasing number of retail businesses was, of course, not the real reason for the decline of small craftsmen's enterprises, but in fact the development of factory—and therefore cheaper—production. This general trend was aggravated in the case of pewterers by a series of other factors, foremost amongst which was the cheaper production of faience ware, stoneware and glass from the 17th century and a hundred years later, of porcelain. In competition with these, pewterers could not match their prices.
12 Even when they repeatedly asked metal merchants to "apply the lowest possible price", the cost of their material continuously increased and could not be compared with that of porcelain. Added to all this woe, popular taste shifted away from pewter goods and in the towns there was scarcely any business to be done since there the more noble porcelain was especially esteemed. An 18th century porcelain plate is inscribed:

"If a pewter plate shall stay bright
One must scour and polish it every day
Yet a porcelain plate
Becomes white and clean by washing
Therefore set upon your table
Ware which is prettily painted and fresh."

If a personal misfortune occurred during these hard times—injury from burns, illness, accident or similar—one's fate was usually sealed. It is true that even in the 19th century the guilds could in part allay the direst need but the promissory note which had to be signed obviously did not put an end to
14 worry. Not infrequently debts had to be settled in conjunction with payment to the guild of the so-called quarterage—a form of subscription. Its amount was pre-determined for a long period and was generally paid annually but now and again at intervals of more than one year. The principal quarterage *(hauptquartel)* to which many masters looked forward with fear and apprehension was additional to this. Originally this quarterage was due on each anniversary of the foundation of the guild. Under pressure of a variety of causes, a day towards the end of the year was increasingly chosen for inviting the master to pay. The assistance of the guild could also be relied upon in respect of payment of the quarterage in as much as payment could be delayed if a workshop had to overcome particularly great need.

As early as 1670/80 complaints about the growing tendency to paper the walls of rooms in the homes of town-dwellers were increasing. Wallpaper now set-off sideboards and coffers upon which in earlier times useful and at the same time decorative pewter had stood. In the trade, with all its other troubles, there was the depressing realization that on this account also less pewter would be sold than in past times. Worry was also brought about by the queries and suspicions of apprehensive or health-conscious citizens that the human life-span had commenced to decline since pewter had been brought into domestic use. As a result, in 1780 Monsieur le Noir, Chief Magistrate of Paris, instigated an investigation into the danger of pewter vessels by three of the most notable chemists. A year later the result was published: a person would have to eat out of a pure pewter dish for 48 years to absorb one grain (0.07 grammes) of poisonous arsenic from 6 loth of pewter. This reassuring report was, however, countered by a certain Monsieur Navier with the comment that in the whole of France one could not come across one hundredweight of clear, i.e. pure, pewter. English pewter increasingly gained a reputation superior to the pewter which the East India Company imported from overseas when just then, a London Doctor, Baker, proved that English pewter resists vinegar, lemon juice and a solution of sorrel-salts even when moderately heated. Disputes of this kind made customers unsure but also led to a preference on the continent of Europe for purchasing everyday pewter originating from England. Because townsmen were next able to buy it more cheaply direct from English shippers and merchants this led to the ruin of many resident masters.

Pewterware was publicized with placards and even with poems. Any pewterer able to affort the cost, made himself new moulds to be able to offer
11 "pewter in the style of silver" (with a fluted surface). Even if one or another master recognized that this new fashion did not altogether suit the simple

Fine pewter! Who will buy, who will buy?
Genuine and not adulterated with lead.
Hardly anywhere beyond England's shores
does it shine like this in a shop;
attractive shapes and modern;
Buy, you ladies! Buy, you gentlemen!
Pottery and porcelain break,
but pewter never in a lifetime.
Children and grandchildren will be able
to inherit it,
and I will take damaged pieces from
everybody
according to weight and test.
Everything can be transformed!
If fashion is against me,
I will not be discouraged
from casting pewter in the future
because who knows how soon
and gladly pewter will be cherished.
Here it stands, you gentlemen!

Sales promotion poem from the 18th century.

character of pewter as a material, economic problems obliged him to conform. There was mutual assistance with moulds and inventiveness in combining parts from separate individual moulds into new whole pieces. Scarcely a single citizen would meet the outlay for pewterware for a great celebration. Even a few decades previously a goodly sum of money was occasionally gathered when someone could afford to invest in a considerable service of pewterware. It was not only changing fashion and the use of tableware of other materials which had caused this source to dry up. Under "regulations to reduce unnecessary expenditure at engagements, weddings, etc." (as for example in Lübeck in 1767) the number of persons at celebrations was restricted, at weddings perhaps to 50.

Worrysome competition from hawkers, bodgers, intruders and patchers has already been mentioned. On the one hand the authorities forbade these itinerant workmen to carry on business and on the other, from time to time, guild pewterers from repairing defective pieces. It was therefore surely inevitable that both town and country dwellers befriend the cheaper pottery. There were also disputes with the potters and glassworkers about pewter mounts; more will be said of this later.

All kinds of expedients were adopted for survival. Prestige prizes of pewterware for shooting festivals were diligently pressed upon the organizers. In Teplitz (now Teplice) in the first half of the 19th century a game of chance was promoted, not for money but for pewterware—perhaps an attempt by a well-meaning authority to support local handicrafts. Monograms, engraving of owner's marks and decoration were hardly ever left any longer to goldsmiths, copper etchers or engravers once the technique of drawing zig zag lines was introduced which did not require so sure a touch as incised engraving. Another decorative technique was also diligently practised, namely dec-
9 oration applied with punches. In addition, pewterers had long since not been
diffident about undertaking simple copper or "yellow alloy" jobs, to make
13 pewter screw-closures for copper flasks and to carry out repairs to copper or
brassware. Ultimately they were only doing what their forebears had done for a long time previously when times were bad: to involve themselves in all kinds of other activities (certainly no longer as at one time, with gunpowder) and to adopt an additional occupation, as for example in Switzerland as gravedigger, cellarman or even military drill instructor. Now and again a master even contrived to obtain permission to deal in "pottery and faience detrimental to his own calling". All these expedients often lessened everyday cares but separation from the pewter trade had likewise begun.

Pewterers make jugs, sheet and all cast work of pewter, brass and bell-metal and also have the right to buy the same in addition to all kinds of lead, also to buy finished work of pewter, brass and bell-metal conforming to their trade and to re-sell them again, also to keep gunpowder for sale.

Regulation of the combined guild (goldsmiths, farriers, locksmiths, spurriers, armourers, pewterers, blade-smiths, braziers and barbers) of the Town of Speyer, 1553.

Products of the trade

The creation of pewterware for display purposes was certainly not the predominating activity and also not of equal importance in every period but yet deserves to be mentioned once more. This is because of the significant artistic value of the salvers, plates, bowls and tankards which were produced during the Renaissance from engraved or etched moulds. Centres for this artistic work established themselves particularly in Lyons, Montbéliard, Strasbourg and, above all, Nuremberg. In a few towns of Saxony lead or bronze plaques by the modeller Peter Flötner were used as patterns for pewter castings. These were then soldered onto undecorated pieces with meticulous competence and ability to blend them in or which also in themselves formed the exterior castings for drinking-vessels. In the case of these artisans there are incontestably valid grounds for designating these items as "noble pewter" in conjunction with pieces of the latter which they produced. The information usually disclosed today even for utilitarian pewterware as to the master's name read from the touch mark serves reliably to date a piece and incidentally makes possible a comparison of styles from workshop to workshop but must basically not be taken as signifying a particular individual's production. Also dedicated to display are those romantic products which appeared in the second half of the 19th century, flagons and tankards in relief, amongst other individualistic serving and drinking vessels, ostentatiously engraved, together with decorated plates and similar articles. They were, moreover, usually given ambiguous marks often borrowed from fantasy.

A certain type of dish which did not require any particular skill either for preparation of the mould or for casting is a peculiarity among display items. These derive their visual appeal from the hand of the engraver who lavishly and pleasingly embellished them all over with coats-of-arms, depictions of flora and fauna amongst other subjects, whereby those decorated at Ulm (Wurttemberg) are outstanding. The name serving or kitchen-dish in fact suggests a utilitarian purpose which is, however, inappropriate.

Pewterware made to the orders of guilds and municipal councils has a display character combined with a functional purpose. The intention here is to symbolize authority, worth, affluence and power and pewterware can indeed perform this. Drinking-vessels in a wide variety of shapes were among the possessions of every guild and took a place of honour at the release of apprentices, installation of masters or the regular meetings of the guild masters on quarter days or on festive occasions. The oldest vessels designed for pouring are the so-called *schleifkannen*, exceedingly richly engraved in a style of particular artistic value which emerged in the late 15th century and of which a few examples survive to the present day. Their German name, in use from ancient times, at first possibly only for wooden jugs permits of several interpretations: it may refer to the need for a powerful push on the handle of the flagon, up to three quarters of a meter tall or the *schleifen*, the escape or release of candidates upon release from articles of apprenticeship or promotion to master. *Schleifen* embraces all kinds of mischief inflicted upon the candidates in which beer and wine play a major role. Because the heavy flagons could only be lifted with difficulty when full they were pulled across the table to the edge or in front of the thirsty participant who could then fill his beaker by means of a tap. This sliding to-and-fro may also have contributed to determine their name. Whilst the *schleifkannen* were serving-vessels from which one could help oneself to beer or wine from a tap—or with handy jugs—a different traditional drinking-vessel was carried direct to the mouth. The name of this container in itself betrays its festive purpose, it is the "welcome". From the beginning of the 17th century increasingly more orders for these drinking-cups came into pewterers' workshops especially as many guilds appeared to be in need of up to half-a-dozen of them. At times also it was fashionable for the guilds to be presented with "welcome" cups by outsiders and many an aspirant solicited "fine weather" for his next master's petition by making a gift of such a vessel to the guild. The "welcome" survived as a ceremonial drinking vessel until the dissolution of the guilds. During the centuries of its history the classic basic shape of the cup was often altered or departed from in curious ways as, for instance, when a butchers' company had the "welcome" fashioned in the form of a sow or that of the fishermen as a pewter trout.

Guilds' arms which were either hung outside or were displayed on the table reserved for special guests in the guild's local hostelry were likewise the guild's collective property as were the drinking-beakers of the individual masters. It is probable that upon admission into a guild the master purchased his own beaker and had it engraved with the name of the guild as owners. Whereas the pewter "welcome" is recognizable by its shape and inscriptions as a typical guild possession, in the case of beakers, *humpen* and tankards this can only be read from the inscriptions. Pewterers produced such items from the same moulds as those for everyday use. The same applies to the so-called *ratskannen* (council jugs) which bear the frequently reproduced town coat-of-arms as an indication of their symbolic function. *Ratskannen* are known from about 1450 and have an importance comparable to the "welcome" and the *schleifkannen*, namely to greet guests of the municipality, at the sealing of official proceedings or for the serving of drink at banquets. Swiss pewterers evolved manifold and pleasing pieces which now and again may well have been cast from moulds previously created for display items.

Among pewterers' products was the plate for ecclesiastical purposes, often in greater, then less in demand. The Church Councils sometimes expressly permitted the use of pewterware by their servants, the next Council banned it from churches and demanded silver or even gold. The use of pewterware outside the churches themselves, as for example when visiting the sick was then, of course, not necessarily forbidden. For this reason the re-

When one day I came to Nuremberg
I went into a shop
In which I saw all the goods
White like silver, so bright and clear,
All kinds of drinking-vessels to be seen
So skilful, artistic and decorative
That I immediately greeted the old shop-keeper
And asked him not to be out-of-sorts with me
But rather to relate to me of
Which craft he was a master,
He answered: Know that I am a pewterer
And make candlesticks and tankards
Of pewter in the round and flat,
Artistically engraved with
Picture-work, foliage and flowers,
Jugs with spouts also come from here,
Pouring jugs with which princes are served
And lights which are suspended,
Bowls, hammered and unhammered
In which one carries food,
Mustard pots and bowls with ears,
Dish plates for those in child-bed,
plates and large chargers
Upon which one carries fish and roast,
And also the English dishes,
Also jugs which stand on three feet,
Flagons together with pewter jugs
Which are only used for beer . . .

"Der Kandelgiessersspruech" (The pewterer's words) by Hans Sachs after a German version of the work of 1560.

peated changes of policy were of no special importance to the trade, particularly as the requirements of the Church were not very great. Orders of course increased significantly during or after times of war as a result of plundering and deprivation. Pewter vessels for the celebration of Holy Communion and for the christening of children were those mainly in demand. These comprised a screw-closured flask for keeping the Communion wine, the cups and their patens, jugs for pouring the water into the pewter baptismal font to be blessed and also for dispensing wine to the assembled congregation. The flask and jug did not differ from those in everyday use and their special function was disclosed only by their engraving. Items having a characteristic appearance were pyxes and ciboria for keeping the consecrated bread, the holy water stoups (which are also found in the households of Catholic families and are utilitarian articles used in everyday family life) as well as oil jugs for anointing the sick. Small measuring jugs can also be recognized as ecclesiastical pieces by their shape.

At various times, particularly during the Baroque period, altar candlesticks were given an appearance differing from that of secular candlesticks. Taken generally, the size of candlesticks indicates their purpose; a further difference between candlesticks for spiritual and temporal use will be discussed later.

The production of functional devices for domestic lighting was one of the exercises of the pewterer from at least the 14th century. For this the candlestick was at all times the most important component but there were also a variety of additional devices. Even chandeliers were produced in a few places. Wall-sconces from whose production various masters hoped for a profitable trade, were also equipped with candles. An economical form of lighting was offered in town and country by the manufacture of oil-lamps, with and without hour-glass.

Amongst functional pewter the variety of eating and drinking equipment may well be historically the oldest and was certainly the most diverse. Plates, chargers and bowls, containers for every imaginable purpose, tureens and dishes, the latter in particularly wide variety for spices which were much used, ladles and spoons are wares typically made for table and board. Added to these in certain decades were dish-stands, heaters, bottle-coasters and even serviette-rings. Tankards, jugs and beakers were available in infinite variety at every period. Much less long-lived were pewter cups and likewise those serving-vessels which could only evolve when the appropriate comestibles became known and available in Europe: coffee-pots and *chocolatières*.

Pewter implements were used in the kitchen. Pots, sieves, colanders, funnels, spoon-racks and a variety of measures are among sought-after items. Kitchen equipment was completed with boxes, flasks, casks and many other storage containers which all represented work for the pewterer.

Those craftsmen are called pewter-founders and jug-founders, Latin stannatores, French potiers d'étain, who make all kinds of ware, house and kitchen equipment and other goods of pewter such as jugs, pots, basins for convenience of washing hands and for soaping linen, deep and flat ones, large and small bowls and plates of all kinds, spoons, forks, salt-tubs, pails, pans, syringes, writing-stands, chalices, beakers, covers, monstrances, crosses, candelabra, lamps, flasks, candlesticks, etc., either themselves or made by others, in order to sell them on or to buy for themselves.

J. H. Zedler, *Grosses vollständiges Universallexikon aller Wissenschaften und Künste*, Leipzig and Halle, 1749.

Functional pewter was even available for hygienic purposes at an early date as, for example, wall water-kegs, soap-boxes and shaving-mugs. Even chamber-pots in many households were of pewter. Bodily care was served by cupping-(blood-letting) bowls, enema-syringes and hot-water-bottles. Pewter buttons and buckles were in demand for clothing, belts and shoes—pewterers supplied them, often in acrimonious competition with button-makers. Roofing-tiles were occasionally of pewter and gutters, pipes and water-taps were made of the same material together with window-fasteners, thimbles and mounts for tobacco-pipes.

Beyond doubt, the production of secular goods determined the nature of the pewter trade in every period. Utilitarian pewter will now be considered, sub-divided into its various—albeit interlinked—functions in the everyday-life of the people, of which festive occasions also formed part.

Tableware

2

When at the time of the declining Middle Ages the discovery and recovery of tin from the deposits of the Erzgebirge offered an opportunity to win tin more cheaply and in greater quantity, a development had taken place at table or board in many of the countries of Europe which greatly favoured the potential exploitation of this opportunity. Numerous rules for "manners and moderation at table" in England, Holland, France and Germany indeed prescribed that each person should have his own bowl and spoon so that too many persons should not each have to reach for one dish of meat and, if feasible, each his own beaker. Breakfast, midday meal and evening supper had established themselves as regular repasts; occasional refreshments were probably taken between meals as part of good manners. There is indisputably a close connection between more refined table habits and an increased use of tableware of which at first only plate, dish and bowl were known. Thus as in course of time tableware became more varied, pewterers' product ranges were also extended. Finally there was hardly an article of tableware which was not produced in pewter. For a long period demand for pewter tableware was encouraged by regulations which particularly guaranteed best quality material in this field (i.e. tableware). In 1770, for example, it was laid down for the entire Kingdom of Bohemia that tableware was to be made of pure tin without the addition of any lead.

Rigid distinctions between plates, chargers and dishes are neither possible nor necessary for early times nor for the present day; in this section flat food receptacles (plates and chargers) will be dealt with first, then bowls and the closely related dishes and tureens as well as further tableware.

Plates and chargers

Today there is probably no longer anything which can tell us when the first pewter plates were used at table. About one hundred years ago the Frenchman, Germain Bapst wrote in his book *Etain* that pewter plates had found admission into monasteries and private households already before the Crusades. Even if this may sporadically have been so, any proof is lacking. Square or round flat wooden trenchers were, however, certainly used until well into the 16th century. Wooden trencher boards originated from the bread slice which was customary for hundreds of years and as *tellerbrote* (breaden plates) served as an absorbent underlay for mealtime dishes. The pewter plates which are rendered in paintings from Gothic times also have the appearance of discs or flat roundels but of these none have survived. These paintings nevertheless reveal that wooden platters were merely imitated in pewter and that independent shapes only developed gradually. The round, as well as the later square flat plates were probably not produced by casting in a mould but were beaten from thin pewter sheet which had itself been cast between two fireproof blocks. At this period, in certain districts even deep plates were made by beating with a hammer. In Posen (now Poznań) they formed part of the masterpiece after an ordinance of 1555. Later,
25 plates belonged generally to what was called by pewterers "flatware", that
24 is, among those vessels which were cast in one piece. The square flat plates of the 16th century are among the oldest surviving flatware.

Although in Gothic times there was already a tendency towards the evo-
27 lution of the shape of plate which is regarded as typical today, its widespread distribution came only in the 17th century. Regional variations were naturally determined by many factors, as for instance in Hungary, where square or polygonal flat plates were still not uncommon even in the 17th century. Which factors combined and above all, how the separate changes in shape developed from the flat roundel or square to the narrow-rimmed plate with deep bowl to the well-known broad-rimmed plates and then to the familiar everyday pattern, is difficult to establish retrospectively today.

Plates are those articles of utilitarian pewter which suffer most punishment and because of this old examples have survived much more rarely than tankards or jugs from early times. Many a thrifty housewife even provided her plates with wooden inserts to protect the pewter from excessively rough knife cuts although because they came to table up to three times daily, severe marks of use necessarily appeared. When the plates then became unsightly, there would be a pewterer ready to scrape them, but the melting pot was nevertheless waiting so that one day they might re-appear in a new shape.

At table, you must not bore your knife into the table-top or your plate, nor scrape it and you must show good manners by moderation . . .

Instruction for behaviour at table, *c.* 1400.

The co-existence of angular and round plates can be established from various documents, as for example in an inventory of 1566 from the monastery of St. Stephen in Strasbourg which mentions "ein Eckecht zinnen dischteller und sechzehn breyte zynen deller uf sohsschissel art und gemach"

(freely translated: "a pewter table plate with corners and sixteen broad pewter plates made in the style of sauce bowls"). "Broad pewter plates" refers
26 to the wide-rimmed serving-dishes, called *kardinaalsschotel* in Holland because they resembled an upturned cardinal's hat. This type of plate appeared in many European countries. It was used in Westphalia as a dish for ham to serve prepared ham on festive occasions and the term "charger", commonly used in England, is indicative in referring to its use as a carrier for food. Owners' coats-of-arms engraved on plates produced even in the 17th and partly in the 18th century mostly indicate a socially well-placed class. Many pewterers specialized in consolidating articles like broad-rimmed plates with systematically applied hammer blows, thus to obtain increased strength. These specialized tradesmen (hammermen) were in Germany called "kandel"-beaters; they were relatively numerous in France. Hammermen struck their master's touch on the readily accessible rim of the "cardinal's hat" which encouraged a particularly deep and clear impression from the punch. When broad-rimmed plates come to light today which have blurred, unclear marks the suspicion of forgery is not far off.

At the time of the "cardinal's hat" pewter plates were still a rarity in the daily life of the people at large; wooden tableware prevailed as in the past. Even in famous hostelries, wooden ware predominated, as for instance in the widely renowned Zurich hotel "Zum Schwert", which in 1611 possessed more than 100 wooden but only 40 pewter plates. However, the rising middle-classes valued being able to dine off pewter plates; even officials travelling in the course of their duty took it amiss if they were not served upon fine pewterware. Communities in the Mark of Brandenburg made it their duty at the time of church visitations to provide the pastor's house with two or three pewter plates and, of course, the tankards to go with them. Silverware would have been preferable but especially after the Thirty Years' War would have been an excessive burden for small rural communities. Only, in fact, about 1700 did it become possible and in the opinion of the well-to-do upper classes, necessary because of the more widespread distribution of pewterware for table and board by then. At that time a plate, a dish and a bowl, all of pewter, were, as in the past, among the valued items specifically mentioned
28/29 in wills whose future owners were precisely stipulated in the often large families. Pewter plates and dishes were among the most honoured prizes at *schützenfests*, the target shooting festivals. In many districts of Germany they were known as *vorteilsteller*—advantage or winners' plates—and as *schiessblättli* (little shooting plates) in Switzerland, whereby in good times even children might win a small pewter plate and adults gain a splendidly engraved charger which usually no longer fulfilled any practical purpose but
282 was a wall decoration. If there was a particular wish to please bridal couples or young parents, plates and chargers or even a tankard were wedding or baptismal gifts. It gradually became customary to have pewter engraved with

Another, who has stolen a pewter plate, shall be put in the pillory for one hour with the plate upon his back and then be outlawed from town and country.

Town Council minute, Dortmund, 1725.

initials or names, dates and depictions appropriate to the occasion; this
35 practice reached its peak among country people between about 1750 and
1830. In many places these pewter plates and chargers were made use of at
one and the same time to encourage a small pecuniary donation for the couple from the assembled guests. For this, the wedding pair sat at a table and
spread a cloth over a plate or charger under cover of which each guest
should contribute his mite.

This custom, formerly known as *weisen* in Germany was intended to alleviate the expense of the wedding. If there was a number of well-disposed
and affluent guests, not only was a significant sum of money collected but
sometimes also, thanks to the chargers and plates which were donated, the
basis of a complete pewter service which consisted of a dozen each of small
and large plates together with twelve dishes of various types.

In England, France and Germany the production of large plates or
chargers was frequently part of the masterpiece. They were sold by pewter-
30/31 ers under the name of roast-plates or roast-dishes and are described as
large plates or flattened dishes with a narrow rim upon which the roast could
be carried and conveniently portioned. Even in less affluent families consumption of meat was greater during the 17th and 18th centuries than in later
times and even venison was relatively easy to come by. This explains why in
about 1650 Parisian pewterers specialized in the manufacture of *plats de ve-
naison*, that is game, which were soon copied elsewhere under the name of
"Louis XIV plates". Fish was served on large oval dishes which were wel-
41 comed at Christmas time for heaping up butter *stolle* (yeast-cake with cur-
42 rants, almonds and peel). Smaller dishes held special accompaniments or
seasonings for the meal. In the centre of many plates and dishes was a
32 raised boss. It has yet to be determined whether plates and dishes with a
boss had any specific function at table; maybe one simply took pleasure in
their attractive appearance which in no way detracted from their functional
purpose. Vessels with a boss in the centre were to be found in every country
with a pewterworking trade from the end of the Middle Ages until the 17th
century; later they become rarer.

To prevent to some extent food becoming cold, from about the Rococo
period pewterers offered two products which enjoyed varying popularity
—plates with covers and hot-plates. For easier handling the plates with cov-
40/43 ers were furnished with a pair of handles, the shape of which was at the same
time purposeful and ornamentally scrolled. The cover, made with a series of
steps, was provided with a detachable handle and was high enough that
when necessary the plate could hold even large portions. Those made in
Karlsbad (now Karlovy Vary) enjoyed a particularly favourable reputation and
became a regularly successful export. Plates and chargers were also produced there, including some with small feet (usually three) which made flat
pieces, which had no handles, easier to lift up and put down. Simply as an ex-

To make sweet gravy for wild boar

Let it seethe in half wine and water, grate into it bread-crust and a little good spiced cake, fry it brown in lard, pour into it the gravy in which the meat has cooked, so that it passes through a strainer, add ginger, pepper, cloves and sugar, let it simmer, lay the game in a pewter dish, pour the gravy over it, the gravy must be somewhat thick.

Cookery recipe, 1724.

To roast green morels

Take them and make them clean, salt and pepper them well / let them stand for an hour afterwards / make clean small skewers and impale them so that some skewers are filled, next lay them on the grill, baste them well with fresh butter / let them become crisp outside and lay them in a warm pewter dish and put a warm pewter cover over them.

Cookery recipe, 1720.

ample of the considerable influence of Karlsbad on the general design of pewter in the 18th century the name of Sebastian Faerber may be mentioned, a journeyman from Mainz: when he returned home after seven years work in Karlsbad and set about becoming a master, he asked the Archbishop of Mainz whether, instead of the usual masterpiece, he might be permitted to carry out his work "in an entirely new way" according to the skills which he had learned.

One must, however, take care that such a fricassé from goat meat comes warm to the table since it may not be put upon any coal fire, otherwise the eggs will coagulate, but safely upon a pewter pot filled with simmering water, by which means one is able to keep it well and warm until later.

Cookery instruction, 1730.

Far less in demand than plates with covers were the products which emerged in the 18th century and were offered under various names as hot-plates. These were of pewter, in the shape of normal plates, chargers and bowls which were double-walled. The double skin allowed them to be filled with hot water, the heat of which counteracted the tendency of food to grow cold. The cost of these was, however, simply too great to make this innovation generally popular in the home. Whilst a single example—often a large
38/55 charger—was sometimes acquired, hardly ever a complete set of plates, because dishes with covers were in fact more useful.

During the Rococo period many pewterers saw themselves as producers of *bürgersilber*—silver for the middle-classes—and imitated the designs then current for silverware. Suitably curvaceous plates and chargers and
33/34 those with gadrooned borders therefore appeared. Many such wavy-edged wares are in circulation today described as "baroque" plates; a great part of them was made before the first World War or wholly at the present time. To some extent there was still profitable business to be done in "pap-plates"
37 even after pottery and porcelain had confirmed their supremacy. Pap means the puree or pulp, especially of vegetables, principally fed to small children. This type of plate is without a rim and with a small standing-ring and its size is smaller than normal eating plates. Their advantage over pottery plates was that they were unbreakable. Influenced by their favourable experience with pap-plates, from the beginning of the 19th century pewterers experimentally produced plates which were comparatively deep with a flat rim parallel to the
39 bottom which closely resemble today's china soup-plates; they were not, however, much used in the home.

Bowls, dishes and tureens

In pewterers' terminology bowls are usually vessels with a deep bottom and more or less steep sides which are used for serving foodstuffs. Tureens are therefore also a kind of bowl. Indeed the term "bowl" is wide embracing in its general meaning. In different regions various special names became established for this kind of vessel or for definite types of them. Soup-tureen is the most frequent description for the largest examples, *assiettes* are the small and shallower pieces. Other names which all stand for utilitarian bowls are (in German) *kump*, *vat*, *kar* or *kerlin*. In contrast to these, "parlour-bowls" or "trisoir-bowls" mean those which were displayed in the living-room as show pieces and virtually never came to table. Because of them many families acquired feather-dusters which were known as pewter-dusters. These were of ostrich feathers tied together in a bundle and equipped with a long handle which were used for dusting pewterware.

The ages and variety of bowls are great; the oldest to survive are from the
44/45 3rd to 5th centuries. There is documentary evidence of their extensive use at banquets during Romanesque and Gothic times. In the year 1600, in spite of strong protests from the local guild, Peter Fischbach, a merchant in Frankfurt-on-Main had a considerable stock of Nuremberg pewter, including seven hundredweight of bowls alone. In the 17th and 18th centuries, military units were sometimes equipped from similar dealers' stocks because one or even two pewter bowls were often included in army equipment, that is among the standard accoutrements of every soldier. Bowls were for a time exceedingly popular as New Year and wedding gifts. In America they were offered by some masters worked in relief, which demanded particular skill and a considerable outlay and which emphasizes the desirability of these products.

46/52 At the present day a type of bowl is frequently encountered which is usually described as a potato- or steep-sided bowl and is often provided with a
47/54 cover. Now and again the cover is either engraved or decorated in relief. In certain areas, for example in Germany in the Bergisches Land and in Estonia they were referred to as rice-bowls or *köngs*. The name potato-bowl came into use early in the 19th century when potatoes became the principal everyday food in many countries. Although they had been cultivated in large quantities in Saxony from 1717, in Prussia from 1738 and in France from about 1760 during the period which followed gruel or pap together with flat bread remained the predominant daily fare. In eastern and southern Europe it was prepared from millet, elsewhere from oats and wheat and was served in Germany as *klinkerkost, klicker* or *klunker*-gruel in pewter pap-bowls of similar
51 type to the steep-sided bowls, which were also made with a segmented rim and from which over a long period the common people used to feed communally.

Originally it was the practice only at princely tables that guests at least shared a pewter bowl in pairs. It was only in about 1650 that people began in substantial farmers' houses to go over to an individual bowl for the chief personages at mealtimes.

Large potage-tureens frequently stood on the table when flat bread was eaten. Potage was a dish of all kinds of ingredients, mainly meat or fish with a variety of spices. From about 1750 bowls were made in France and Belgium
55 which were also *réchauds*, that is, which kept food hot. *Tinnen fatts* (pewter tubs) came into use in Westphalia. The knife marks on these bowls indicate how diligently morsels of the boiled smoked meat, bacon and sausage were cut-off as they went round the table. In more affluent circles sugar-cake was
50 sometimes laid out in pewter bowls for dessert.

In most households there is concern to keep all the bowls of the same size. It is better to have some larger, some smaller ones. Foodstuffs which are not liked for eating must be served in the latter. Because those who are being served become immediately discouraged by the appearance of their customary larger bowls filled with unpopular food, their first thought is that they will be emptied as little as usual. If, however, a smaller bowl is arranged for serving such food, people are pleased in a certain way because they can see in advance that it will be possible for them to finish the dish.

Allg. System der Hauswirtschaft (General system of domestic management), Berlin, 1790.

24 Rectangular flat plate; 15×11 cm ($5\frac{7}{8}'' \times 4\frac{3}{8}''$), 16th century.
Stedelijk Museum, Alkmaar (Netherlands)

25 Rectangular flat plate; length 15.7 cm ($6\frac{1}{4}''$), 16th century.
Museum Boymans-van Beuningen, Rotterdam

25

26 Broad-rimmed plate, so-called cardinal's hat, with owner's coat-of-arms and initials on the rim; diameter 35 cm ($13^{7}/_{8}$″), *c.* 1690.
The pewter marks on this kind of piece are usually struck on the edge.
In private ownership

27 Round plate with narrow rim; diameter 20.5 cm (8″), 15th century.
Stedelijk Museum, Alkmaar

28/29 Records of inheritances with an exposition of the pewter goods and their contemporary value; *c.* 1760.
In private ownership

27

83.

... zeigen 13 Loth
das Loth à ...
gerechnet . . . | 5: 10 —

Serre

Cap: III.

Arbeiten und Kün-
ste

1. Sechs Mittelschüsseln
2. Drey kleine Zimmer
schüsseln
3. Eine ... und ...
Kalte Teller
4. Eine Leuchter
5. Ein Zimmer ...
6. Ein dergl. ...
7. Ein ...
zusammen ...
... 62 Loth ...
... daran
ein Zimmer ...
und 3. dergleichen
Teller ...
... Küchen
abgegeben ...
... welche 6 Loth
zeigen ...
...

Fr: Maria Elisabeth Schä-
...

ex Cap: 7.

Item

2 fl. 14 gr. — 1 Dutzend Teller 12 Loth.
à 4 gr.

3. 4. —. 6 Küchenschüsseln
10 Loth.

3. 17. —. 2. ... Kannen
und 2. ...
... 20 Loth.

—. 14. —. 2. ... 2½ Loth.

—. 20. —. 1 Leuchter und 1 ...
... 5 Loth.

11 fl. —. —.

Hr. ... Gottlieb
und ... Jungfer
...

ex cap: 7.

Item

2 fl. 14 gr. — 1 Dutz. Teller 12 Loth à 4 gr.

3. 1. —. 6 St. Schüsseln 10 Loth.

—. 20. —. 2 St. Leuchter 1 ...
... 5 Loth.

6 fl. 14 gr. —

G L

30 French venison dish; diameter 50 cm ($19^{5}/_{8}''$); 17th century.
Musée communal, Huy

31 Roast-plate and cylindrical tankards; diameter of the plate 41.5 cm ($16^{3}/_{8}''$), 18th century.
In private ownership

32 Bowl with centre boss and plate with wide rim; diameters 34 and 25 cm ($13^{3}/_{8}''$ and $9^{7}/_{8}''$), *c.* 1700.
In private ownership

32

33

34

33 Plate with spirally gadrooned rim; diameter 22 cm ($8^5/_8$″), *c.* 1780.
In private ownership

34 Wavy-edged plate, so-called Baroque plate; diameter 23.5 cm ($9^1/_4$″), 2nd half of the 18th century.
In private ownership

35 Plate with vernacular engraving, executed by the technique known as wriggle-work; diameter 34 cm ($13^3/_8$″), dated 1823.
In private ownership

1823

36

37 38
39 40

36 Bowl with arched bottom and four spoons; diameter 41 cm ($16^{1}/_{8}''$), dated 1851. In private ownership

37 Pap-plate; diameter 21 cm ($8^{1}/_{4}''$), *c.* 1780. Staatliches Heimat- und Schlossmuseum Burgk/ Saale

38 Hot-plate; diameter 25 cm (10″), *c.* 1840. Schlossmuseum Altenburg

39 Deep plate; diameter 23.5 cm ($9^{1}/_{4}''$), dated 1829. Städtisches Museum Halberstadt

40 Detail of Fig. 43: So that the sometimes heavy covered plates can be carried safely, the handles are joined to the edge of the plate with separate fillets. A strut gives rigidity and a pleasing appearance to the handle itself.

41 Oval multi-purpose charger for roasts, fish, Christmas cake and so on; length 52 cm ($20^{1}/_{2}''$), dated 1848. Kreisheimatmuseum Grimma (Saxony)

42 Multi-purpose dish; length 38 cm (15″), dated 1799. Museum "Schloss Moritzburg", Zeitz (Saxony)

43 Two plates with loose tiered covers, cast in Karlsbad (Karlovy Vary); diameter 32 cm ($12^{5}/_{8}''$), *c.* 1750. The handles on the edge of the plate are solidly cast on, the one on the cover swivels. Staatliches Heimat- und Schlossmuseum Burgk/ Saale

44

45

46

44 Bowl with wide rim; diameter 11.3 cm ($4^1/_2$"), A.D. 300–500. British Museum, London

45 Footed bowl; diameter 19.5 cm ($7^5/_8$"), A.D. 300–500. British Museum, London

46 Steep-sided bowl; height 9.8 cm ($3^7/_8$"), diameter 31.5 cm ($12^3/_8$"), 1st half of the 19th century. Städtisches Museum Halberstadt

47

48

49

47 Covered steep-sided bowl with a sphinx to adorn the cover; diameter 13 cm ($5^1/_8$″), *c.* 1820. Traditionsstätte Erzbergbau, Aue (Saxony)

48 Porringer; diameter 15.5 cm ($6^1/_8$″), *c.* 1600. Museum Boymans-van Beuningen, Rotterdam

49 Porringer; diameter 11.5 cm ($4^1/_2$″), *c.* 1782. One of the two ears is in the form of a ring to enable the porringer to be hung up when not in use. Nordiska Museet, Stockholm

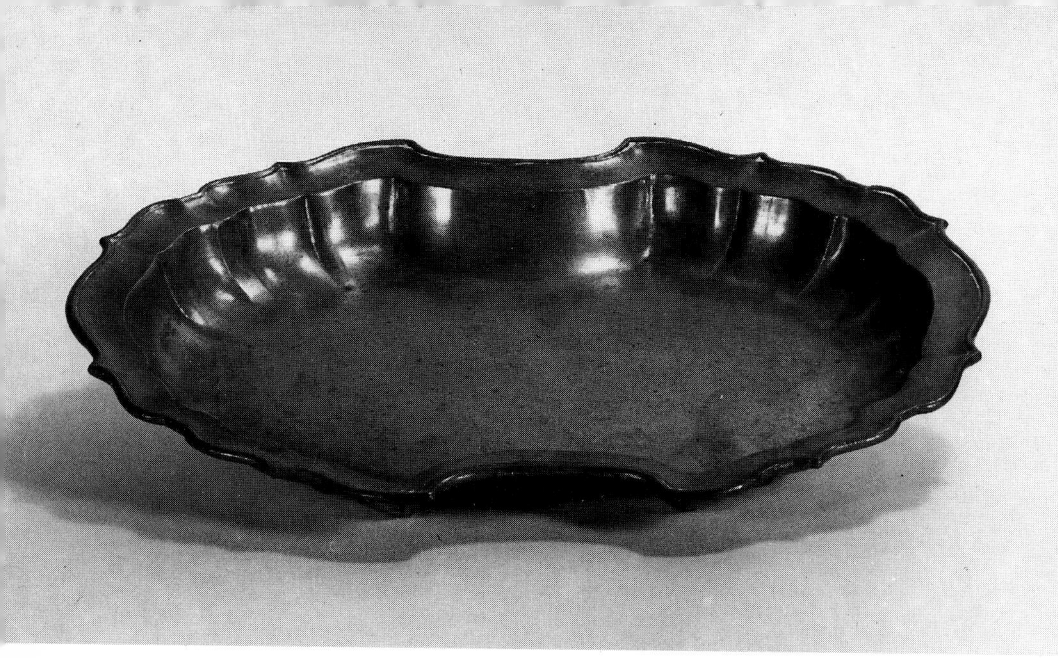

50 Dish for pastries and other dainties; length 28 cm (11″), 2nd half of the 18th century.
Staatliches Heimat- und Schlossmuseum Burgk/Saale

51 Pap-bowl with segmented edge; diameter 19 cm ($7^1/_2$″), dated 1832.
Heimatmuseum Mühlhausen/Thuringia

52 Steep-sided bowl; diameter 36 cm ($14^1/_8$″), dated 1819.
In private ownership

53 Serviette ring; diameter 5 cm (2″), 19th century.
In private ownership

54 Covered straight-sided bowl; diameter 32 cm ($12^5/_8$″), *c.* 1820.
Gedenkstätte Crimmitschauer Textilarbeiterstreik 1903/04, Crimmitschau

55 Hot-water dish; diameter 33.8 cm ($13^3/_8$″), 1st half of the 19th century.
Vogtländisches Kreismuseum Plauen

53

56 Midwife's bowl with cover-plate and decorated knop-feet; length 34.5 cm (13$^{5}/_{8}$″), *c.* 1743. Kunstindustrimuseet Oslo

57 Midwife's bowl with cover-plate and knop-feet; diameter 21.3 cm (8$^{3}/_{8}$″), *c.* 1735. Nationalmuseet Copenhagen

58 Midwife's bowl with hinged cover and stay; height 19.8 cm (7$^{7}/_{8}$″), *c.*1745. Norsk Folkemuseum Oslo

57

59 Bowl with one ear (porringer); diameter 14 cm ($5^1/_2$″), *c.* 1775. Virginia Museum of Fine Arts, Richmond

60 Porringer; diameter 18 cm (7″), dated 1792. In private ownership

61 Hospital-bowls and spoons; diameter 21 cm ($8^1/_4$″), *c.* 1800. Museum "Schloss Moritzburg", Zeitz

62 Scandinavian porringer with base-ring; diameter 22 cm ($8^5/_8$″), *c.* 1746. Suomen Kansallismuseo Helsinki

61

62

63

64

65

63 Small tureen; height 18 cm (7″), *c.* 1800. In private ownership

64 Sauce-boat; height 10.5 cm ($4^{1}/_{8}''$), *c.* 1830. Kreisheimatmuseum Grimma

65 Basin with handles; diameter 16 cm ($6^{1}/_{4}''$), *c.* 1830. Traditionsstätte Erzbergbau, Aue

66 Four-tiered food-carrier; height 29 cm ($11^{3}/_{8}''$), *c.* 1817. Nordiska Museet, Stockholm

67 Tureens; height 28 and 26 cm (11″ and 10 1/4″), end 18th/beginning 19th centuries.
Staatliches Heimat- und Schlossmuseum Burgk/Saale

68 Pastry pan; diameter 14 cm (5 1/2″), end of the 18th century.
Kreisheimatmuseum Grimma

68

69 Round tureen; height 21.5 cm ($8^1/_2$″), dated 1804. Kulturhistorisches Museum Rostock

70 Round tureen with a boss on its lid and drop-handles; height 31.5 cm ($12^3/_8$″), *c.* 1790. Kulturhistorisches Museum Rostock

70

71 Sugar-bowl with spoon-rack; height 20.3 cm (8″), 18th century. Österreichisches Museum für angewandte Kunst, Vienna

72 Stand with four scallop-shaped dishes, on ball-feet; height 28 cm (11″), dated 1786. Museum "Schloss Moritzburg", Zeitz

73 Epergne; height 23 cm (9″), *c.* 1750. Museum des Kunsthandwerks, Leipzig

71

72

74 Sweet-dish with segmented edge; height 6.8 cm ($2^5/_8$"), dated 1798.
Heimatmuseum Mühlhausen/Thuringia

75 North German brandy-cup, known as *kolleschal*; height 12 cm ($4^5/_8$"), 18th century.
Museum für Deutsche Volkskunde, West Berlin

75

76 Sweet dish *(schauer)*; height 15 cm ($5^{7}/_{8}$″), 2nd half of the 18th century.
Museum "Schloss Moritzburg", Zeitz

77 Sugar-dish; height 12 cm ($4^{3}/_{4}$″), 1st half of the 19th century.
Vogtländisches Kreismuseum Plauen

78 Sugar-dish; height 14 cm ($5^{1}/_{2}$″), *c.* 1790.
Gedenkstätte Crimmitschauer Textilarbeiterstreik 1903/04, Crimmitschau

76

79

80

79 Cheese-dish; height 14 cm ($5^1/_2''$), *c.* 1800. Gedenkstätte Crimmitschauer Textilarbeiterstreik 1903/04, Crimmitschau

80 Butter-dish; diameter 20.5 cm (8″), 2nd half of the 18th century. Kulturgeschichtliches Museum Osnabrück

81 Plate with cup-shaped cavities for ten eggs, in the centre a container for salt; diameter 31.5 cm ($12^3/_8''$), 17th century. Nationalmuseet Copenhagen

82

83

84

82 Salt-box with hinged cover, the figure in the form of a lion; 15th century.
Museum Boymans-van Beuningen, Rotterdam

83 Thuringian salt-box; height 5.5 cm ($2^1/_8$"), late 18th century.
Vogtländisches Kreismuseum Plauen

84 Salt-pot, footed; height 6.4 cm ($2^1/_2$"), *c.* 1500.
Stedelijk Museum, Alkmaar

85 Egg-cup; height 7.8 cm (3"), last quarter of the 18th century. When inverted the egg-cup can also be used as a small dish for eating soft-boiled eggs out of their shells.
Vogtländisches Kreismuseum Plauen

86 Salt-box; height 4 cm (2"), dated 1816.
Kulturhistorisches Museum Rostock

87 Spice-dishes, on feet; height 6 and 3.5 cm ($2^3/_8$" and $1^3/_8$"), late 18th century.
Museum "Schloss Moritzburg", Zeitz

88 Sugar-sifter; height 14 cm ($5^1/_2$"), *c.* 1815.
Vogtländisches Kreismuseum Plauen

89 Spice-dishes, each with two compartments with hinged covers; length 7.5 cm (3"), 2nd half of the 18th century.
In private ownership and from the Kreisheimatmuseum Grimma

90 Salt-shaker and salts on feet; height 4.5–8 cm ($1^3/_4$"–$3^1/_8$"), 19th century.
Museum "Schloss Moritzburg", Zeitz

86
87

88
89

90

91

92

91 Spice-stand with three inserts; height 5 cm (2″), 1st half of the 18th century. Gedenkstätte Crimmitschauer Textilarbeiterstreik 1903/04, Crimmitschau

92 Spice-box with eight containers; 1760. Gewerbemuseum der Landesgewerbeanstalt Bayern, Nuremberg

93 Spoon with flattened handle and oval bowl; length 36.2 cm ($14^1/_2$″), dated 1769. Kulturhistorisches Museum Rostock

94 Four spoons, one with engraved bowl; length 16 cm ($6^1/_4$″), *c.* 1800. Museum Weissenfels

95 Spoon with rod-like handle; length 17 cm ($6^5/_8$″), 17th century. Städtisches Museum Halberstadt

93

94

95

96

97

98

96 Mustard-pot with openings for the mustard-spoons on the edge of the cover; height 12 cm ($4^3/_4$″), 1st third of the 19th century.
In private ownership

97 Spice-dish with booted feet; length 17 cm ($6^5/_8$″), dated 1830.
Traditionsstätte Erzbergbau, Aue

98 Footed small spice-bowl; diameter 16 cm ($6^1/_4$″), dated 1721.
Traditionsstätte Erzbergbau, Aue

99 Cruet for vinegar and oil-bottles together with salt-shaker; height 28 cm (11″), late 18th century.
Musées royaux d'Art et d'Histoire, Brussels

100

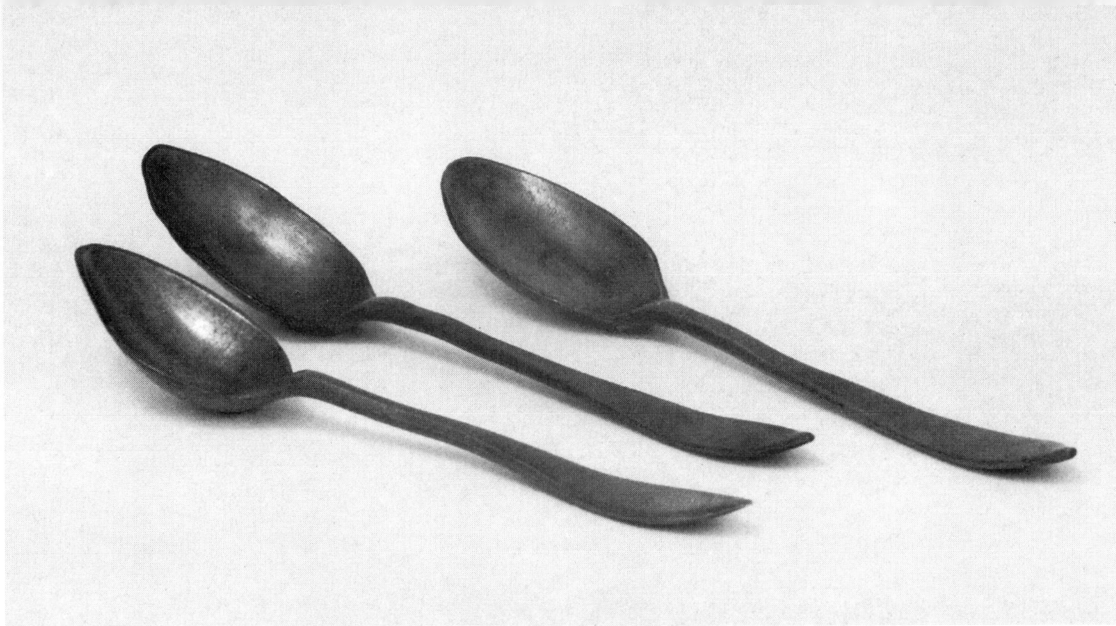

101

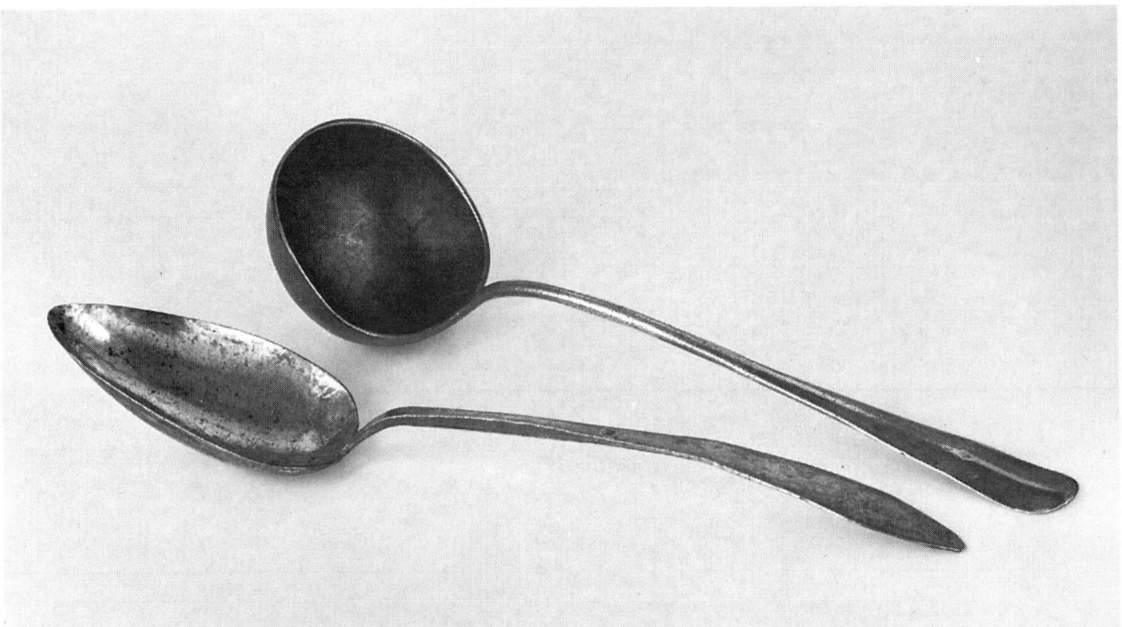

102

100 Children's spoons; length 13.4–14.6 cm ($5^1/_4$"– $5^3/_4$"), 2nd half of the 18th century. Vogtländisches Kreismuseum Plauen

101 Gravy spoon and ladle; length 35 and 33 cm ($13^3/_4$" and 13"), *c.* 1840. In private ownership

102 Spoon-mould of brass; 2nd half of the 17th century. The Henry Francis du Pont Winterthur Museum, Winterthur, Delaware

103 Detail of Fig. 93: owner's engraving in the bowl.

Following page:

104 Basting or serving-spoon; length 17.2 cm ($6^3/_4$"), 18th century. Vogtländisches Kreismuseum Plauen

105 Pastry-slice; length 30.5 cm (12"), *c.* 1840. Heimatmuseum Mühlhausen/Thuringia

106 Soup-ladle; length 34.5 cm ($13^1/_2$"), *c.* 1810. Museum Waldenburg/Saxony

Sophia
Margreta

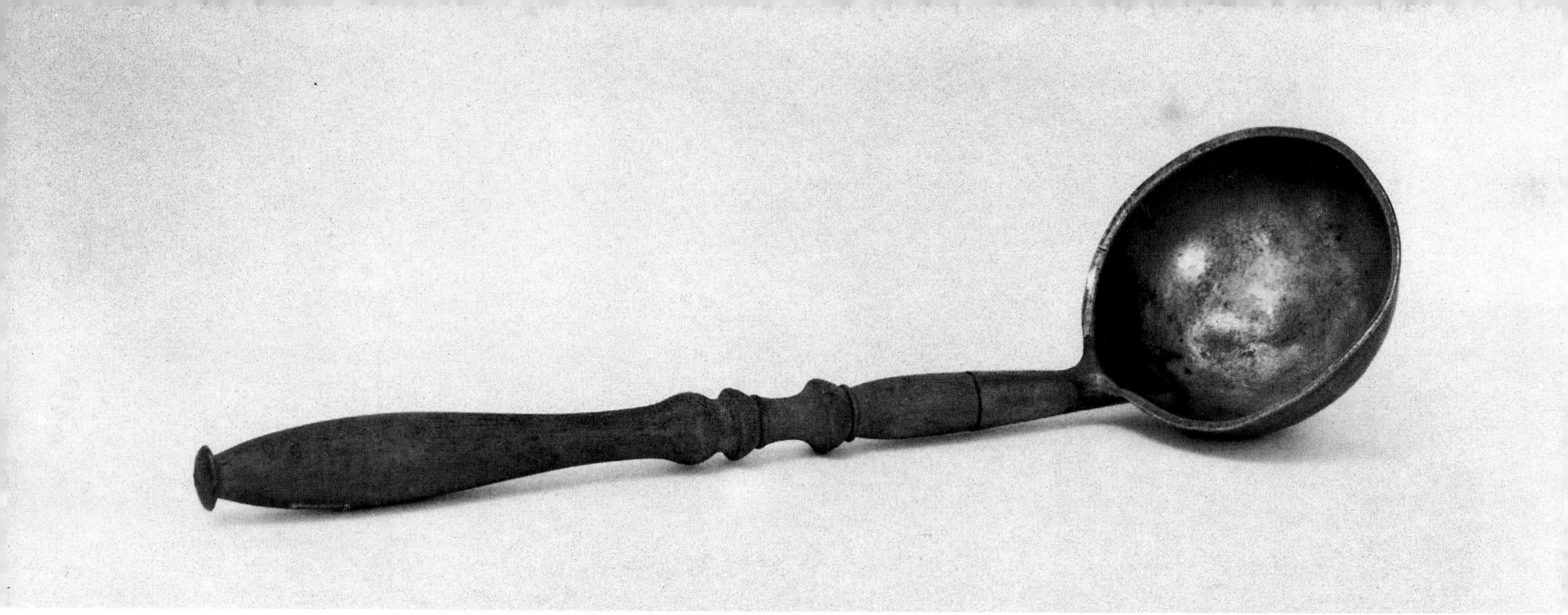
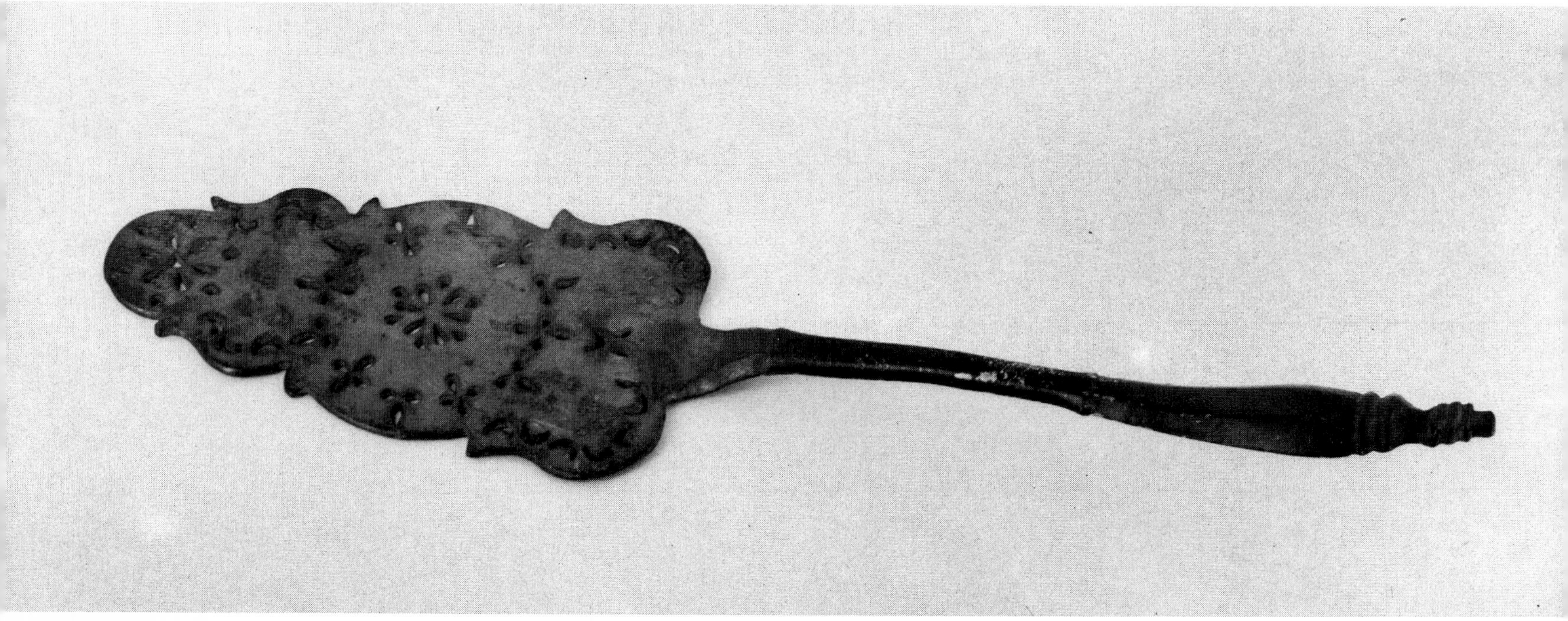
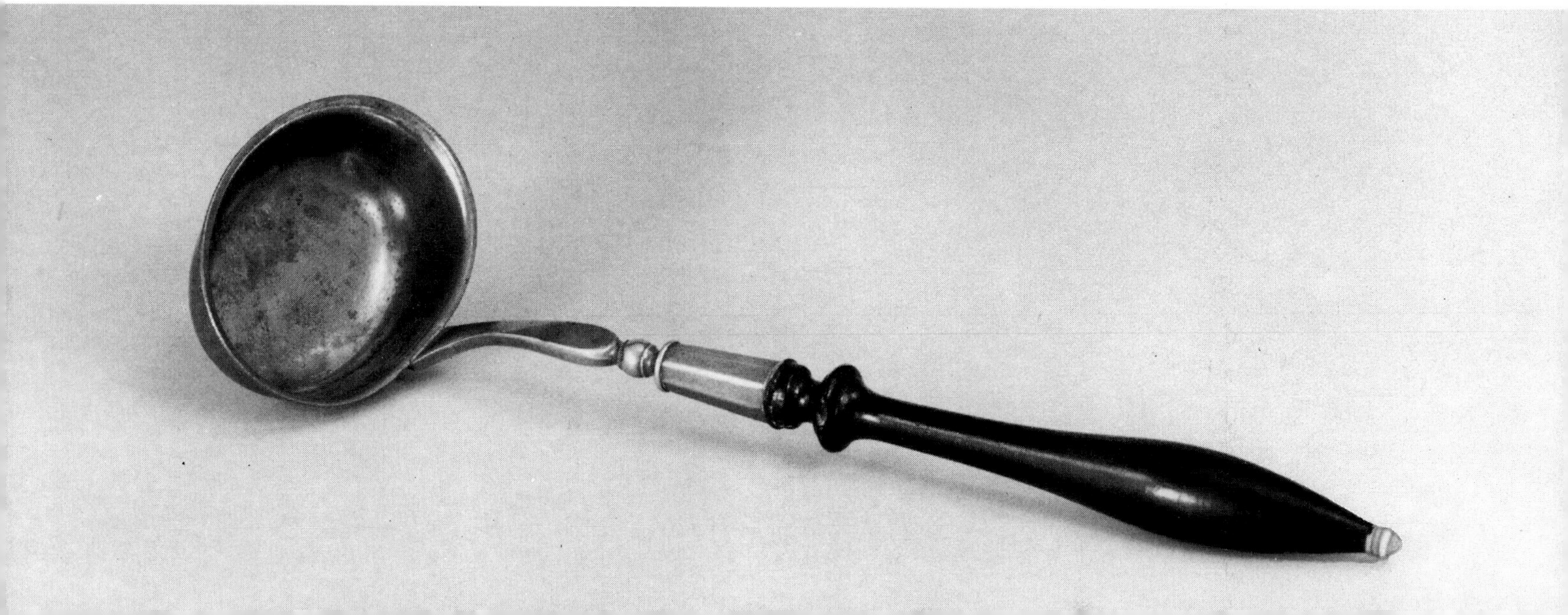

Because a great deal of pewter reached the table direct from the cooking stove it left marks upon the wooden surface. When in the 16th century fashion required that leather coverings be replaced with white table-cloths the sooty marks were so displeasing to the eye that pewterers discovered a great opportunity of selling bowl-rings (bowl-wreaths, hollow rings or saucepan-wreaths). It is true that table surface and table-cloth could also be protected with a wooden underlay, by pieces of wood laid side-by-side, an iron grid or a plaited ring of straw, juniper bark or wicker. Because, however, the pewter trade—and in competition with it, that of the brass-founders who made rings of copper and brass—offered bowl-rings with movable handles, its products were better than all the others. They thus also became a means of transporting hot bowls from stove to table. Pewter bowl-stands were later displaced by dishes placed underneath and table protectors which soon lost their functional purpose. When the trade at large tried to derive business from the growing use of serviettes among wide circles of the populace (in the 19th century) by the production of serviette-rings, it brought in nothing; silversmiths found them more profitable.

Bowl-ring, hollow ring
It is a round, turned and pierced wreath of silver, pewter, copper or brass, either flat or resting on three button feet, upon which bowls are placed to keep the tablecloth clean. Persons who do not like, or are unable to spend a large sum but are fond of cleanliness, use bowl-rings of the same kind made of neatly plaited peeled osier.
Explanatory definition, 1743.

In eastern Europe bowls which had a flat bottom but were otherwise hemispherical in shape were called *kauss* or *kauschen*. Their usefulness increased when during the 16th century they were provided with handles in
48 the style of projecting ears. Thus under the German name *ohrenschüssel* (eared-bowl) the familiar type of porringer was born which survived until the last century in Europe and overseas. At first these bowls were intended to contain gruel and belonged to the equipment of hospitals; later they served as soup-bowls and for taking special drinks, in sick rooms probably also for coffee. Peculiarly enough the use of porringers was for centuries largely linked to the sick-bed. Thanks to their convenience of handling and manageable size they were introduced everywhere as midwives' bowls. Their usual description in old documents is *breikachel*, a further reference to gruel which emphasizes that even in childbed it predominated as a foodstuff for a long time. In Austria it was a neighbourly good deed to call on a young mother for a few days after the confinement with "child-gruel" or pap, which was presented in pewter "goden" bowls. If the circumstances of the mother-to-be were particularly good, further gifts were also brought in the so-called "midwives-basket". This custom also existed in Sweden and in addition to a box made from decorated matchwood the local community provided a hot meal, in a wooden groats tub rather than a pewter bowl. It is probable that here, as elsewhere, porringers were in everyday use; after a meal, they would again be hung-up on the wall for decoration, for which purpose they were provided
49 with a ring.

When people were able to afford to bring the mother-to-be nourishing soups of chicken, capon or veal instead of gruel, larger numbers of double-walled hot-plates from pewterers' workshops came onto the market than

previously. It was in Lyons, Bordeaux and Rouen that the *écuelles à bouillon* were probably first devised whose removable cover became a flat eating-dish when it was turned over. In order that the dish thus created would stand firmly, the cover was embellished with three figurines which provided feet for the bowl in its upturned position. This design was adopted far and wide, whereby Strasbourg masters produced particularly accomplished pieces.
56/57 Characteristic forms were developed in Denmark and Norway. The variants from these countries were also to be found a little later in Central Europe as small soup pots with button feet. In another design the cover was secured
58 with a hinge and when it was open a stay stabilized the bowl while the contents were being consumed. Clearly the child-bed bowls with removable covers—the "bauchkumps mit drei füsschen aufm deckel" (bellied bowls with three little feet on their covers), as they are described in 19th century catalogues, proved better.

59 Porringers were also used everywhere as general purpose soup-bowls whereby in America and England those with only one "ear" were esteemed. Morning soups were popular until long into the *Biedermeier* period in Europe, even supper often centred on a soup. Small porringers were the most suitable vessels for it and were particularly popular in rural areas where they could also be used for field-workers who at harvest time were very fond of "brown soup" at intervals. This was prepared from plums, raisins, currants, syrup and eggs, frequently enriched with a measure of ginger-beer and was a welcome source of energy during hard physical work. This "brown soup" formed the main meal together with thick rice. The unbreakability of pewter bowls was still regarded as advantageous in agricultural pursuits in the second half of the 19th century as, moreover, also in hospitals, educational institutions and even prisons, whose requirements sustained many a pewterer at this period, as for example in Ratibor (now Racibórz, Silesia), the master
61 August Wanke, active in business only from 1888. Such bowls had of course to be of wider general-purpose use than porringers and were accordingly larger. The food-carriers—canteen-bowls—which one finds in Hungary, used there mainly for women in child-bed, the Scandinavian countries and Switzerland were of general utility. These usually comprise three or four eating-bowls stacked on top of each other of which the uppermost is provided with a cover which can be used as a plate. This set of bowls was normally carried by an iron handle and the separate containers were held together with a
66 leather strap. The strap was led through eyes which reveal a possible kinship of food carriers and porringers.

On the Baltic and even more on the North Sea coasts and indeed deep into their hinterland, porringers were regarded as the ideal dish for *mährten* or *coltschall* (caudle). Mährten is a dish for which bread, pretzel, rolls, gingerbread or other ingredients are crumbled into a liquid. *Mährten* of brandy, wine or beer were popular; in times of extreme need, a mother-to-be had to

In the morning, a soup or vegetables,
milk for the workers,
for the others a soup.
At midday soup and meat,
cabbage, peppered or salted meat.
At night, soup and meat,
turnips and fresh meat or pickled meat,
vegetables or milk.

Regulation for the diet of servants, issued by Count Joachim von Öttingen, *c.* 1515.

be satisfied with a *mährte* of water enriched with a few drops of rape-seed oil.
The description *coltschall*-dish suggests that these small bowls were popu-
60 lar for brawn and jelly; in the colloquial speech of Northeast Europe at that
time, brawn was called *coltschall*. In contrast, between Mecklenburg and
East Frisia *kolleschall* was understood to mean a type of brandy-cup which
was in general use there. A gastronomic treat which made a name for itself
was Frisian bean-soup *(sienbohnensopp)* which contained raisins, lemon
peel, ginger root and candy as its invariable ingredients in a proportionate
quantity of rum or brandy. For this, as well as for more simple concoctions a
75 type of vessel was used which has a certain relationship to the *kovsh* of Russia and Scandinavia which, however, are mostly of silver. Whilst the *kovsh*
was a drinking-vessel, the contents of the brandy-cup were served out of it
62 with a ladle. In Finland a porringer with a stand-ring was used for this purpose
which was also made in Holland *(brannwinskoppe)*, Sweden *(brännvins-
skal)* and even in America. To the annoyance of the clergy, secular porringers were now and again used to hold holy water for christenings at
home—it was said with a wink, of many a person all too clearly excessively
devoted to the brandy-cup that they were very likely to have been christened
from a porringer.

Development of the tureens which emerged in the 18th century was initiated by the covered bowls which during the Middle Ages and the Renaissance comprised two similar bowls, one upturned upon the other. On tureens the cover became more recognizable as such and was, moreover,
provided with a handle to lift it. They were mainly used for carrying-in foodstuffs, principally soups. The cover sometimes has a cut-out for the handle
of a soup-ladle. At first these new vessels were not readily accepted in simple households, because the tureens were shaped like those of silver and
not only radiated an unaccustomed formality but were also expensive.
63/67 When, however, simpler and therefore cheaper forms became available
69/70 they were accepted everywhere as articles of general use. In 1830 in many
Thuringian towns a "tureen shaped in contemporary taste after the drawing
provided" still belonged to the pewterer's masterpiece. Tureens naturally
could be and had to be used in the home for a variety of purposes, thus the
68 small ones, known regionally in Germany as *suppenkümps* (soup-bowls),
for example, as pie-dishes. According to a description from the year 1808
this is a "pretty pot with a cover, in which meat pie is carried to the table. It is
an oval round and hollow container made of pewter." Pies were sometimes
baked in pewter tureens in the oven but because of the danger of melting
contemporary cookery books recommended tinned copper dishes.

64 Gravy-boats or sauce-boats (German *salzer*) had to be made from particularly pure pewter. The *salzer* contained *salz*, a sauce prepared from various
spices to accompany meat and flat bread. Sauce-boats were also handed
round the table as butter-servers from which molten or brown butter was

The pewterer displays most outstanding skill with gadrooned jugs and tureens which are shaped in the style of silverware. He calls vessels gadrooned when they have in their length half-cylinders or curves next to each other, which also spiral round the vessel and are hollow internally.

Handwerk und Künste in Tabellen (Synopsis of crafts and arts), Berlin, 18th century.

poured onto viands. Housewives were expressly warned against melting butter and browning it over coals in pewter bowls because the salt in the butter attacked the pewter, absorbed it and would thus be ruinous to health.

71–78 The wealth of variety in pewterers' wares in the early 18th century expressed itself among other things in those dishes which appeared from time to time under the German collective name of *schauer*—for display. *Schauer* are dishes on a high foot of which those intended for sweetmeats found entry into more affluent families. Similar articles out of the ordinary products include salvers on feet, sets of dishes and sugar-bowls with integral spoonholder (of which the basic shape was that of a tureen). For the majority of the populace plain bowls were the norm; even a sugar-bowl in the form of a swan was an exceptional creation. The long arched swan's neck served as a convenient handle to open this extremely functional and particularly appeal-
81 ing type of container. Egg-holders for communal use are an oddity. Usually
85 each person at table had his own egg-cup from which to partake of a soft-boiled egg. "For convenience sake" (as is stressed in contemporary writings) the egg, having been boiled for two or three minutes was placed in the egg-cup, the shell opened with the point of a knife and the egg consumed from out of it. Other common German names for the egg-cup were *eiermüldchen* (trough, tub, bowl), *eiernäpfchen* (basin, bowl, dish, cup) or *eierschüsselchen* (little egg-bowl).

Egg-cups

are small bowls cast in pewter, inversely vaulted, standing on three button feet, in which one puts soft-boiled eggs to eat them from.

Frauenzimmerlexikon (Women's lexicon), Leipzig, 1715.

Butter-dishes, butter-boxes and spice containers

In Scandinavia and North Germany there is a common article of tableware which today is known exclusively as a butter-dish. In former times and other
79/80 regions it was, however, also called a cheese-dish: "Is generally of pewter, in the form of a round plate and rests on a low foot, cast and turned kitchen ware, on which cheese is borne to the table." It was nevertheless mainly used for butter. In northern Germany they were always made of pewter, elsewhere principally of wood. In each case, the intention was always to give a tempting appearance to piled-up butter. In Sweden it was made into attractive shapes in a mould before being brought to table on a wooden platter with small feet *(ostol)*. Pewter butter-dishes were slow to emerge and, as in Germany, were closely linked with the traditions of rural marriages. Two opposing slices were cut from a conical mound of butter and the two flat surfaces thus created were decorated with depictions of the bride and groom in raisins or currants. The rounded surfaces of the butter-cone were decorated with cloves and pepper corns and it was popular to write the names of the bridal pair with these spices. At an advanced hour these figures provoked numerous jokes. It was also the custom to pass a full butter-dish round the marriage table so that each guest might conceal a coin in the mound of butter which would help the young couple to start their married life.

Whereas butter-dishes were regionally relatively circumscribed both as to manufacture and use, butter-cans were included in pewterers' product ranges far and wide. They are known from at least the 16th century. Generally, a butter-can is understood to mean a round container, more rarely square or rectangular and closed with a lid. The lid can be loose, hinged or screwed. The German names *butterdose*, *butterbüchse*, *butterbus* were all current. In Holland the description *boterdozen en gortlkokers* was used for the screwed containers because groats were also cooked in them. However, the main purpose of butter-cans was to bring butter to the table at meals. At many periods a Scandinavian meal without a butter-box on the table appears almost unthinkable. In France, England and America they were made from carefully refined pure tin. Their size is arbitrary, determined by the dimensions of the patterns belonging to the masters who produced them. In contrast, pewterers in East Frisia usually made two sizes, namely for a half-pound and a pound.

Furthermore, no person in this guild of pewterers shall make storage bottles, casks, bowls, butter-boxes or salts other than from pure material as formerly customary and shall mark it twice with his mark.

Scroll of the Stralsund Pewter Guild Authority, 1586.

At latest by the beginning of the 19th century, butter was becoming less plentiful as a foodstuff. The by-products of milk-processing, thin curds and whey, predominated increasingly in the households of working people. On the land, mainly in harvest time, when reapers of grain and hay and diggers of potatoes and beet toiled all day in the fields, these containers were used to keep butter which was taken from it at breakfast, midday meal and supper. As in the case of porringers, their robustness was of value and assured an advantage over earthenware and faience. Complaints from the pewter trade became increasingly more loud as attractive porcelain became more and more plentiful, fashionably produced in the towns—there was naturally at this time much pessimism current among pewterers about their trade. But even if frequently in conflict with the potters, pewterers were always expert at making pottery butter-jars and dishes more attractive and robust with pewter mounts and to profit accordingly. Potters indeed protested that this was not customary in the trade and pewter mounts served no purpose but in spite of this, pewterers gained their share of the trade. The introduction of porcelain gradually put an end to this because it was much too fine to be adorned with pewter bands.

. . . indeed even the countryman on the land who formerly still included a pewter butter-basin in his children's humble dowry, now buys one of porcelain because it is the fashion. . .

Letter of complaint, Osnabrück, 1786.

Spice containers were of an importance which today hardly seems imaginable and for three decades were mainly made of pewter. The high esteem attaching to these containers stemmed from the spices which they housed. Therefore even the salt container and mustard-bowl sometimes became display pieces because of their function. Salt has always been the most important of condiments. In the Middle Ages, at an appropriate social level, salt containers were embellished with precious stones which were said to change their colour if there were poison in the salt. Display and notional purpose were thus combined. The fear of a deliberate admixture of poison was not so pronounced later on but practical persons were anxious by then lest pewter itself could yield poison into the salt. On this account, in many towns it was expressly decreed that only pure tin must be used for the manufacture of salt containers. As will be related later, from time to time pewter salt containers were totally condemned.

The oldest surviving salt vessels date from the late 15th to the early 16th
century. Many of these containers have an elongated finger-piece on the lid
82 which supports it when open. It seems that they were also made with hollow
handles which enabled the salt to be strewn but this is not typical of early
patterns. It was said of the little salt-boxes (which, moreover, were popular
as shooting prizes among other things) from the workshops of Swiss pew-
83/86 terers that they were convenient to take salt from. The salts which were
widespread in Thuringia were also designed to be easy to use. These salts
were relatively small containers from which the condiment was taken with
thumb and forefinger. Salt-shakers only emerged in the 18th century. They
were used not only for salt but also for pepper and sugar. The pear-shaped
containers consisted of two parts which were screwed together, the upper
one with holes or slits. If with slits, the container is always only suitable for
88 sugar because even when shaken carefully relatively large quantities of the
contents are strewn about.

Most frequently to be met with in all countries with a pewter trade are little
84/90 bowls upon feet which were used in northern Germany to catch drips. This
was their function when *dröppelminnas* (dripping Minnies) were used; more will be said on this subject later. In other districts superstitions associated with salt led to a variety of entertaining practices. For instance, in Bohemia and the Erzgebirge on Christmas Eve a pewter salt, full up, would be turned upside down. If the salt retained the blunt tapered shape of its container one might hope to go on living in good health and spirits. Woe, however, if the heap of salt turned out incomplete or if it fell apart entirely—then old hands round the table prophesied certain specified illnesses for the coming year or if the worst came to the worst—the end.

Until long into the 19th century shapes were evolved which, whilst basi-
87 cally governed by the utilitarian function of the ware, nevertheless enable an
effort to create something unusual to be acknowledged. Almost all these
forms as applied to salt containers remain dependent on the age-old basic
construction—foot and bowl; a cover is exceptional. It was only in the early
Rococo when containers were first produced which would hold both salt
and pepper that a cover became a normal part of these vessels. Now and
again a nutmeg-grater is cast in between the two hinged lids; grated nutmeg
was used in incomparably greater quantities than today on foodstuffs and
91/92 even drinks. Indeed spice-stands which sometimes have numerous parti-
tions indicate that even at table it was not only salt and pepper which were
used.

Small bowls as well as dishes, often with small feet, held spices in a dry or made state, principally mustard. Mustard (German: *senf)* seeds were ground into a paste with wine-vinegar or *most* (must or new wine) which was

A cruet stand with a mustard pot, sugar and pepper containers, also a small basket for lemons as is fashionable.

Regulation for the preparation of a masterpiece in the Electorate of Brandenburg, 1797.

96–98 valued at table as *möstling*, *möstrich* or *mostert*. Mustard-pots mainly appeared in the early 19th century and in many places they formed part of the obligatory masterpiece from time to time. In the lid of a mustard-pot there is almost always a small cut-out for a mustard-spoon.

99 Not all too often pewterers produced stands for oil and vinegar containers of glass which were called *karafindl* in Switzerland. Their limited production is explained because on the one hand it led to strife with the glassworkers who regarded trading in these goods as their own privilege. On the other hand, in the eyes of the public this kind of pewterwork was regarded very much as "mock silver" so that substantial business could in any case not be expected. Pewter vinegar and oil dispensers also exist, which, painted white, were used as tableware. Because, however, most of the "best arranged and generally useful cookery books" pointed out that vinegar ought never to be stored in pewter vessels these goods also proved a failure.

It is to be noted that one must put no vinegar into a pewter vessel, not even for one hour, if one intends to keep it because it will become quite thick and mere skin, indeed if one leaves a jug of vinegar standing all night in pewter and afterwards puts it into a cask of good vinegar, the whole will be spoilt.

Practischer Ratgeber (Practical adviser), Halle/Saale, 1778.

Spoons, forks and ladles

Prior to about 1700 when in most countries the invariable components of a setting of table cutlery became clearly defined as spoon, knife and fork, it had undergone a long development. The case (German *besteck*) was originally the holder for the man's side-weapon, the knife, which played a dominating role at table for a long time. The case was often provided with a steel and occasionally with a two-pronged fork.

Metal spoons—although known from early historical times—probably appeared at table among the higher classes during the Middle Ages but were seldom used directly for eating because the liquid constituents of a meal were mopped up with bread.

Even in the 15th and 16th centuries spoons were not yet in general use in Europe but nevertheless in sufficient numbers that pewterers took up their production and various masters made a speciality of them, for instance in Böhmisch-Leipa (now Česká Lípa), in Emden and in Leyden where there was a guild of pewterers, spoon-makers and tankard lid-makers. At times many pewterers had of necessity to specialize because on the grounds of competition masters who had moved in from elsewhere were only permitted to make spoons like, for example, Jürgen Metzker, who came to Kolberg (now Kołobrzeg) in 1659, who was also allowed to repair old pewterware. In the 18th and 19th centuries spoon-making became the main source of income for many pewterers, especially after a steel rod was incorporated into the handle to prevent it bending. In spite of this, rapid wear due to the softness of the material was a perpetual problem. In early times there were efforts to achieve greater strength by hammering after casting but effort and reward were not profitably related. The fact that moulds for casting pewter spoons were also in the possession of many families so that they could produce their own is revealing. This was naturally particularly the case in remote
102 areas; in Canada almost every rural household owned a spoon-mould.

The shape of spoons demonstrable from the 15th century was with round bowl and flat-sided or round handle. This shape, like a type of stalk, was the most practical because at that time the handle was gripped in the fist. This
95 shape of spoon to some extent survived until into the 19th century and in certain rural areas even into our own time, although it is likely that many spoons made recently are only hung up for decoration. The shape of those in use changed from about the second half of the 17th century and was brought about by refinements in eating habits. The bowl assumed an oval shape and the handle became wider, akin to a strip, so that the spoon could be held
93 more elegantly between thumb, middle- and forefinger. A slender rib on the back of many spoon-handles—the rat's tail—made them more rigid. Owners' cyphers engraved on the handles or bowls of individual pewter
94/103 spoons indicate that they were always important possessions. They were welcome gifts from god-parents, to the infant as well as to the mother or to the bride.

At times many types of spoon were produced by the trade. Straining spoons were already produced at a relatively early date, of which probably none have survived. At first they were probably for straining broth, later they became merely sugar-casters. During the 18th and 19th centuries they were mainly to be found in English homes. Marrow-spoons from there must also be mentioned, whose elongated scoops were used for scraping out the marrow from bones. In East Frisia cream-spoons were a favourite accessory for drinking tea. Gin spoons from Holland could hold so much gin in their deep bowls that these spoons were even bought as drinking-vessels. A
100 pewterer from the Duchy of Berg was still offering vegetable, milk, soup, eating, children's and tea-spoons in 1837 and was thus enabled to withstand competition which had adversely affected spoon-makers in particular for a long time and came from various directions.

The office of shop-keepers forbids a stranger born in Saxony to cast pewter spoons and sell them to townspeople but is allowed by the Council.

Council minute, Soest, 1667.

In Prague in the 16th century Italian pewterers were already permitted to manufacture and offer for sale spoons and similar domestic articles in the precincts of the Teyn church. Whilst the derogatory epithet *bönhasen* meant botchers everywhere, in Austria a name soon emerged for the Italian craftsmen which was closely linked to the production of spoons—*katzelmacher* (from the Italian cazza = spoon). This was generally understood to mean makers of metal implements for ladling out fluids. *Katzelmachers* were a continuous worry and aggravation to the resident masters in the pewter trade. There were also disputes about spoons with tinmen, cutlers, needle- or pin-makers and the makers of spoons from sheet metal. Tinmen subsisted by making and being able to sell "composition" spoons, the needle- and pin-makers claimed the same right for spoons of Britannia-metal. In both cases alloys were involved which were principally of tin but did not consist of the mixture normally used by pewterers. Meanwhile the latter had long since discovered that the addition of antimony instead of lead for spoons produced a much desired hardening effect so that the normal alloy was naturally no longer adhered to. Disputes went now in favour of one side, now of the other. There were similar problems in quarrels with the cutlers. Competition from the makers of sheet-metal spoons was quite different. These spoons, formed by die-stamping and afterwards tinned were made in enormous quantities in factories with an intensive sub-division of processes (up to 23 operations). In Saxony alone, in the first half of the 19th century 3.6 million spoons of 70 different types were produced annually, whose low cost could not be achieved by pewterers. The trade endeavoured in a variety of ways to find customers for pewter spoons. They were, of course, prizes at target shooting meetings and in Hildesheim were even offered as prizes in games of chance. A pewterer by name of Heinrich Carl Friedrich Speer from Esens in northern Germany had the original idea of drawing lots for pewter spoons to increase turnover. Three dozen lottery tickets included six winning ones, namely for 12 spoons, a soup-spoon, six, four, two and finally one spoon as consolation prize. A ticket could be bought for $4^1/_2$ *stüber*; business went well but the lottery was quickly forbidden after complaints from other masters.

For more than thirty years faience and pottery have taken the place of pewter, spoons are now only of real or imitation silver.

Report of the Council of the town of Harburg, 1846.

In the "inventory of the entire contents of the house in which died" in 1760 Alderman and Licenciate Hoedt of Düren (Rhineland), two pewter forks are listed and some are also mentioned as in the possession of the goldsmiths' authority in Riga but these were nevertheless not included in the normal manufacturing programme of pewterers. The material is too soft to give stability to the prongs of a fork. Therefore only handles for iron forks were made and these only in the 19th century. At different times forks of Britannia metal were marketed but not very frequently.

101/104 The dipping or scooping-spoon with a deep round bowl is not only the predecessor of today's normal eating spoon but also of the ladle. The ladle appeared considerably later than the spoon because the partaking of soup was not yet general during the Middle Ages. It is possible that ladles came before gravy-spoons of which those which may well be the oldest date from
105/106 the end of the 17th century. Soup-ladles (known in many places as *schleif*) were available both entirely of pewter and also with a wooden handle. Pewterers also made those with wooden handles in their entirety, turning the wood on a lathe. In the 19th century there were even numerous attempts to produce a kitchen slice entirely of pewter; as with forks, the softness of the material did not favour sales.

Cooking-spoons
are what cooks call the large spoons with which they prepare food in the kitchen.

Explanatory definition, 1743.

Pouring Vessels for Serving

3

Drink has always been taken with meals and to a greater or lesser extent in certain periods eating, serving and drinking-vessels of pewter have formed part of a properly laid table. Further to this, however, drinking is not only a necessity of life but frequently a pleasure. Its high esteem is illustrated by the fact that at times one of the worst things one could say of a person was that one would not drink a glass of beer with him. Drinking was so popularly and frequently so immoderately pursued that the forceful term "boozing" was used and declaimed against from many sides. Yet the lust for drinking continued, not only for alcoholic beverages together with whey or buttermilk and apple juice but also from the 17th century for coffee and chocolate. Having regard to the importance of their purpose such a variety of types of vessel for serving liquids was evolved by pewterers as was only surpassed by the tankards and vessels from which to drink. Tankard generally means a drinking-vessel and jug one for pouring. The etymological root of the German name *kanne* (Latin: *canna* = pipe) indicates their distinguishing characteristic, namely an outlet in the form of a pipe or spout. Naturally, such a distinction between jugs and tankards was at no time adhered to in everyday speech or in the actual performance of pouring-out or drinking. Included among pouring vessels for serving, to be described in this chapter, there will be many, formally regarded as drinking-tankards which were really used as pouring jugs, a kind of jug without spout.

Beer and wine containers

Pewter jugs evolved gradually from the second half of the 13th century. Because they did not rapidly cease to be impervious like the wooden ones and were not so easily broken as those of pottery it seemed likely that they would become articles in general use in the long and short term. At first their high material cost was against them but illustrations dating from the following century, for example the Manessian manuscript, show that jugs were not in-

frequently used for pouring at table. Material survivals from the 14th century
are rare and very few have come down from the following century. Jugs upon
feet (Burgundian jugs) enjoyed great popularity. This is evidenced amongst
other things by their portrayal in seals and pewterers' marks. Possibly in some
instances they were shaped from hammered pewter formed over a spherical
anvil. During the Gothic period, however, the technique of jug production
generally practised was neither hammered work nor the casting of the body
in one piece, but two halves were cast. The vertical seam resulting from their
soldering together is a basic recognition feature of old work, produced be-
107/108 fore about 1550. This can be seen very clearly in two flagons of Swiss origin.
When on the 18th October 1356 an earthquake destroyed the Schloss Hom-
burg in the Fricktal (Aargau) they were buried in earth and thus preserved to
be dug up centuries later relatively little damaged. The 14th century jug
found during the castle excavations in Buda may have had a similar fate and
is distinguished as the oldest item of pewterware found in Hungary. In
Sweden jugs are also the oldest surviving pewterers' work but date only
from the 15th century. Finally, it is thought that in England none survived by
native masters made before the beginning of the 16th century.

In the time of Albrecht Dürer and Martin Luther in Germany, there existed
containers for beer and wine with the notable names of *grosstender* (great
flagon) and *stuczen* (flagon) and to which the name *keller* (cellar) was also
given. In both cases these were large flagons with hinged covers which were
placed under a barrel which was usually kept in the cellar and filled from it.
The *stutzen* (flagon) which was also known as a *spann* in northern Germany
sometimes had an outlet tap for convenience in use and handles on both sides
19 of the tapered body. Large flagons or jugs for domestic use held a good 5 litres of liquid. Their purchase price was naturally high and they remained
carefully looked-after possessions through many generations. In spite of
110 careful handling signs of wear first appear on the hinge of the cover which
becomes looser and looser. Such indications of use can be taken at the
present day as evidence of considerable age in a tankard or jug. Another
type of pouring container of large capacity—the German *kellerflasche* (cellar
flask)—has a screwed lid and frequently a closure for the spout. It served not
only for fetching beer and wine but also for storing oil or as a water container.
One can readily assume that large beer and wine containers were only to be
found in more affluent and therefore only few households; only in later times
131 did they become more plentifully available in the form of the cylindrical flagons which were not quite as big. Even smaller slim jugs, for which often only
the name flask or bottle (German: *flasche*) was used were more widespread.
In 1699 the pulpit orator, Abraham a Santa Clara described pewterers as
tradesmen in racy, popular terms: "But most of their wares serve the human
gullet; for bowls, plates, beakers and basins find an all the year round market
111/117 for the mouth which likes no flask better than a pewter one." Wine from the

And because flasks are made in more than one type, for ordinary large flasks, which are normally used in guild parlours, one shall give eight pfennigs per pound for their making. But for the other serving-flasks, which are now and again found in households and which contain three-and-a-half up to seven litres one shall be made to pay ten pfennigs per pound but as regards small flasks under one litre, a schilling per pound.

Regulation for pewterers, Fribourg/Breisgau, 1511.

inn across the road would be fetched in flagons if there was none at home.
The jugs used to fetch beer were only a little taller than wide. In wine producing districts there was often one or more small casks in the cellar; from about
127 1750 resourceful pewterers had manufactured a "wine-lifter" for these to be
emptied suitably. The long suction-tube of this device, which resembled a
large enema-syringe, was inserted into the middle of the cask through the
bunghole and a measure of wine drawn off carefully. One could thus be certain that one had obtained the best in the cask. On the top, it was too weak
because it would have lost strength by evaporation, at the bottom of the cask
it would be sharper and stronger because this was where the lees collected.
Such was popular belief which favoured the sale of wine-lifters as a necessity. The wine-lifter usually drew off barely three-quarters of a litre. When
guests were being entertained, a well organized man-of-the-house made
sure that he wiped the full flagon with a cloth as it came from the cold cellar to
remove condensation and to restore the pewter's pleasing lustre. He then
served it in goblets, glasses, beakers or small tankards or the guests helped
themselves.

During the Gothic and Renaissance periods one of the most common
pouring vessels in central and northern Germany was a jug with a slight belly
112/113 and narrow neck, for which the name "baluster jug" has been coined in our
own time because of their appearance. When Matthaeus Friedrich sent his
book *Wider den Saufteufel* (freely translated "Against a Boozer") for printing
in 1557 in Frankfurt-on-Oder he endowed it with an intimidating woodcut on
the title page "Der Saufteufel" ("The Boozer"). One is enabled to see from
this that baluster jugs were used for drinking directly out of when carousing
109 was at an advanced stage. The use of Hansa jugs, so called because of the
area of their currency, which were known in Hamburg as *standen*, was governed in the same way. One cannot generalize as to whether these jugs
(which strictly speaking are tankards) were used more for wine or for beer or
indeed whether they are linked with the serving of any particular drink. Whilst
a vine tendril in low relief or simply a leaf on the handle suggest a wine jug,
drinking habits on the North Sea and Baltic coasts more a beer jug. On this
subject, the beer brewed in Gouda in the Netherlands from the water of the
Issel enjoyed great popularity from the end of the 16th century and that of
Breda was described as of excellent flavour about 1590. In Groningen where
a renowned beer was also brewed, pewterers produced Hansa jugs in considerable numbers until well into the 16th century. The special role of beer as
a drink was due not only to enthusiastic descriptions of its qualities of taste
and to such epigrams as "Bier und Brot ist gut für Hungersnot" ("Beer and
bread are good for hunger's need") but in northern Germany also to the expression *kindelbier* (christening feast). This refers to the feast after a christening, a family festivity on a large scale. The importance of this feast as one
of the high points in everyday-life is illustrated by a regulation in accordance

If any person is drinking out of a jug and sneezes into it, he shall be allowed to drink the rest of it and afterwards have the vessel rinsed out but under no circumstances to hand it to anyone else.

17th century drinking rule.

with which even childless couples were allowed to arrange one *kindelbier* during their married life. At an advanced hour many jugs passed from mouth to mouth and jokes were made about "the luck of the jug": to have found just enough drink in the jug as it passed round to quench one's thirst.

In accordance with a directive of 1375 in Hamburg *standen* had to be cast of pure tin. In other parts and as a general rule in later times this was altered: knobs, handles and feet might sometimes be made of an alloy of one pound of lead to one pound of tin. Because products were sold by weight, heavy handles and knobs made their appearance but also caused friction among masters themselves. Thus in 1649 the Oldenburg pewterer Gerdt Schlömer made a complaint against his fellow master Johannes Vorlage because he had "shown him up atrociously" in front of the public in the market. After a householder had bought a three-pound jug, master Vorlage advanced, seized the jug and said to the purchaser: "How you have let yourself be taken by the nose! This is a second-quality jug which I sell for 9 groschen per pound and you have had to give 12." It was not only that his products were denigrated as second-grade pewter with a high lead content (in German *en-negut*), complained Gerdt Schlömer, but the other master had definitely dented the jug which made it unusable. As frequently happened in such cases, the dispute ended by their coming to terms.

By the 17th century Hansa jugs were no longer in general use. This was moreover a time when brewers were starting to fill beer into earthenware bottles and to sell it in them. Contemporary accounts tell how the Bobbel Beer of Delft sprang foaming from its earthenware bottle into the gullet. Where better manners prevailed, beer was served in tankards which narrowed
176/178 towards the bottom, the *rörken*.

In the whole of France and the southern and southwestern regions of Europe, preference for wine inspired the production of suitable jugs. The French *cimarres* are emphatically containers for wine. They are reminiscent of the jugs with feet from the workshops of the German pewterers. A strap-handle helped when pouring and a pivoted handle over the top was fastened
116 close to the rim of the *cimarre* on two studs, for carrying. Whilst viticulture and the retailing of wine were encouraged, the government of France unhesitatingly prohibited beer brewing during times of high grain prices, as for example in 1693, 1709 and 1740. The following statistics throw a revealing light upon the inferior status of beer drinking: in 1750 40 Parisian breweries sold about 75,000 barrels of beer; a good 30 years later there were only 23 breweries which produced only 26,000 barrels; viticulture expanded proportionately. It can readily be understood that during this evolution pewterers were already striving at an early date to introduce special forms of vessels for the transport, serving and drinking of wine. Wine has been generally marketed in bottles only since about 1800, before that it usually left its cellarage in casks. Because even in France itself only more affluent famil-

ies in wine producing areas were able to purchase a full cask of wine, the *cimarre* was popular as a means of transport from wine-shop to dwelling but whose numbers were nevertheless probably considerably exceeded by
162 special small tankards called *pichets* (which were still also used for carrying). The larger vase-shaped jugs, popular particularly in the 19th century, with a moulded ring round the body—the *brocs*—were provided by French pewterers with a handle with a denticulated profile on the inside so that the jug could be firmly grasped for pouring.

Upper Franconian wine jugs became a distinct type, characterized by a spherical belly above a short cylindrical foot and beneath a slender concave neck. They have appeared in Würzburg, Gunzenhausen, Hassfurt and Mainz. It is questionable whether they were actually made by pewterers in Mainz. At the time when the first pewterers started to work there in the 16th century Upper Franconian jugs were no longer in fashion and those from Cologne, which may well have been related to them, were slowly becoming popular.

It is quite exceptional that the production of masterpieces was only introduced for Mainz pewterers on the 25th April, 1754 and amongst other items,
119 a *birnkanne* (pear-shaped jug) had to be produced. Pear-shaped jugs or tankards often stood on a plate-foot with the stalk towards the top. The name plate-foot stems from recent times and refers to the fact that the foot often provided on pear-shaped jugs and tankards had the configuration of a plate when viewed from below. In the 18th century pear-shaped jugs became a product characteristic principally of Silesia but they were also popular in Hungary. In Tyrnau (now Trnava), for example, people were fond of bringing wine in them as a gift after the so-called *tischrecht* (table due) had not been practised for a long time. In Central Europe this was understood as a custom whereby a boarder (paying guest) brought his landlady a pewter jug (or a silver spoon) upon his arrival which he then left behind upon his departure. Paying guests or visitors who were obligated to produce a special gift natu-
120/122 rally opted for small serving-jugs, of which the bellied ones (*krumme* or
114 crooked work) were more expensive than those which were cylindrical or became wider at the base. Costly "crooked" work was assiduously very skilfully practised in southern regions, even after cylindrical jugs had be-
115/128 come the norm in the north, the largest of them being called columnar jugs. It indeed appears as if rationalization commenced in those parts much sooner than elsewhere. The fact that the handle was soldered-on is symptomatic of this. Following general practice from early times, elsewhere it was incorporated into the vessel by casting until into the 19th century. To do this, the pewterer pierced the body of the jug, positioned the mould for the handle in the opening and sealed off the interior with a piece of linen. When cast the handle was therefore very securely attached to the body. Even the bottom of the jug was often cut away for casting-in a handle when the latter's mounting

A newly to be initiated master pewterer before his actual acceptance must make the following masterpiece consisting of four parts, namely:
a) a 4-pound flat dish
b) an oval fluted wash-basin and can
c) a hand-cask with sub-tray
d) a pewter pear-shaped jug
for which 4 pieces the candidate master may make the moulds in clay, fired in the oven.

Pewterers' regulation, Mainz, 1754.

started at the base in substantial vessels. As a result of this technique the impression of the linen or "rag imprint" may be a recognition mark of old solid
craftsman's work. Soldered handles were already popular with pewterers in
northern Germany and Silesia in the 18th century. Efforts towards rationalization are also apparent in the work of American pewterers who did not, in-
121 deed, shun "crooked" work but shaped many sizes of jugs in such a way
that small plates, themselves made as tableware, could be soldered on as
bases.

131 In Germany and eastern Europe the *rohr-flaschen* (spouted cans) or *loosskannen* which emerged at a later date and which have already been mentioned had a similar function to that of the French *cimarre*. They were relatively large cans with a screw-closure and a tubular spout and were intended for carrying and pouring wine and beer and which had evolved from the heavy cellar flasks. Because of their size they were also used in the kitchen as storage vessels for all kinds of liquids including water.

The spout which gave their name to this kind of cans was produced by pewterers by a process which according to an 18th century description was as follows:

"The spouts or pipes are cast in a special mould. This spout mould has no core by which a hole through the spout would be created, consequently it is not cast hollow but is in fact blown hollow after casting. It is commonly made like a handle mould for lead or pewter and both halves put together form a cavity which is exactly similar to a spout and which is open at both ends. The pewterer stands the heaviest end of the two parts of the mould put together upon a fustian cloth which lies upon wet clay or loam and he fills the cavity with molten pewter. After familiar laws of nature the pewter which is in close contact with the mould cools earlier than that in the centre. A few moments after casting, when the pewter against the mould has already solidified, the pewterer raises the mould so that the fustian no longer stops the lower hole of the spout mould and blows onto the pewter from the top. The pewter in the centre runs out underneath because it is still fluid but the pewter against the mould stays behind and a hollow pipe is then naturally created. Afterwards a hole or circle is chiselled in the belly of the can and the spout fitted in and soldered in place."

In the 17th century in certain areas of Thuringia a variation of the spouted
118 can appeared with a cranked spout formed at the outlet as an animal's head.
It is likely that the so-called "harvest cans" developed from these. Another
125 distinct shape of spouted can is the Bohemian *lirl* or *lidl*-jug which may well
have been intended principally for wine. It was discovered by chance that a
little bismuth on the bottom of the jug enhanced the palatability and keeping
quality of wine and this once again favoured the sale of pewter jugs because
bismuth could not be incorporated in the bottom of pottery jugs—to wit, the
competition.

In no other country was the pewter trade so accomplished in developing such varied and at the same time characteristic forms of jug as in Switzerland. In the 16th and 17th centuries many journeymen who aspired to the dignity of master were required to devise an unusual form of jug and to cast it. The young master then frequently suffered loss in that the piece did not sell and what was worse, the often costly mould would be of no further use. As a result of such experiences it was decided, for instance in Basle in 1610, to stipulate only pieces currently fashionable. In so doing there was continuous awareness that certain forms were almost always in fashion, as for example
288 the *glocken* (bell), the *stitze* and Walliser (Valais) cans. The term *glocken* (bell) can, coined in the 19th century and referring to its appearance established a name for one of the very earliest shapes of pewter can. In a window in the Church of St. Elizabeth in Marburg (Upper Hesse) from about 1250 is depicted a can resembling a bell which was used by the Thuringian landgravine Elizabeth (died in 1231) to take comforting drinks to the sick. A bell-can appears upon probably the oldest pewterer's seal of 1270. Finally, it is also illustrated in the Manessian manuscript of songs, dating from about 1300. In spite of their early existence and obviously considerable numbers none made before the 16th century has survived to the present day. Most of those which have come to light are measuring-jugs, that is jugs which held a fixed quantity; of these measuring jugs and also of the *stitzen* more will be written later.

In consideration of the fact that the masterpieces are good for nothing and no longer saleable, but were in an old style, in future the masterpiece shall be determined to be in a current fashion so that such can be of value and saleable for a beginner.

Resolution of the master pewterers, Basle, 1610.

Stitzen were used for serving wine, but also for milk and water as kitchen equipment. This type of vessel which tapers towards the top also appeared in southern Germany and in Bohemia, there mostly in Eger (now Cheb). The spouted *stitzen* originating from Eger were known as *pitschen* or *peschen*. They were introduced only in the 19th century. In Thuringia this kind of vessel was even occasionally produced in pottery between 1695 and 1720. The South German *stitzen* differ in detail from Swiss work. The knobs on the covers were not hollow but were always cast in the solid by Swiss
124/126 masters; bands round the rim or small feet were omitted. In Austria a type of
130 *stitzen* with a long spout, stemming from the base, were sometimes produced which resemble the *steg*-cans popular in Switzerland as wedding gifts. The long spout derives its necessary stability from a stay connected to the body. Stays were not only given the appearance of a clothed arm but the clothing was sometimes different for "ladies" and "gentlemen". In Germany these cans were also produced occasionally, for example in Ulm. A jug is sometimes found in the Altmark, the *rahn*, which in appearance seems to have been influenced by Swiss *steg*-jugs. On Sundays and feast days, beer was fetched in them from the inn for the table at home, sometimes to the annoyance of the clergy. Finally, *steg*-jugs in the style of those from Swiss workshops were also produced in Austria in the 17th and 18th centuries, for example in Wels and Linz.

Last Easter Day, an equal number of local young lads together with others from the tavern, went across the alley to the skittle ground with a fiddler, carrying a beer jug in front of them.

A parson's complaint, 17th century.

Preceding page:

107 Tankard with vertical casting-seam; height 29 cm ($11\frac{3}{8}$"), pre-1356. Historisches Museum Schloss Lenzburg

108 Jug with vertical casting-seam; height 19 cm ($7\frac{1}{2}$"), pre-1356. Historisches Museum Schloss Lenzburg

109 Hansa jug; height 20 cm ($7\frac{7}{8}$"), 16th century. The description "jug" has established itself for this type of vessel although they never have a lip. Suomen Kansallismuseo Helsinki

110 Detail of Fig. 19; The hinge jaws have become substantially thinner and considerably separated as a result of prolonged use. The thumb-piece on the cover has worn a dent in the handle over the course of years.

111 Jug with profiled lip; height 20.7 cm ($8\frac{1}{8}$"), *c.* 1670. In private ownership

112 Baluster jug; height 29.5 cm ($11\frac{5}{8}$"), 15th century. Suomen Kansallismuseo Helsinki

113 Baluster jug; height 37 cm ($14\frac{1}{2}$"), 2nd quarter of the 16th century. Statens Historiska Museet Stockholm

114 Serving-tankard with slightly flared base; height 22 cm ($8^5/_8$"), *c.* 1700.
Österreichisches Museum für angewandte Kunst, Vienna

115 North German columnar jug with profiled band; height 32 cm ($12^1/_2$"), dated 1789.
Städtisches Museum Halberstadt

116 Cimarre; height 30 cm ($11^7/_8$"), 17th century.
Museum Boymans-van Beuningen, Rotterdam

117 Slim, slightly lipped jug on ball-feet and with escutcheon; height 34.5 cm ($13^1/_2$"), dated 1740.
The escutcheon often bears the owner's name.
In private ownership

114

115

118 Jugs with screw-closures and cranked spouts; height 32 cm ($12^1/_2$″), *c.* 1700. Staatliches Heimat- und Schlossmuseum Burgk/Saale

118

119 Bellied or pear-shaped jug; height 24 cm ($9^1/_2$"), 1st half of the 18th century. In private ownership

120 Bellied jug with curved spout; height 27 cm ($10^6/_3$"), 18th century. Städtisches Museum Halberstadt

121 Bellied serving-tankard with plate-foot; height 20 cm ($7^7/_8$"), 2nd half of the 18th century. The Henry Francis du Pont Winterthur Museum, Winterthur, Delaware

122 Jug; height 21 cm ($8^1/_4$"), dated 1646. The pouring outlet is closed particularly well by the projecting nose which shuts into the spout. Museum Waldenburg/Saxony

Following pages:

123 Octagonal beaked flagon; height 28.2 cm ($11^1/_8$"), early 18th century. Musée gruérien, Bulle (Fribourg, Switzerland)

124 Jug with stay in the form of a strap between neck and spout; height 37.5 cm ($14^3/_4$"), 18th century. Kulturhistorisches Museum Rostock

125

126

127

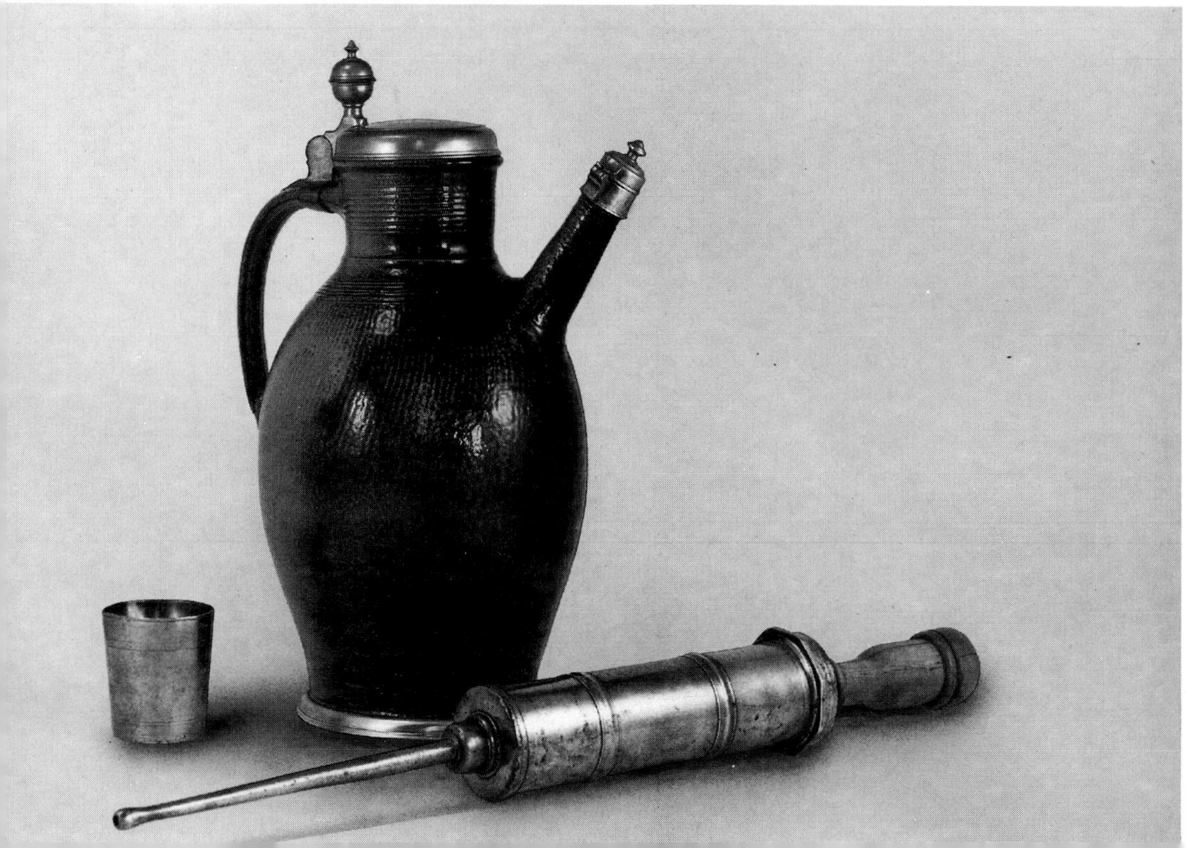

125 Spouted jug, known as *lirl* or *lidl*; height 29.2 cm ($11^1/_2''$), dated 1851.
Vogtländisches Kreismuseum Plauen

126 Wine-can with stay; height 34.5 cm ($13^1/_2''$), 17th century.
Museum des Kunsthandwerks Leipzig

127 Siphon together with pottery jug and pewter drinking-beaker; length 64.5 cm ($25^3/_8''$), *c.* 1825.
In private ownership

128 North German columnar flagon with profiled spout; height 37 cm ($14^1/_2''$), dated 1706.
Kulturhistorisches Museum Rostock

129 Swiss "chain" can; height 35.2 cm ($13^7/_8''$), early 17th century.
Schweizerisches Landesmuseum Zurich

Following pages:

130 *Stitze* flagon with spout; height 22 cm ($8^5/_8''$), dated 1695.
Tiroler Volkskunstmuseum Innsbruck

131 Spouted can; height 27 cm ($10^3/_8''$), *c.* 1800.
In private ownership

MR

132
133

134
135

132 "Walliser" (Valais) jug, so-called "belly-jug"; height 26.5 cm ($10^3/_8$"), 18th century. Museum des Kunsthandwerks Leipzig

133 Belly-jug with extended collar-lip; height 27 cm ($10^5/_8$"), *c.* 1700. Museum "Schloss Moritzburg", Zeitz

134 Jug from Bunzlau (Silesia) with pewter-mounted handle, foot and rim; height 25.5 cm (10"), dated 1751. In private ownership

135 Basle coffee-pot, known as *rundele*; height 22 cm ($8^5/_8$"), 2nd half of the 18th century. Historisches Museum Basle

136 Coffee-pot, strap-handle wound with leather; height 24 cm ($9^1/_2$"), 1st third of the 19th century. In private ownership

137 Coffee-pot engraved with floral decoration, known as Turkish pot; height 24.5 cm ($9^5/_8$"), 2nd half of the 18th century. In private ownership

138 Bottle-stopper; diameter 4.2 cm ($1^5/_8$"), *c.* 1850. There is a pouring spout under the cap. In private ownership

139 Detail of Fig. 20: The pewter-mount on the handle is artistically decorated. To achieve a more pleasing appearance the hinge jaws have little scalloped indentations.

140 A selection of tankards (Bunzlau, Altenburg, Bürgel) with pewter mounts; height 24–31 cm ($9^1/_2$"–$12^1/_4$"), 18th century.
In private ownership

141 Coffee-pot with applied wooden handle; height 40 cm ($15^3/_4$"), 2nd half of the 18th century.
The Henry Francis du Pont Winterthur Museum, Winterthur, Delaware

140

142

143

144

145

142 Cylindrical tea- and coffee-pot with hinged cover; height 14.5 cm ($5^{7}/_{8}$″), *c.* 1830. In private ownership

143 Cylindrical coffee-pot and milk-jug with loose lids; height 21.5 and 14 cm ($8^{1}/_{2}$″ and $5^{1}/_{2}$″), *c.* 1830.
In private ownership

144 Coffee-pot with wooden handle and wooden knob on its lid; height 24 cm ($9^{1}/_{2}$″), *c.* 1810.
Traditionsstätte Erzbergbau, Aue

145 Coffee-pot with wooden handle; height 22 cm ($8^{5}/_{8}$″), dated 1846.
Heimatmuseum Mühlhausen/Thuringia

146 Bolted cans with bent spouts; height 35 cm and 31 cm ($13^{3}/_{4}$″ and $12^{1}/_{4}$″), 1st half of the 19th century.
Schlossmuseum Altenburg

146

147 Globular multi-purpose small pot; height 6 cm ($2^{3}/_{8}''$), *c.* 1800. Heimatmuseum Mühlhausen/Thuringia

148 Bolted jug with straight spout; height 30 cm ($11^{1}/_{4}''$), *c.* 1820 and bolted jug with curved spout; height 30 cm ($11^{1}/_{4}''$), *c.* 1868. Museum "Schloss Moritzburg", Zeitz

148

149 Small milk-jug; height 14 cm ($5^{1}/_{2}''$), dated 1855.
In private ownership

150 Coffee-pot; height 27.5 cm ($10^{7}/_{8}''$), dated 1814.
In private ownership

151 Milk-jugs, so-called *melkgütten*; height 9 cm ($3^{1}/_{2}''$), dated 1830.
Gedenkstätte Crimmitschauer Textilarbeiterstreik 1903/04, Crimmitschau

152 ·Multi-purpose pots; height 13 cm and 11 cm ($5^{1}/_{8}''$ and $4^{3}/_{8}''$), *c.* 1780 and 1800.
Traditionsstätte Erzbergbau, Aue

153 Multi-purpose pots; height 12.5 cm and 16 cm ($5''$ and $6^{1}/_{4}''$), 1st half of the 19th century.
Heimatmuseum Geyer/Erzgebirge

151
152
153

149

150

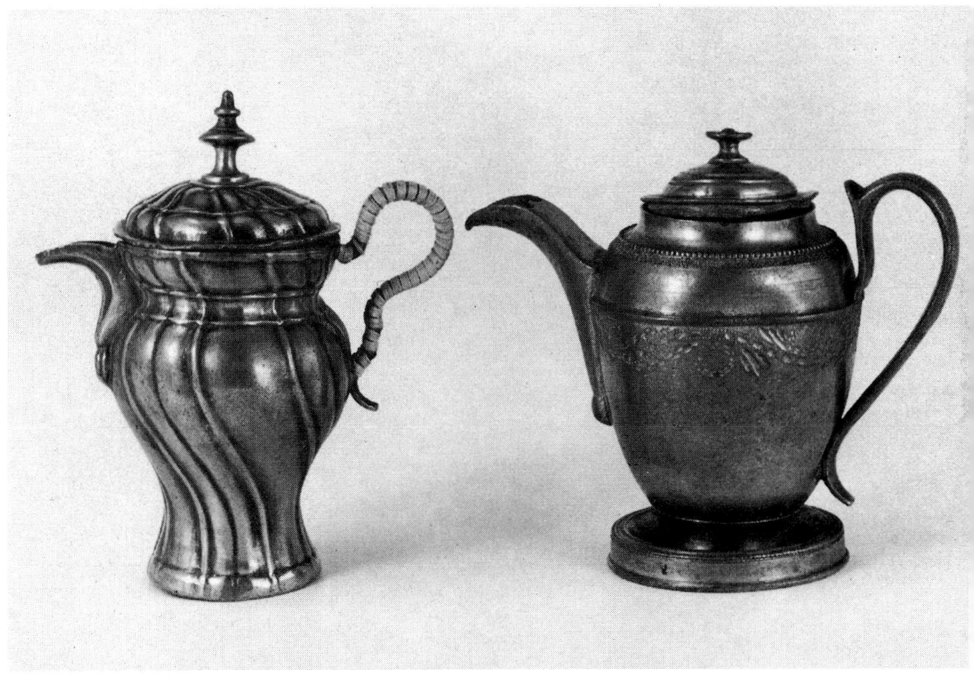

154

155

156

154 Tea-pot; height 17 cm ($6^5/_8''$), 19th century.
Traditionsstätte Erzbergbau, Aue

155 Tea-pot with internal strainer at the outlet for the spout, the handle bound with willow-bark; height 11 cm ($4^3/_8''$), *c.* 1830.
Schlossmuseum Altenburg

156 Multi-purpose jugs; height 13, 22 and 14 cm ($5^1/_8''$, $8^3/_8''$ and $5^1/_2''$), dated 1862.
Heimatmuseum Geyer/Erzgebirge

157 Jug, drawn in towards the base; height 22 cm ($8^5/_8''$), dated 1825.
Heimatmuseum Mühlhausen/Thuringia

158 Tea-kettle with stand and burner; height 30 cm ($11^3/_4''$), 2nd half of the 18th century.
Vogtländisches Kreismuseum Plauen

Following page:

159 Globular jug with stalk-handle, known as chocolatière; height 10.5 cm ($4^1/_8''$), dated 1776.
This type of chocolatière was also used for sauces.
Heimatmuseum Mühlhausen/Thuringia

160 Small tea-pot with wooden stalk-handle; height 15 cm ($5^7/_8''$), *c.* 1810.
An internal strainer indicates that it is for use as a tea-pot.
Kreisheimatmuseum, Grimma

161 Pots with stalk-handles, known as chocolatières, one of them ribbed in the style of silver; height 14–22.5 cm ($5^1/_2'' - 8^7/_8''$), dated 1780, 1813 and 1841.
In private ownership

157

132 The Wallis (Valais) can—belly-can—was distributed throughout the French-speaking part of Switzerland; it has a certain resemblance to the jugs of Cologne. Bellied pouring-cans of this type, on which the pouring out-
133 let is formed solely by a slightly extended lip on the rim, are also found in
135 France in the form of *pichets* and occasionally in England. The *rundele* ("little round one") is bellied but provided with a spout and is mainly associated with Basle. It is exclusively a serving-vessel. Other containers which could also be used for carrying drinks across the street or into the fields were for preference provided with a pewter carrying-chain which was led through two soldered eyes. Many of the jugs and tankards with chains made by Swiss
129 masters are clearly related to the *cimarre*. On another vessel which was also made in large numbers in Swiss workshops—the flattened flask *(platt-flasche)* used predominantly for drinking from—a carrying-strap or arched handle was introduced in place of a chain.

For centuries serving-jugs were made not only of pewter and of other metals but also of pottery. On the one hand, therefore, pewterers were potters' competitors and on the other, valued business associates because they purchased large quantities of pottery and faience. In the regulations laid down by the authorities it was expressly permitted to pewterers that they could sell pewter-mounted pottery in markets, which provoked the displeasure of shopkeepers who were adversely affected. Pewter mounts had been used on vessels in most countries since the beginning of the 16th century. These were understood to include not only the lid, cast to fit exactly, but in addition parts which gave protection from damage. This was necessary mainly round the base of the jug which was not infrequently put down on the table with a heavy hand. Equally, the rim had to absorb many a hefty slamming down of the pewter lid. Pottery bottoms usually had a band round the rim, the base of the more fragile faience jugs was more often provided with a pewter underlay. The quality of material used for mounts was subject to less stringent controls than for jugs made entirely of pewter. A higher proportion of lead in the alloy for bottom plates increased their weight and gave the jug enhanced stability. At certain periods, it was popular with pewterers to link the mounts round the base to the cover with a pewter strip running down the
134 back of the handle. The pewter strip on the handle-back had both strengthening and decorative qualities; on certain pieces, for example artistically
20 painted narrow-necked faience tankards, the pewter mount of the handle was mainly decorative. In such cases the hinge-jaws were not of the usual
139 pattern but workshops took the trouble to file small teeth out of the semicircular jaws.

Potters also considered themselves competent to ensure the rigidity of pewter mounts on their vessels. They pierced a hole in the upper part of the handle for insertion of the hinge-stud and often provided a number of circum-
140 ferential grooves for protective belted pewter bands. This took place only as

All work shall have a proof of the same kind, except pottery ware, which must be mounted with proof or common pewter, so that each purchaser can judge the value for himself accordingly.

Pewter regulation in Bayreuth, Kulmbach and Hof, 1689.

long as price allowed an abundance of pewter mounts; from the second half of the 18th century they were increasingly reduced simply to the lid and band round the foot.

When with the start of industrialization large numbers of bottles were
138 produced, various pewterers experimented with the production of bottle-stoppers incorporating a spout. It is unlikely that any of these stoppers still survive.

Coffee- and milk-jugs

"La bottega del caffè"—this unusual and curiosity-provoking name was displayed in 1647 upon a building in Venice which thus became the first European coffee-house. In 1650 one followed in Oxford, two years later one in London and from 1677 and 1683 respectively coffee could be drunk in premises specially dedicated to it in Hamburg and Vienna. Very likely many a citizen went only unwillingly into this kind of public establishment and preferred to savour the novel beverage at home. In many places there were disputes with the authorities who declaimed forcefully against the new fashion and pointed out that one's forebears had fared well with beer and brandy in moderation. How were pewterers to react to the increasingly popular drink when clerical dignitaries spoke against persons who made "boozers' ware"
137 for it? Obviously they went on producing "boozers' ware" for coffee, which had at first been used likewise for chocolate and tea.

The shape of coffee-pot now established world-wide was made by pewterers from the beginning of the 18th century and offered under the description "Turk's can". This has reference to the colloquial term "Turk's drink", used popularly for coffee because it had become widely known owing to the sacks of coffee left behind by the Turks after the siege of Vienna in 1683. The dome-like cover of these vessels may have contributed to "Turk's cans" becoming popular in Europe specifically for dispensing coffee. Pear-shaped pots were used principally for serving alcoholic drinks solely in Russia. In 1800, when porcelain was already widely distributed it was said: "The well-known Turkish pots or those entirely of pewter as well as those of good Bunzlau (Silesia) pottery are held to be the best for making coffee." The long-lasting equal esteem or even preference for "pots entirely of pewter" may stem from the increasing practice of taking an everyday drink hot or at least warm. Beer, *kofent* (a half-beer), wine, new wine and the like are heated only exceptionally whereas in contrast the drinks then coming into fashion tasted best when they were hot. Word quickly went round that pewter pots would keep coffee hot for a particularly long time. In comparison with competing materials, pottery and porcelain, pewter has significantly lower heat conductivity and insulates against heat loss correspondingly. It is un-
136/141 equalled even by silver in this respect. Once the handle of a pewter pot has become hot it can be uncomfortable for pouring. The trade therefore studied to obtain wicker or bast with which to bind the handle. Carefully plaited and

Coffee-pot
It is a small container, round and tall or short, with a handle and spout, sometimes provided with feet, of silver, brass, copper, sheet-iron, porcelain, terra sigillata or serpentine, which is used for infusing coffee.
Explanatory definition, 1748.

144/145 gleamingly lacquered it also enhanced the appearance of the ware. From about 1790—even somewhat earlier in America—handles increasingly came to be made of wood and pots to be fitted with them. In many cases pewterers used their own lathes for turning the wooden handles. Even the knob for the lid, otherwise cast on directly in a two-part mould was sometimes made from wood. The maxim—if you want something done, do it yourself—naturally applied to these as well.

At the beginning of the 19th century the pear-shaped coffee-pot custom-
142/143 ary until then was joined by the cylindrical pattern which very soon became popular. Because it was easier to make, the trade was pleased by this development. A most varied assortment of sizes became available in progressive increments; the small jugs were used for serving milk. Now and again small compact versions were made which could be used as tea-pots as well as coffee-pots. The cylindrical pots partly retained the curved handles of the pear-shaped ones, in part they were rectilinear. They always stood comparatively well away so that the hot body would not be touched when pouring.

In about 1830 coffee became a morning drink as well as tea in many European countries. Even in England many families still preferred it to tea in the morning even if reservations against it were meanwhile greater than on the Continent. At that time the long-term after-effects resulting from a pamphlet of 1674 in which English women inveighed against coffee because it made men weak, withered and quite impotent were still being felt. One year later the Government had closed coffee-houses, which had increased enormously in numbers in a few years, for a short period. Nevertheless in about 1700 coffee was drunk more and more and in much wider social circles than, for instance, in Germany. Reservations about coffee only revived when tea became increasingly plentiful and was on sale considerably more cheaply. In spite of an otherwise extensive range of jug, can and pot production, in point of coffee-pots English pewterers were at all times restrained. It was quite different on the Continent. Although the middle classes were never able to afford coffee every day, coffee-pots were an important part of pewterers' production ranges and readily saleable because instead of genuine coffee the people grasped at substitutes. Foremost among these was lightly malted barley which housewives in the Netherlands and Germany were fond of enhancing with chicory. This was now and again added even to genuine coffee. Roasted chestnuts, peas, nuts and beech-mast were also used as substitutes for coffee. Because it was brewed in the pot, pewterers positioned the spout fairly high up on the neck. In this way the coffee grounds did not come out into the cup or beaker when it was poured out but remained at the bottom of the pot. Malt-coffee was taken to daily work outside the home and when possible kept hot or re-heated. For carrying and pouring workmen's coffee—"wretches' coffee"—the pewter trade put on sale a tall pouring can which was provided with a rigid carrying-handle. The handle

The first plea:
Dear Wife! Please do rise earlier in the morning so that the cook does not put too much chicory in the coffee . . .

From the 7 pleas of husbands to their wives in a Neuruppin picture sheet, 1825.

spanned the cover and lifted off with it. This required that the cover should be
fastened for carrying. The problem was solved by a pewter bolt which was
148 pushed into a retainer soldered to the neck of the can. Bolted cans have
straight cylindrical spouts but also some which are curved and terminate in
188 an animal's head which are reminiscent of the so-called harvest-cans. A regionally distributed variation in the German provinces of the Vogtland and
146 Thuringia are bolted cans with a long spout starting almost at the base and
sharply bent at the top. When a worker took coffee with him in one of these, it
was prepared beforehand in another container. These cans were more frequently used for milk and sometimes also for water.

Neither the trade (nor coppersmiths) was able to do any considerable business in coffee-trays. They were round, oval or square in shape and were designed to carry a coffee-service. This purpose, current in more affluent circles could not be extended into simple everyday-life although pewterers made coffee-services available at favourable prices at the expense of quality of material. A higher proportion of the poisonous lead was acceptable inasmuch as direct contact with food and drink was not involved and therefore no harm to health could result. In contrast, great care was bestowed on the composition of the material of the vessels which would contain the fluids to be served. Sometimes no lead at all was included but in its place admixtures of copper and bismuth. To improve resonance many masters even added iron to the alloy for "plate for households of the nobility and coffee- and teapots".

Whilst coffee-pots have survived into our own day in impressive
numbers, this is much more rarely the case with milk-jugs. Clearly this is
linked to the growing preference for faience and porcelain as materials for
these wares from the second half of the 18th century onwards. It is possible
that small pottery jugs were already more popular for milk even when small
pewter jugs were in use for a variety of purposes. Thus the serving vessels
described by many collectors today as mocha-pots were also used for serv-
147/153 ing milk and may well also have been used as chocolatières. The reduced di-
157 ameter of the lower part of many of these pots from the European Rococo
356 period points to their relationship with the somewhat earlier so-called *hefe*
(yeast or barm) pots but also to the fact that they were not usually used as
152 tea-pots (see below). A type of milk-jug was made by only a limited number
of pewterers which derived from those fired in porcelain and was thus clearly
149 recognizable as intended for serving milk. There is a type which was more
151 widely distributed which was described as a milking can *(melkgütte)* in a few
German regions and which, like the majority of containers primarily intended
as milk-jugs, has no cover. Because of their name, *melkgütte*, there is a notion
that they were used directly as receptacles when cows or goats were being
milked. This is a misconception because they were always of very small size and
could at best be used for scooping milk out of a milk-pail and to drink from.

Tea-pots and chocolatières

Like milk-jugs, viewed overall, tea-pots are rarer than those designed for the preparation and serving of coffee. In England, America and the northern parts of the European Continent, however, a preference for tea encouraged pewterers to very active production and especially in rural areas they were to some extent able to hold their ground for a long time against competition from porcelain. When it became general practice in the pewter trade in the 19th century to demand a piece of work from a journeyman this was often a tea-can or tea-pot. The distinction between can and pot for the preparation of
160 tea was observed very precisely in many places—the tea-can is a smaller
18 vessel, intended for at most two persons, the tea-pot is larger. At English and American weekly markets pewterers put on sale tea-urns which differed considerably from tea-pots because they had no spout but, instead, one or more taps. These tea-urns resemble the *kranenkanne* (from *kran* = North
276–278 German for tap or cock) produced in America, Denmark and northern Germany which were favoured as coffee containers and about which more will be written later.

Many masters enjoyed the reputation of being specialists in moulds for wares connected with the taking of tea like, for example, Stephan Furckel of Augsburg in the first half of the 18th century. If a pewterer had to make a mould for casting large or small tea-pots he had to take into account the fact that only a wide and low style could hope to find public favour. In households word had quickly gone round how important it was to allow the leaves which came from a distant land to draw in hot water for a few minutes after infusion and for this they must be widely distributed over the bottom of the pot. It would be a positive outrage to prepare the new drink in a tall container because thus its fine aroma would not unfold and its wonderfully stimulating powers would not be activated. However this may be—the thickset bellied pots with their spouts let-in low down in contrast to coffee-pots were the style which was most popular with customers. Due to their wide bottom area, with care they were also suitable as kettles in which water could be brought to boil. Damage quickly followed, however, if the water boiled dry or the coals were too hot. Thanks to itinerant pewterers it was everywhere possible to have a new bottom patched in. To prepare water for tea there was of course also an internally tinned copper kettle or a container of some other fire-resistant material. Al-
158 ready in about 1760 tea-kettles with an associated oil or tallow-burner, very much in the style of those of silver, were now and again on offer. They did not enjoy any popularity worth mentioning for any length of time because they may well have entailed too much fuss to use.

Tea-kettles and tea-pots respectively almost always had a folding-handle which extended well above the hinged lid when upright. Its horizontal handpiece was of wood. Small tea-cans were provided with wicker-wound pewter strap-handles or a wooden stalk-handle projecting from the body. The trade far and wide generally favoured plum tree wood for the wooden

Tea-pot
It is a small rounded vessel of brass, sheet-iron, porcelain, terra sigillata, serpentine or pewter, with a handle and spout, in which tea is infused; it is usually designed for only one or two persons because if it is intended for more persons and is provided with a little tap, it is called a tea-urn.

Explanatory definition, 1748.

parts of tea-vessels. Hand-pieces and handles were often turned on their own lathes by pewterers themselves. It was worthwhile to achieve a certain dexterity for this inasmuch as wooden parts were also called for for coffee-pots and likewise for completing chocolatières.

"Tea-strainers with fine holes" announced many a pewterer at the beginning of the century and looked forward to good business. But even when tin was alloyed with antimony instead of lead and therefore became harder these strainers do not appear to have stood up to much use. At least for a time greater commercial success came to those ingenious masters who soldered a strainer to the interior of the pot where the spout emerged and who
154/155 also still extolled the somewhat altered but still stocky bellied shape as yet the most modern. The convex shape was only relinquished after the 1850s
156 when the trade hoped for fresh success with a kind of multi-purpose pot.

Tea had already come to be considered a daily drink and the enjoyment of coffee on Sundays and feast days attainable for wider levels of society while chocolate still remained a luxury out of reach. As early as the 16th century, Spanish seafarers brought cocoa home with them from Mexico, a century later it had become known and esteemed in England, then in France, Germany and finally the whole of Europe. At first, however, this exotic drink was to be found only at Court. Thus it was of little use to the public at large when in 1684 an aspiring doctor of the medical faculty, Monsieur Bachot, advocated to the venerable University of Paris the thesis: well-prepared chocolate was a most excellent discovery which the Gods would have preferred to nectar and ambrosia. One might consider that chocolate was better than the drink of the Gods which bestowed immortality. The candidate managed to convince the audience of his extravagant claims and one or another of them will have remembered them when two years after the thesis and then again in 1689 silver chocolatières were made at the French Court. These events were only of interest to the pewter trade because a special shape of pot was introduced for the new drink. Naturally the style of those in silver was looked to when by and by both town and country people were able to savour cocoa. By about 1800 it had largely lost its luxury character in all European countries. For some decades previously pewterers had already been selling chocolatières which were shaped in the style of the silver ones. In general, chocolatières are taller than they are wide. If they approach a spherical shape in appear-
159 ance they were also used at home as small pans for sauce. Chocolatières were made until about 1850. The latest of those produced no longer had a gadrooned body but in spite of simplification the socket for the wooden handle was not soldered-on but cast in. The linen imprint in the interior of the pot ought to be present in chocolatières of this date in contrast to stirrup-handled pots of the same period. In addition there are very rare examples with a hole in the cover, closed with a flap, through which a twirling stick could be introduced to stir the chocolate prior to serving.

"Chocolate" or "succolate" is made from a fruit / which is often brought from Guatemala / and closely resembles almonds . . . It is not only succolate which is prepared from it / but the Indians are said to produce a universal drink from it (like beer with us). It is agreeable to a chilled stomach / exceptionally strengthening, however, to the restorative balsam / and conducive to sexual intercourse.

C. Vielheuer, *Gründliche Beschreibung frembder Materialien und Spezereien* (Fundamental description of foreign substances and spices), 1676.

Drinking-vessels

From the declining Middle Ages onwards certain drinking-vessels were produced which played a considerable role in the everyday-life of the people and yet for a long time were only rarely found in domestic households. This was due to festivities which took place more in public than at home and were popularly celebrated in the local tavern. Festivals included taking of office, end of shepherd's hiring, tilling of the common fields, fishing the ponds and the numerous religious feasts. The tavern was always to a great extent the focal point. Tavern-keepers were accordingly among pewterers' best customers. Dozens of tankards, either entirely of pewter or of pewter-mounted pottery must have been melted down from one time to another or ordered afresh as they became the victims of unruly guests. The landlord would arrange for individual numbers to be engraved upon the covers so that tallies could be more easily kept when the party became lively; he chalked up on a slate how many times each tankard was emptied and refilled. To do this, he necessarily had to give the same tankard to each guest each time and therefore evolved the "regular's" tankard used by only one individual. Convivial gatherings of journeymen of a particular trade (tankard days or *krugtage*), which consisted of a comparatively unvarying circle of people led to the engraving of their owners' names or monograms on tavern tankards. If anyone managed to afford a pewter tankard for the home it would be engraved with the initials of the head of the family as soon as possible. It was a special honour for it to be handed quite full to a visiting guest—custom required that the guest then emptied it in a single draught.

Beakers also developed from communal drinking-vessels to everyday use. They are associated with the tavern in a similar way to tankards. Their own beakers were carried by many of the wandering journeymen; this practice may have originated to some extent on grounds of hygiene. Pewter cups were essentially more stylish than beakers. These were never to be found in taverns and were not very common in private households. Taverns of course possessed none of the drinking-vessels which pewterers designed specially for children. Because babies' feeding-bottles made of pewter were eminently practical they became an article of everyday use at an early date.

Flasks and tankards

Even after the sound of the wine-bell had announced that the tavern was closing, festivities not infrequently continued "behind the shutters". Some time previously lentil-shaped flat flasks, made of pottery, wood or leather would have been filled in preparation. At the beginning of the 15th century, pewter flasks *(gurten)* appeared in Switzerland which completely displaced those of leather whilst in Hungary the wooden *kulacs* predominated. A pyramidic truncated foot indicates that these flasks also stood on the table for pouring from. Mainly, however, they served as portable containers for drinks—sometimes they were also known as pilgrims' bottles. Pewterers
21 provided them with eyes through which a leather strap could be passed for convenience of carrying. They could thus easily be taken across country. When these containers were also intended for serving and pouring, the
165 lidded neck of the flask had a slightly protuberant lip and the rounded oval body of the flask was provided with a handle. Drinking-flasks which could be closed with a stopper were put at the bottom of a well on hot days to cool the wine. For those who could afford them, pewterers also offered large, usually
175 basin- or bucket-shaped coolers which were filled with cold well water and stood immediately adjacent to the table during a meal. In spite of its functional usefulness the flat pewter flask was not in demand after the 17th century.
166 Its place was partly taken by one with a considerably larger neck, gourd-shaped body and screw-closure which was carried by the hand with a chain. In Switzerland this type of container was known as *feldflasche* (field flask), in France as *bouteille*.

During the festive meals at the time of the wine sales the flask was generally passed from mouth to mouth. This was understood to set the seal on transactions or agreements which often took place in high spirits and at a very late hour. All those who were present at the negotiations and overheard the outcome were considered witnesses to the proceedings because they had participated in the festive meal. Even betrothals were announced and sealed in a similar way and because this resulted in a great deal of mischief these kinds of event were expressly and emphatically forbidden. The authorities also tried to regulate the quantity of wine to be consumed at these festivities. Thus, for example, in 1625 in Hesse it was decreed that a quarter of wine might be drunk when 500 gulden value was sold and bought. Such

and similar ordinances encouraged amongst other things the gauging of
pewter drinking-vessels which was often done in pewterers' workshops
(more will be said later on this subject).

Whilst flat flasks were evidently not yet gauged for a specific volume this
was now and again the case with early tankards. The few surviving examples
163/164 from the Gothic period to some extent display such a notable elegance of
form that it is difficult to come to terms with the bucolic role which they had to
109 fulfil at many festivities. The easily handled Hansa jugs fit this kind of picture better, the oldest one of which (1331) discloses a Crucifixion scene in
the lid. It has already been mentioned that Hansa jugs were used as drinking-vessels and not just to pour from when a party became lively. When, as is
suggested today, a tippler saw a depiction of the Crucifixion (which in old
jugs is usually on a medallion on the interior of the base) he would be cau-
tioned to moderation. The bantering comment "he has seen the Lord" followed if someone had drained the jug too often. The medallions on the bottom were a normal decorative feature occasioned by a practical manufacturing purpose. They covered the hole through which a rod was inserted to hold
the body of the jug when it was being worked on the lathe. When the medallion was soldered in position (sealing the bottom) work on a jug or tankard
was essentially complete. Pewterers most frequently used small roundels
for this, in the form of rosettes in relief.

In many places low, wide tankards were known as *fletsch*-tankards and
sometimes had raised bands round them. Sometimes, also, the body of
171 the tankard is concave-sided. It is possible that the raised bands derive
from those which were of importance to strengthen wooden vessels but
which serve a purely aesthetic purpose on pewter tankards. A *humpen* made
in Münster bears the interesting inscription: 1.5.9.4.: ELSEKE PENE-
KAMPVS + BADEMODER. THO MONSTER. This piece may therefore well
have belonged to the proprietress of a public bath-house. In the bath-
houses of the 16th century many pleasures could be pursued, a taste for drink
amongst them and one can imagine that an enterprising bath-house keeper
("bath mother") required an impressive number of drinking-tankards. Similar surviving tankards from this region have a pierced hemisphere on the
bottom upon which a bayonet-locking mating part can be fastened. In England and northeastern Europe, craftsmen occasionally made tankards
which incorporated a hollow knob (for mace) which could be screwed off.
The hollow half-ball as well as the hollow knob were to contain spices, principally to give an agreeable flavour to beer. In England there were spiced
beers at a very early date but also in many years stringent prohibition against
brewing with hops, as for example in 1530 by Henry VIII. It is possible that
during these times spices were used to try to correct the flavour. "Braket"
(ale, pepper and honey) and "ale-berry" (sugar, beer, pepper, nutmeg,
bread) were two drinks which enjoyed special popularity and which it was

likely were already filled into the flat flasks. It cannot, nevertheless, fairly be assumed that for the preparation of braket and ale-berry the devices in or on tankards were used. It is different with medicated ales. To make this, herbs following a particular recipe were put into the capsule in the base and the beer was left to stand a while before drinking. Sage-beer was held to strengthen the stomach and prevent trembling of limbs and knees. A tankard of wormwood beer taken in the evening was supposed an effective remedy for unfruitfulness in women. Those of the female sex who were melancholy could be restored to good humour with balm-mint beer. So was quoted in generally popular household recipes. Anyone who put cloves in the pewter spice capsule was hoping to cure stomach illnesses and finally, it was recognized that bay-leaves induced sweating.

Anyone who has hiccoughs should put a bare-bladed knife into a tankard of beer and drink a good draught from it in one breath.

"Rockenphilosophie" (Petticoat wisdom), Chemnitz, 1759.

Cloves, cinnamon and mace were used by many a pewterer in his work-
174 shop in co-operation with a cooper for the production of Lichtenhainer tankards. This refers to a drinking-vessel made up of wooden laths and decorated with pewter intarsia and with a pewter cover. The Lichtenhainer tankard derives from the *birken-meyer* (birch section) which is understood as a drinking-vessel made principally in Thuringian districts from one piece of birchwood complete with bark or of some other wood finished off with birch bark. The name also refers to the fact that the vessel was cut out of one limb or trunk—German *meien* (cf. mow) was in former times a colloquial word meaning to cut. In the 18th century *birken-meyer* were still in use in some places but were known as *lanzen* or *stübchen*. As pewter tankards decorated with intarsia became more plentiful they were adopted for use by a tavern in Lichtenhain, situated at the gates of the Thuringian town of Jena. From about 1700 the tavern was well known for late and copious toping in its rooms. Until that time barley beer with the highly descriptive name of "Jenischer Dorfteufel" (Jena Village Devil) was served which people went out of their way for whenever possible and which was specially to the taste of the "regulars" of Jena. Then the Lichtenhainers brewed a better beer. When the topic of conversation was beer drinking, students from Jena rapturously spoke solely of "Lichtenhainer". The German author Otto Julius Bierbaum wrote in the 19th century in one of his works about a voluptuary who was so "Lichtenhainized that student bloods went into fits of admiration". The name Lichtenhainer tankard was naturally gradually applied to the new *lanzen* and *stübchen*. As regards the use of cloves, cinnamon and mace in the manufacture of wooden tankards, this is linked to the application of pitch to the interior of the tankard. Pewterers themselves often applied the pitch to wooden tankards bought for them to embellish. Like rosin, pitch was always on hand because it was used to join the pewter and pottery on pewter-mounted pottery, above all when applying display adornments. In the course of "improving the economy in country and town" attempts were repeatedly put in hand to do away with pitch in beer containers and pewterers were also urged only to ac-

cept delivery of wooden ware which was tight without the use of pitch. In Saxony, moreover, the authorities promised brewers an incentive of 50 thalers if they did not use pitch in their casks for two years but nevertheless supply good beer.

The majority of drinking-vessels were of such a size that they could not be emptied at one draught. If they were of small size they were made for
167/168 brandy or water and perhaps also for milk. The *rörken* made in northern Germany and Scandinavia were certainly drinking-vessels of which relatively
170/172 small versions are known and which undoubtedly served almost exclusively
176 for the consumption of alcoholic drinks. The German name *wein-kroos* (wine tankard) indicates that *rörken* were not only used for beer drinking. The great passion for gambling in the 16th century and especially the widespread and most frequently pursued practice of dicing stimulated pewterers to manufacture tankards which could be used for both drinking and dicing. *Glücksrörken* had a pierced double bottom in which there were one or more dice. In northeastern Europe the trade conceived the wheel-of-fortune tankard. These are drinking-vessels which have a wheel-of-fortune, usually of brass, upon the cover. When seated in congenial company each drinker rotated the wheel. The number of tankards, beakers or glasses to be emptied or to be handed round the circle was determined by the number to which the
178 hand on the wheel pointed when it stopped turning. Dicing *rörken*, wheel-of-fortune tankards and puzzle-jugs (*rörken* with a hollow tube round the lip, the outer wall pierced with one or more outlets) had their place in everyday convivial company but needless to say, they were almost never found in the home. The popularity of puzzle-jugs is indicated by the fact that they were also made in pottery.

A vessel quite decidedly intended for the consumption of beer is the *wal-*
169 *zenkrug* (cylindrical tankard), so called because of its appearance (German *walze* = roll or cylinder). Its shape originates from wooden examples and it was made in pewter as early as the 16th century. The *walzenkrug* only achieved general popularity one or two centuries later. Even in the period of its greatest acclaim it was barred from the refined tables of the upper classes as being too coarse. If beer was drunk instead of wine, glass tankards were preferred. In contrast, pewter *walzenkrüge* enjoyed an unusual measure of
282 popularity amongst the people. They were prized as marriage or christening gifts. Even though about the year 1800 only something approaching a quarter of the population of Central Europe were literate, the custom of having legends and pictorial representations engraved on marriage and christening tankards gained increasing currency. In many districts a "house tax" was usual when marriages were contracted. This meant a gift for the household goods and often included a cylindrical pewter tankard. In certain instances prosperous Swiss citizens gave their daughters a marriage gift consisting entirely of pewter. In Graubünden pewterware was engraved with the name

If a beer tastes of the barrel take a tuft of 35 grains of wheat, hang it in the barrel and the beer will become fit to drink.

Fünff Bücher von der göttlichen und edlen Gab, der philosophischen hochthewren und wunderbaren Kunst, Bier zu brawen (Five volumes on the godly and noble gift, the philosophic, precious and wonderful art of beer-brewing), Erfurt, 1575.

Divine blessing,
happy times,
I wish to you both
as godfather.

I would not part with the front of my wife for everything in the world.

Maiden, love and wine shall be my pleasure.

Just see how my sweetheart laughs because the stork brought a baby.

We are joyous
as Heaven disposes.

Inscriptions on tankards, *c.* 1800.

of the bride and the marriage date. There and elsewhere if guests were expressly invited to a "gift" wedding, they were fond of donating a drinking-vessel. When a guest was invited to a "coffee wedding" he expected only coffee and pastries to be served and his gift was determined accordingly. At a "cold wedding" there would be no hot food. "Gift weddings" were great events which every young couple would have liked to celebrate but which economic hardship often did not allow. The donor of a pewterware gift would not hesitate to have his own name engraved upon it to keep his memory green. Frivolous inscriptions on cylindrical tankards were always a common practice.

Walzenkrüge were in fact included in the production range of pewterers in every country but were produced particularly plentifully in the regions of Saxony and Thuringia. In Saxony tankards were often engraved with the Saxon coat-of-arms which was gratifying to the authorities. Prior to 1807 in addition to five bars crossed diagonally by a bend of rue it included crossed Electoral swords and the Electoral crown. However, after the Elector of Saxony had concluded peace with Napoleon in 1806 and had joined the Rhenish Confederation he adopted the style of King of Saxony. A king's crown was then included above the coat-of-arms and can also be found upon engraved tankards. Awareness of this detail is useful for recognizing fakes.

The swelled base-ring of Saxon and Thuringian *walzenkrüge* is not present on those from northern Germany which have a flat bottom. In Denmark
180/181 and Scandinavia the profiled base-ring is sometimes replaced by three ball-feet. Scandinavian, as also now and again Austrian and German pewterers
179 made pleasingly tall *walzenkrüge*. The attractiveness of these was surpassed by those from Southeast Europe (Transylvania) whose tall and slim appearance promoted the German name *flötenkrüge* (flute tankards). *Flötenkrüge* are not infrequently richly engraved and provided with a handle decorated in relief.

162 In France *pichets* were what *walzenkrüge* were in Saxony and Thuringia, namely drinking-vessels widely popular among the people but nevertheless not for beer but for wine. Whilst *walzenkrüge* had only a few unimportant differences within separate German regions, there are clearly distinguishable variations among *pichets*. Thus, for example, they are found with and without covers, with a parallel or tapered lower portion and with constricted or cylindrical neck. All, however, stood directly upon their bottoms and had a slightly drawn out pouring lip at the rim. *Pichets* could therefore be used as vessels for pouring. They are frequently gauge marked and could accordingly be used as wine measures. The popularity of *pichets* endured from the early 16th century until about 1750; they have been copied until the present day, provided with an artificial patina and fake marks.

It has already been mentioned that in certain circles glass tankards were preferred to those of pewter. This did not please pewterers. Because, how-

182 ever, glass tankards were often provided with a pewter band round the base and with a pewter cover, efforts were made to derive some profit at least from these. For pewterers it was by no means only a matter of casting and mounting the metal parts—their right to this was not and could not be seriously challenged by anyone. It was far more a question of selling the pewter-mounted glassware, concerning which there was repeated litigation. An exclusive right was claimed by shop-keepers as well as glaziers and pewterers. During the complaints, each of these propounded an "age-old right in law" and the law courts awarded the right now to one, now to another. Conflict frequently reached such a level that a royal decree became necessary to restore a certain measure of order. A few pewterers, like for example Alois Reil, who worked in Upper Bavaria from the beginning of the 19th century, even requested the right to sell unmounted glassware. Sometimes this also led to legal action, for instance in 1864 against the master Anton Burger in Upper Palatinate who traded in unmounted glass vessels. A pewterer from Urach, Johann Georg Büchner the Younger, who worked as a "transparent glass painter" also provoked anger. A situation similar to that with glass tankards existed concerning the retail sale of pewter-mounted pottery and faience. Since the beginning of the 16th century pottery and the occasional
183 tankard of serpentine had been taken into pewterers' workshops for mounting. There are even instances when the manufacture of tankard mounts with cover and strap formed part of the masterpiece. Relations with the potters were often good. Thus during the course of centuries the pewterers and the potters in Munich established a common guild. Separation came about by agreement only in 1805. Because pewter covers were not sold loose, potters made no endeavour to intervene to any great extent in the pewter trade. There were, however, conflicts about the right to sell with the shop-keepers' guilds which also led to varying outcomes. In Stettin (now Szczecin) in 1700
184 even a ship's master secured for himself the privilege of selling faience which was just making its appearance. The pewterers of Prenzlau protested against this and declared that the most important part of the tankards was certainly their pewter covers and because of this they ought to retain the right of retail trade. The chamber locally responsible for matters of war and administration proposed a compromise.

In the households of the people pewter-mounted pottery and faience were carefully handled and treated as articles of such value that they were
173 listed in detail in wills. The value put upon pottery is shown by the sometimes
185/186 outstandingly engraved pewter covers, some of which were produced by professional engravers. If a pewterer learned of an intention to commission a showy engraving he may well then have used particularly good-quality material. Generally he was free to decide for himself how much lead he would add to the tin when it was intended for casting covers for pottery and faience tankards.

The display parts with which principally the covers of beer tankards are decorated are of English pewter. They depict portrait busts of princes, decorative motifs, historical scenes with superscriptions; they are pressed out in Nuremberg by means of polished dies engraved in steel, distributed throughout Europe, sold by the hundred and turned into the rim of the cover.

J. S. Haller, *Werkstätten der heutigen Künste oder die neue Kunsthistorie,* Brandenburg and Leipzig, 1761.

Harvest-cans and feeding-bottles

It has already been mentioned that country people still preferred pewter wares long after they had been displaced by cheaper materials in the large towns. In these circumstances those in the pewter trade had to consider what to produce, taking into account special rural needs. There were not, in fact, many new individual products to be found since most pewterware had always conformed to the wishes of country people whilst the harvest-cans which emerged in the last third of the 18th century in Thuringia, Saxony, in the Vogtland and in the Erzgebirge make it clear from their name that they were emphatically for a rural purpose.

In principle this has reference to a can in which a drink could be taken out into the fields, from which liquid would not easily be lost and from which one could drink directly when required. The unusually heavy physical labour on hot harvest days of necessity demanded occasional breaks for recuperation. Indeed the authorities were sometimes of the opinion that more profit could be derived from the labour force if this kind of thing was forbidden and not even the *vesperbrot* (afternoon meal) allowed between main meals. Thus, for example, an ordinance of the Electorate of Brandenburg in 1687 stipulated that persons in good health must not eat more than three times a day either in summer or winter. The ruling classes quickly learned, however, that more was to be gained if the heavy work of harvesting was mentally and materially stimulated. In many places country people then said that the arrangements at harvest times were like those for weddings and christenings.

On very hot harvest days during which country people must perform their work without shade or intermission, it must be considered that they very much long for recuperation and refreshment of their animal spirits.
Then is the right time to come to the aid of the body with cooling fare.

Recommendations for the owners of manors, gentlemen, etc., Berlin, 1786.

Pewter harvest-cans had a screwed lid with a rigid semi-circular stirrup-handle cast integral with it. Its diameter was such that it could be securely held in the hand when carried. So that as little liquid as possible would be
190 lost from the relatively long spout it was provided with a small flap-cover. This cover opened when a refreshing draught was quickly taken from the can as was usually done at harvest time. For this reason further development abandoned the flap-cover and instead the end of the spout was extended
187 somewhat, horizontally at the level of the can's shoulder. When the can was standing in a basket or similar receptacle the end of the spout then projected over the edge and was readily accessible. To create a pleasing appearance it
188 was given the shape of an animal's head with a tube in its jaws. This tube could be taken into the mouth when drinking.

What was drunk from harvest-cans? In accordance with a contemporary account of about 1800 the harvest drink in the Netherlands was wretched coffee, in Austria apple juice or skimmed milk and in France perry or cider, generally, however, apart from water, *covent*. *Kofent*, a small beer, is mentioned as early as 1423 and was recommended for harvest time with the comment that it quenched the thirst, restored failing strength and reduced the need for foot. So that it would flow readily from the can pewterers drilled a hole up to half a centimetre in diameter in the screwed lid so that a strong
189 draught could be taken even with the lid secured.

As drink, nothing but good, genuine beer, all of which must be given to them by the master of the house and mother of the family, cleanly prepared, without displeasure, grumbling or sullenness.

Outline for an order by the authorities of Anhalt for community feeding, 1614.

Harvest-cans were not used exclusively for the purpose which gave them their name but also as pouring and storage vessels in the household and on festive occasions. In contrast, the number of possible uses for children's pewter feeding-bottles was much more restricted although they were often used in the care of the sick. In spite of their restricted function they were to be found in most families, which may well have been connected with the numerous children customary at that time. Pewter feeding-bottles are rendered in paintings as early as the end of the 15th century. They were made in pewter in every country and their names are various and colloquial. In Germany they were called *lutsch* or *zutschkännchen, kindernonnen, ludeln, warzenflaschen,* also *saughörner* and now and again *krankenflaschen* (mostly in America) for those who were sick. Pewterers offered feeding-bottles inessentially two types. The older and possibly most numerous form
191–193 has the shape of a truncated cone with a screwed cover from which projects a small sucking tube resembling a nipple. The other type has a spherical belly extending into a slender neck on which fits a more or less long sucking tube which can be screwed off. The spherical belly had the effect of making it easy to keep milk warm when a hot-water bottle was used; from about the
373–377 second half of the 18th century pewterers had made hot-water-bottles with one or more recesses in the body in which feeding-bottles could be placed. This impelled many frugal young housewives who had previously used a stone heated in the oven to warm the bed, to make an effort to buy a hot-water-bottle instead.

These easily cleaned and unbreakable feeding-bottles were principally offered for sale "for the good of those children who are being reared without a mother". Every now and again it was also stressed that they could be used to "teach small children how to suck and drink". They therefore fulfilled in every respect the function of today's feeding-bottles with a rubber teat. Glassmakers also produced feeding-bottles of the same shape as those of pewter which were subsequently fitted with a closure which was tubular or in the form of a knob. The "goose-bill for children" offered in some lists was possibly an attempt to earn some money from pewter dummies. The usual dummy was a piece of bread and sugar wrapped in a small piece of cloth which was dipped in milk or water and given to small children to suck.

Vessels to be used both for feeding and for pouring were the biberons made in the Netherlands and neighbouring German districts *(schapenkannetje)* as well as the Swiss *brunnenkesselchen*, literally small spring or well
196 kettle (also called *sugerli* = biberon). Biberons were already in existence in the 16th century; they are much rarer than feeding-bottles and may well have been intended more for the use of the sick. Dutch and North German
125 biberons bear a certain relationship with the *lirl*-tankards of the Egerland which have already been mentioned as serving-vessels. A closer connec-
195 tion, however, exists with the *brunnenkesselchen* made in the workshops of

Swiss pewterers. This name alludes to the use of these vessels after they
had themselves been filled from a water-keg in turn to dispense water into
354 their associated washing-bowls. Whether and to what extent they were used
for this purpose is disputed. On the other hand, they were certainly used as
drinking-vessels for children. This is confirmed not only by the widely used colloquial term *sugerli* but principally by children's tooth marks on the outlets of
the containers. For ease of use the biberon hung on wire loops by their pivoting handles, upon which they could be tilted without having to unhook them.
The outlet pipes usually reached right to the interior bottom; a child would
therefore be able completely to empty a *sugerli* which was standing upright
in front of it.

At this point, brandy-flasks must lastly be mentioned as a type of drink
container, because it is sometimes assumed that feeding-bottles were also
used as pocket flasks for spirits. Needless to say, this is not out of the question in principle, but probably would only have been in emergencies, an exceptional expedient. There is hardly any written evidence of their use for this
purpose whilst a great deal exists for the popularity of glass spirit flasks with
pewter closures. The smaller ones served as pocket flasks, bigger ones for
194 storage in the cellar. Regardless of their size and material all flasks which
were bellied-out towards the base with a narrow neck at the top were known
in Germany and in France as *bouteille*. Pewterers were not always successful in achieving a permanently tight joint between the glass and the pewter on
flasks with a screw-closure. It was therefore recommended to draw a pig's
bladder over the top as a safety measure. This, of course, refers to the closures on large flasks.

Storage of brandy is, so far as the ordinary kind is concerned, best done in small barrels, fresh from wine, or those in which brandy has already been kept for some time:
The strongest and most frequently drawn is most safely kept in glass bottles, because in those of pewter it becomes stale and in those of pottery, if it stands for a long time, it acquires an earthy taste; yet even in the glass ones, it is necessary to take great care and because pewter screws do not seal all that tight with each other and their cement, with which they are attached to the neck, is not do durable that nothing can evaporate out, one must tie over it a double thickness of bladder previously wetted in water.

Der Oeconomische Tausendkünstler (A thousand economical tricks), Frankfurt and Leipzig, 1760.

About 1800 in England pocket flasks were occasionally made entirely of
pewter which followed the shape of those of glass. In Bulgaria also — where
copper otherwise predominated — a few craftsmen sold pewter flasks. Those
197 designed for rose brandy *(pavur)* also resembled those of pottery and like
them were provided with a screw-closure. The large versions found in Austria were used to carry apple juice "for rustics and work-people" at field
work.

Beakers and cups

Beakers are found in pictorial representations as early as the late Middle
Ages and are accordingly to be counted among the oldest of pewter table-
279 ware. They are already mentioned in written works of the 14th century. Despite such documentary evidence of their existence, none have survived
from that period. This may be for two reasons. One is indicated by surviving
evidence that they did not appear in all too great numbers in taverns and
households. Plates and bowls, for example, are mentioned in considerably
greater numbers than beakers. The other is that they were easily damaged.
Beakers are vessels which have to stand up to multiple drinking bouts. Any
one of them might suddenly fall to the floor and be trodden on. Beakers

Preceding page:

162 Pichet; height 24 cm (9 1/2″), *c.* 1500.
Museum des Kunsthandwerks Leipzig

163 Baluster-shaped English tankard and dish; height of tankard 22 cm (8 5/8″), diameter of dish 34.5 cm (13 1/2″), 16th century.
Victoria & Albert Museum, London

164 Tankards; 14th–15th centuries.
Nationalmuseet Copenhagen

165 Flattened flask; height 20.7 cm (8 1/8″), 15th century.
Museum des Kunsthandwerks Leipzig

166 Chain-flask (field-flask, bouteille); height 33.5 cm (15 1/8″), dated 1720.
Gedenkstätte Crimmitschauer Textilarbeiterstreik 1903/04, Crimmitschau

164

165

17 20
TH

167
168

169
170

167 Barrel-shaped tankard; height 18 cm (7″), *c.* 1840. Heimatmuseum Geyer/Erzgebirge

168 Brandy-tankard; height 14 cm ($5^1/_2$″), *c.* 1780. Heimatmuseum Mühlhausen/Thuringia

169 Cylindrical tankard with the cover-knop modelled as a human head; height 25 cm (10″), dated 1778. In private ownership

170 Drinking-mug (without cover); height 15 cm ($5^7/_8$″), *c.* 1770. Virginia Museum of Fine Arts, Richmond

171 Tankard with concave sides and raised band, known as *fletsch*-tankard; height 12.8 cm (5″), 2nd half of the 16th century. Oberösterreichisches Landesmuseum Linz

172 Small drinking-tankard; height 17 cm ($6^3/_4$″), dated 1750. In private ownership

173 Account of a will in which two small pewter-mounted beer-kegs are mentioned; *c.* 1760. In private ownership

173

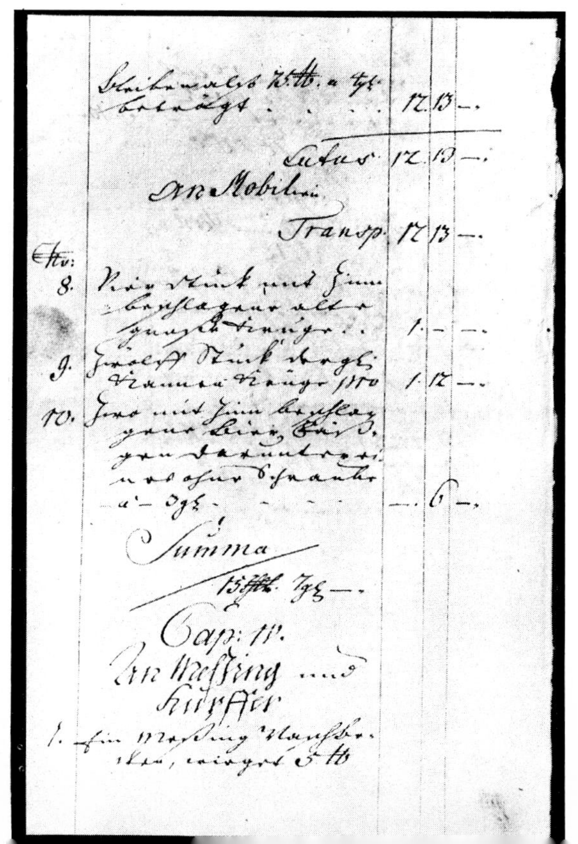

174 Tankards of wooden laths with pewter mounts and pewter inlay, known as Lichtenhainer tankards; height 15.5 and 18 cm ($6^1/_8$" and 7"), 18th century.
Staatliches Heimat- und Schlossmuseum Burgk/Saale

175 Wine-cooler; length 57 cm ($22^1/_2$"), dated 1761.
Museum des Kunsthandwerks, Leipzig

174

175

Following pages:

176 Two tapered tankards, known as *rörken*; height 21 and 25 cm ($8^1/_4$" and $9^7/_8$"), 17th century.
Kulturhistorisches Museum Rostock

177 Tankard with accentuated long neck; height 22 cm ($8^5/_8$"), dated 1764.
Kulturhistorisches Museum Rostock

178 *Rörken* with pierced wall, known as puzzle-jug; height 22 cm ($8^5/_8$"), *c.* 1750.
Museum des Kunsthandwerks Leipzig

179 Tall cylindrical tankard; height 30 cm ($11^3/_4$"), dated 1830.
Traditionsstätte Erzbergbau, Aue

177
178
179

IOCHM MIREKE 1629

180 Detail of Fig. 181: cover.

181 Tall cylindrical tankard with double-domed cover; *c.* 1629.
Historiska Museet, Göteborg

182 Pewter-mounted glass-tankard; height 25 cm (10″), dated 1775.
Heimatmuseum Mühlhausen/Thuringia

183 Tankard of serpentine with pewter mounts and pewter handle; height 13 cm ($5^1/_8$″), 1st half of the 17th century.
Städtisches Museum Halberstadt

184 Pewter-mounted faience tankards; height 25.5 and 26.5 cm (10″ and $10^1/_2$″), 1st half of the 18th century.
In private ownership

184

185 Detail of Fig. 186: cover engraving

186 Pewter-mounted Westerwald tankard; height 20.5 cm (8″), dated 1750. In private ownership

185

186

187 Thuringian harvest-can; height 28.5 cm (11 $^{1}/_{4}$"), dated 1854. In private ownership

188 Detail of Fig. 187: the end of the spout in the form of an animal's head with the drinking-tube in its jaws.

189 Detail of Fig. 187: vent in the screwed cover which permitted a free flow of liquid while drinking.

188

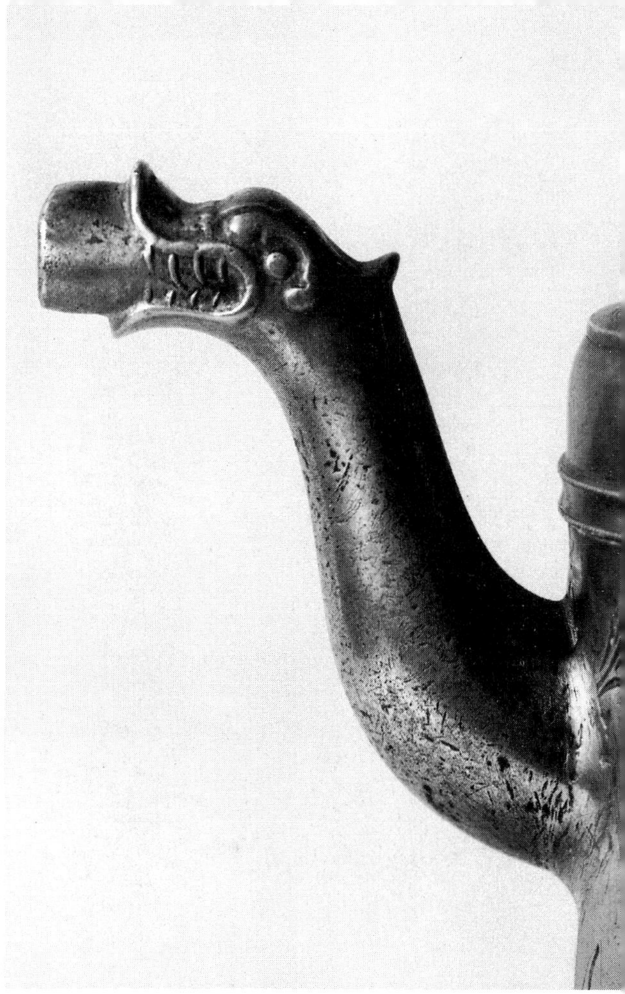

189

187

190 Harvest-cans with flap-covers for their spouts; height 12.5 and 16 cm (5″ and $6^1/_4$″), dated 1793 and 1847. Heimatmuseum Geyer/Erzgebirge

191 Feeding-bottle for an infant; height 11.9 cm ($4^5/_8$″), 17th century. Museum des Kunsthandwerks Leipzig.

192 Feeding-bottle for an infant with outlet in the shape of a teat; height 11 cm ($4^3/_8$″), dated 1832. Schlossmuseum Altenburg

193 Feeding-bottle with globular belly and elongated feeding-tube, for an infant; height 21 cm ($8^1/_4$″), *c.* 1820. Kreisheimatmuseum Grimma

191
192
193

194 Glass brandy-flask with pewter screw-closure; height 13.5 cm ($5^{1}/_{4}''$), *c.* 1800. In private ownership

195 Swiss biberon *(brunnenkesselchen)* with incised iron pivoting handle; height 16.3 cm ($6^{3}/_{8}''$), *c.* 1800. Schweizerisches Landesmuseum Zurich

196 Netherlandish biberon with long feeding-tube; height 11 cm ($4^{3}/_{8}''$), early 17th century. Museum Boymans-van Beuningen, Rotterdam

197 Pewter-mounted pottery brandy-flask; height 17.5 cm ($6^{7}/_{8}''$), *c.* 1650. In private ownership

196 197

198 Beakers; height 9 and 10.5 cm ($3^1/_2$″ and $4^1/_8$″), dated 1807 and 1830.
Vogtländisches Kreismuseum Plauen

199 Beakers showing the owners' names from two generations in the same family; height 5.2 and 7.7 cm (2″ and 3″), dated 1780 and 1836.
In private ownership

200 Beakers with pronounced flare to the rim, known as *staufs*; height 6 cm ($2^3/_8$″), dated 1793.
Traditionsstätte Erzbergbau, Aue

201 Beaker with reinforced base; height 8 cm ($3^1/_8$″), *c.* 1800.
Museum "Schloss Moritzburg", Zeitz

202 Lightly swamped beaker; height 10.5 cm ($4^1/_8$″), dated 1837.
Heimatmuseum Mühlhausen/Thuringia

201
202

203 Footed beaker; height 16.8 cm ($6^{5}/_{8}''$), *c.* 1840.
Städtisches Museum Halberstadt

204 Beaker with handle; height 8 cm ($3^{1}/_{8}''$), *c.* 1800.
Museum Weissenfels

205
206
207

203
204

Preceding page:

205 Footed beakers on short stems; height 17 cm ($6^{3}/_{4}$″), dated 1839–1841. Gedenkstätte Crimmitschauer Textilarbeiterstreik 1903/04, Crimmitschau

206 Beer-warmer; length 18.4 cm ($7^{1}/_{4}$″), 2nd half of the 19th century. Vogtländisches Kreismuseum Plauen

207 Cups with handles of differing shapes; height 6.8 cm ($2^{5}/_{8}$″), 18th century, and height 7.8 cm (3″), *c.* 1800. Vogtländisches Kreismuseum Plauen

208 Cups with saucers; height 6 cm ($2^{3}/_{8}$″), dated 1803. Kreisheimatmuseum Grimma

209 Cups with saucers; height 7 cm ($2^{3}/_{4}$″), dated 1810. In private ownership

210 Cups with saucers; height 6 cm ($2^{3}/_{8}$″), early 19th century. In private ownership

210

also suffered damage when they were put down with a heavy hand. Many thus found their way back into pewterers' melting pots, afterwards to re-appear at table as new drinking-vessels. Although there is documentary evidence that not only silversmiths but also pewterers made nesting beakers (those which fit one inside the other in a column) in fairly large batches, it seems none have survived. Service was generally made from large flagons or smaller jugs and tankards.

It is worthy of notice that it was sometimes expressly prohibited to fetch beer from the cellar direct in a beaker. "Let no-one fetch a beaker of beer out of the cellar" — this or the like is contained in many documents.

Amongst ordinary people pewter beakers were popular in the 16th and
17th centuries as "morning gifts". This refers to the gift which a bridegroom
gave to his bride on the morning after the marriage "to requite her for the taking of her virginity"; the morning gift was nevertheless customary on the re-
marriage of widows. The bridegroom had his bride's name engraved upon it,
often framed in a garland or flowers or similar. The shape of these early beakers tended to follow those of glass; in northeastern Europe pewter beakers,
especially those which were somewhat bellied were also called glasses. In
205 France tulip-shaped stemmed cups were made with a ring round the base
decorated with studs. Their name, *timbales à coco* points to their being favoured for the enjoyment of liquorice water. Tulip cups were still presented
as gifts at engagements and marriages in the 18th century when the "morning gift" had become customary only among the high nobility. In England,
corresponding vessels were called "loving cups". After the Gothic period
198 tapered beakers were generally more widespread than those of tulip shape
or which were bellied. It was only in the 18th century that they tended more
and more to a cylindrical shape. In that same century beakers were still valu-
199 able possessions which were bequeathed from father to son.

In North Germany and Scandinavia two-handled cups held a special
place and were passed round during convivial drinking. The somewhat large
cup would then be grasped by the handles with both hands and raised to the
lips. The name for the two-handled cup was a *stop*. It is possible that this
term derives from an old fluid measure which was valid in Sweden until 1883
and originated from a unit of volume, the *kanna*. One *kanna* contained two
stops or four quarters which were equivalent to 2.617 litres. In old Russia a
fluid measure similar in volume and name was the *stoof*. From the 17th cen-
204 tury *stops* were no longer made. The *rörken* which have already been mentioned became fashionable in their place and can be generally regarded as
successors to two-handled cups as well as those with only one handle.

In Switzerland and southern Germany at the time of the *stop* the pewter
trade made a type of beaker which flared towards the top and which was of-
200 fered for sale under the name of *stauf*. A number of pewterers embellished it
with three small feet which were popularly given the appearance of animals,

pomegranates or even the human torso. The *stauf* later went over to a
203 straight tapered or cylindrical shape which, however, did not find by a long way so great a circle of customers as in the north. Sometimes voices were raised against the use of pewter for drinking-vessels for children. Thus in 1780 there were repeated complaints that at night, mothers were in the habit of warming milk or beer over a lamp for their children. Because now as a result of insufficient care in cleaning there were deposits from the previous drink, these were dissolved by the effect of heat. Children consumed these deposits with the fresh drink and thereby suffered great harm. It would seem that in northern Germany and Scandinavia no-one was particularly impressed with these theories because not only was there a brisk production —and corresponding market— but also until into the 18th century the widespread habit of drinking warmed beer in fairly large beakers. Relatively large beakers were to be found in the households on many handicrafts masters' families as a reminder of their initiation into the guild. In some districts the *hänsel* beaker had to be emptied on the occasion of such an initiation, the name stemming from entry into a "hansa" (company or association). Although it was a commemorative gift the *hänsel* beaker was put into use and there was no hesitation about standing it on a stove to prepare warm beer.

An effective remedy for colds

Take half a litre of beer, 1 egg, a knife-point of flour, some butter; ginger, nutmeg and salt to taste. Let it come to the boil and drink it hot.

Household remedy, 1723.

Heated beer was also prepared and served outside the home. A chronicler writing in the declining years of the 18th century reported that it was still an esteemed drink "when travelling and in inns where one cannot expect good
206 coffee". An incidental item which must be mentioned are the beer warmers with which a few pewterers tried their luck. These tubular vessels were filled with hot water and then stood in the tankard of beer until, cold from the cellar, it reached the desired temperature. The manufacture of such devices, needless to say, brought no significant return. In contrast, those who made small brandy beakers *(liekedeeler, strieker)* had more success. They sold well on the North Sea and Baltic coasts. It seems that dice beakers, which were shaped after the "lucky" *rörken*, having a pierced double-skinned base, were not a proven success.

Cups, like beakers, were intended for the use of only one individual. These emerged in the 18th century, not only in pewter but also in other most frequently used materials as the new "foreign liquors" became established and the production of chocolatières, coffee- and tea-pots began. Certainly there were included in an inventory from Saxony as early as the 17th century "two Waldenburg cups, mounted with pewter". Waldenburg cups meant pottery vessels but the word "cup" must not yet be taken to mean the shape
207 later to be considered typical. The appearance of early cups made entirely of
208–210 pewter clearly indicates that beaker casting moulds were used: saucers were still usually lacking and only became customary at the beginning of the 19th century.

Cup

A bowl, small bowl, a plain drinking-vessel from which one drinks tea, coffee, chocolate or other exotic liquid.

Explanatory definition, 1744.

Cups or bowls with handles are known in pottery from very early times. Amongst the pewter bowls with handles which resemble cups the most widespread in northern Germany were the *tröstelbierschalen* — drinking-vessels for condolence beer. Mourners were served with solacing beer in these containers after funerals. They largely disappeared in favour of cups when, from about 1800, coffee was served after the obsequies instead of beer. In central and southern Germany the *köpfgen* was a drinking-vessel for beer resembling a cup: *köpfgen* or *koppchen* fired in porcelain were always intended for the new drinks from the start.

Although cups were made in every country with a pewter-working trade they never really became fashionable. Only the Russian *tsharka* — a simple round cup with a strap-handle — was used with some frequency for drinking tea from a samovar. Pewterers went to great trouble to imitate silver cups
208 with gadrooning or to follow the shape of those of porcelain so as to reflect the "outstanding character" of chocolate, coffee and tea but porcelain had already achieved predominance in this field at an early date. Those who were as yet unable to afford porcelain often used pewter beakers instead of cups.

Kitchenware and Storage Vessels

5

In his historical novel *Vittoria Accorombona* which appeared in
1840, Ludwig Tieck told of a party who were besieged and, lacking
musket balls, rapidly melted down pewterware from the kitchen.
There was indeed manifold utilitarian pewter to be found in the
211 kitchen, for example, bowls, pots, funnels, strainers, moulds and
other items. In Austria and Germany, kitchenware was often called
häfen—pots and pans. In addition to the pots and pans used directly
for the preparation of food and drink were pewter storage vessels.
Because households were predominantly arranged to be self-sufficient, storage containers were of particular importance and their number was proportionately great. Of pewter containers, screw-top flasks which could be closed so as to be almost airtight were very practical but likewise boxes, together with cans for oil and water. Urns which served to keep coffee hot were another type of storage receptacle.

The kitchen was also the place where pewterware was washed and cleaned. Two scouring pails were normally used, one for pottery and one for pewter. After meals, washing-up was done either with pure sand boiled in lye or with sand alone. Now and again a straw scouring pad was used to make dull pewter bright again. After scouring, the ware was rinsed in clean water. At weddings and other occasions when a number of guests were invited, women dish-washers from the neighbourhood stood ready to ensure that there would be no shortage of pewterware at table. From time to time the usual scouring and washing no longer sufficed to restore the characteristic pewter shine. The metal takes on a patina for whose removal even the pewterer took part at the Grand Ducal Court at Moscow. Otherwise this was done within the domestic circle and namely with "pewter herb"—horse-tail or shave grass. When the patina had not been removed for a long time, shave grass would no longer put it to rights. In this case filings of brass,

In addition to the vessels which pewterers produce there are . . . further a thousand-fold kitchen devices among which there is almost nothing to be found which some all too greedy women do not demand to have in their frivolous display kitchens; even the broom must have a pewter stick and the dusting whisk a pewter handle.

C. Weigel, *Abbildung der gemeinnützlichen Hauptstände* (Account of the main professions of public utility), Nuremberg, 1698.

copper, iron or even pewter were glued to a piece of leather. The pewterware was then polished with the previously prepared leather until it was gleaming bright. If while doing this a housewife discovered signs of decay in the metal (pewter sickness) the affected piece was promptly sent for melting. It was simpler to do this rather than as would, of course, be done today, namely to etch out the diseased parts with dilute hydrochloric acid, use an abrasive if necessary, then conscientiously remove all acid traces in a hot-water bath and, when dry, solder up the hole or missing piece.

Strainers, funnels, spoon-holders and moulds

It was relatively seldom that a housewife had to scour any item of kitchen equipment which did not come into contact with a hot stove or even direct with a naked flame. Such pieces were rinsed and now and again cleaned like all other pewter. Usually they were left to dry in the air after rinsing. This was also the procedure for strainers which until the middle of the 19th century
214–216 were made in the shape of pierced pots with feet. The softness of the material forbade fitting of a handle and thus to do away with the feet; only very small strainers with stems were offered by a few pewterers for tea or milk about 1840 and even rarer are the fish drainers current about 1700 in the form of round dishes with handles and rhomboid pattern lattice. In use a straining pot was placed in a bowl or similar vessel if the drained liquid was to be retained. So that they could be moved easily even when full, they had two handles soldered on in a similar way to those on jugs and tankards. For stability many straining pots were stepped in reducing diameters, most, however, were not. They were used for tammying milk to make cottage cheese and also for straining boiled cabbage and other vegetables. Some even had covers. In addition they were also suitable for pressing apple pulp through. If there was no more robust piece of pottery or cast-iron equipment available, pewter strainers were also used to prepare peas. Boiled peas were rubbed through and separated from their hulls with a wooden spoon. Swiss so-called "onion baskets", which were also used for flowers and were very seldom made had a certain likeness to strainers. These were pierced, almost spherical containers which were hung from a chain and from whose holes onion shoots could sprout.

Füllhals (fill-neck) is the widespread term for the type of funnel which was cast in the solid until about 1800 and subsequently usually soldered up from sheet pewter. Even the handle is of pewter strip cut from sheet. The term
212/213 "fill-neck" indicates the purpose for which it was normally used, to which was added a special purpose as the availability of coffee became more widespread. Lined with a linen cloth or better still, a piece of absorbent paper, the funnel was used for the preparation of filter coffee then, of course,

Purée of elder-flowers

Take elder-flowers, strip them off, wash them clean and let them simmer in good thick milk, force them through a pewter sieve, break 4 or 5 eggs into them, salt them, pour butter to it and let it simmer well. Mix sugar and raisins with it and serve it.

Cookery recipe, 1732.

uncommon. It is possible that mainly small mocha-jugs were filled in this manner.

Spoon-holders are among the earliest products of the pewter trade. When wooden spoons were not actually carried on the person, after meals they were put in a drawer, at the edge of the table, in leather pouches on a rack or on the wall or into cut-outs in the table surface. After acquisition of the more costly pewter spoons, these had to be visible to everyone after meals and displayed for the enjoyment of all. To achieve this, at first a wooden stand was used which was known in the alpine regions and southern Germany as a *rehm* (cf. *rahm* = frame). From the 16th century onwards, howev-
217/218 er, pewter spoon-boards under various names existed in almost every Euro-
220/222 pean country with a pewter trade. The "spoon-wreath" which was made in northeastern Europe is more rare. This was in the form of a circular wreath —conforming to its name—into which spoons could be inserted. It was probably no longer produced from as early as the 18th century. Spoon-boards, in contrast, were made until well into the 19th century. Whereas they at first hung in the living room, at this date they had for a considerable time
219/221 hung only in the kitchen. So-called spoon-bags into which cutlery was put after washing-up were always exclusively kitchen equipment. A small outlet, usually in the form of a short tube, allowed water to drip away so that spoon-bags only had to be taken off the wall at times when there was a general cleaning of all the pewter.

224/225 From the 17th until the 19th centuries pewter moulds were part of the equipment of many kitchens. They were used for shaping pastry and marzi-
230 pan before these were put in the oven. Half- or single-sided moulds created images of fruits, plants, human figures, animals and similar subjects. In the first half of the 17th century various pewterers—influenced by the sculpturing of the master of "noble" pewter Enderlein and others—endeavoured to
226–229 transpose popular themes into their small half-moulds. This required considerable skill in the production of the mould; the actual casting operation it-
231–233 self was less complicated. Full or whole moulds were more complicated to design because they had to be sectional in such a way that they could be separated without disturbing the surface of the pastry or marzipan after it had been shaped. Many of these moulds were probably also used for sweetmeats or confectionery. In Germany the workshop of the Biberach (Wurttemberg) pewterer Friedrich August Gutermann in the 19th century came to specialize in moulds for the production of Easter bunnies, snowmen and the like which were supplied to confectioners and chocolate factories.

Baking attractive decorative-edged marzipan.

Take a pound of good almonds, soak them and take their skins off, dry them again, pound them until they are like milk, add as much sugar and rose-water as is good; next put the whole into a brass beaker, roast it upon coals, as dry as possible. When it no longer sticks and can be pressed into the mould, take some good starch in a small piece of cloth, dredge the mould well with it, then press the paste into it so that it is perfectly even, then put it from the mould onto a sheet or plate, place it upon the oven, let it get thoroughly hot so that it dries and becomes nicely white, afterwards gild it.

Confectioner's recipe, 1784.

Kitchen-bowls, boxes and canisters

Bowls not only took their place upon the table at mealtimes but were also
234–236 used for tasks in the kitchen. In them the dough for bread or pastry were mixed, vegetables and other accompaniments to meals prepared, food kept hot and so on. Even cooking was done in bowls, especially soup. For this,

the trade produced deep rimless containers which had two small handles. This kind of bowl was occasionally provided with three ball-feet, a feature which did not in fact attract any special popularity in the household. For practical reasons bowls were kept in the kitchen. During the blossoming period of the pewter trade most households possessed a bowl-board upon which
237 bowls could be hung and also set out. Many kitchen-bowls have a ring for this purpose, often soldered on at a later date. Before they were put away on the bowl-board after use, the bowl-boy was at the housewife's disposal. This was a wooden stand upon which bowls (and plates) were dried after being washed. The large oval basins already mentioned which served as wine-coolers and which scarcely still exist today were also extensively used in the
175 kitchen from the 15th century. They are frequently to be seen in woodcuts and etchings of an early date. It is possible that washing of bowls, plates and similar articles was once speedily performed in one of these large wine-coolers because now and again documents refer to pewter wash-tubs although their function for keeping cool is clearly recognizable from the depictions in which they appear.

Like wine-coolers, butter-troughs are rare survivors. These containers were in fact first produced by the trade only in the 18th century but clearly only in very small numbers because otherwise they would be found more frequently. According to a contemporary description, butter-troughs were "pewter vessels, round in their length, shaped like a small trough, which had four feet and a cover". They were used for keeping baked butter-plaits or butter-rolls whereby attention was drawn to the fact that the plaits and rolls could be reliably protected from vermin and dirt in these containers.

Pewter boxes and canisters were found at various times in almost every kitchen. Today there is a somewhat retrograde distinction between the two terms that for canisters, the height is greater than the diameter but for boxes it is less. This kind of differentiation was made contemporaneously neither by pewterers nor in everyday usage but both terms were used at random for this kind of container. However, these always mean a container with a cover. Closely associated with the term canister is indeed a type of butter-cake, in Germany called *büchsenkuchen* (canister-cake) which the family may often have been lucky enough to enjoy. To make it the housewife stirred flour, milk, eggs, salt and nutmeg together, put the dough into a canister thickly spread with butter which was then closed with a cover and placed in a bath of boiling water. Once the dough had become firm in the can, it was taken out, cut into slices and finished by baking in hot lard. The preparation of "canister-cake" seems to be the only instance of such containers being used directly to prepare a foodstuff. Otherwise they were used as typical storage containers, also outside the kitchen, for example for tobacco. Among the products kept in the kitchen would be fat, tea, coffee, cocoa, spices and
240 soap. Large containers, with and without screwed covers or handles were

Fricassé of roast meat.

Cut a veal roast into fairly small pieces and perhaps some roast chicken and mutton all mixed together, extract the marrow from the bones if you have any beef bones with marrow in them, put it into a pewter bowl with the previous ingredients, pour onto it three parts of water and one part of wine, take two small onions, peel them and cut them up, put them into the pewter bowl and cook until the onions are tender.

Cookery recipe, 1741.

241 used for fat, principally lard but also butter, oil and sometimes curds. The
canisters which were used in the 19th century for the preparation of ices
238 were likewise of considerable size. These canisters had a screw bayonet-
fastening cover which was spanned by a rigidly soldered stirrup-handle.
Once filled, the canister was agitated to-and-fro in a mixture of salt and ice
when the contents gradually became frozen and could then be enjoyed.

Smaller containers housed the constituents for drinks and also spices. At
an early date the frugal housewife already attached importance to storing
roasted coffee beans in a canister or box with a screw-closure. She would
239/240 normally have several containers for tea. This was determined by the many
242 kinds available, each of which was reputed to possess some beneficial quality. Because among the people it was necessary to cure oneself, health teas
were brewed from every possible strongly scented plant and the results
passed on from generation to generation. Camomile, lime-blossom and
peppermint teas were among those normally kept which were supplemented
by herbal teas which are still familiar today but also some such as oat-straw,
cherry-stalk and pansy teas.

Tea herb

Store it / in pewter containers / so that no damp comes to it / nor any fragrance out of it.

C. Vielheuer, *Gründliche Beschreibung frembder Materialien und Spezereien,* 1676.

Saffron was used as medicament, spice and colouring. The old rhyme
"saffron makes the cake yellow" refers to its role in baking; housewives
dyed cheese and butter yellow with it. A pewter box or canister with an en-
243 graved inscription was usually at hand for the storage of saffron. In addition
there were those for cinnamon, cloves and nutmeg. These boxes were usually the same in appearance and were differentiated only by their inscriptions
which were sometimes executed by a pewterer himself. In America in about
1800 characteristic tall slender canisters made their appearance which were
exclusively for the keeping of nutmeg. For salt, which of necessity had to be
available in every kitchen, pewterers at all times produced storage containers and it has already been mentioned that every now and again doubts were
expressed about possible danger to health. In the 18th century a doctor of
medicine by the name of Büchner, working in Halle on the Saale (Saxony)
caused great turmoil and agitation among pewterers because he wrote
against pewter salt-boxes in widely distributed publications. Even if soups
and broths were salted and then brought to the boil in pewter vessels over
open coals it could be harmful—at least, this was alleged by the dedicated
doctor from Halle. Whether significant loss was engendered by such allega-
tions can no longer be determined today. They certainly upset pewterers
and many housewives afterwards only used pewter salt-boxes for the storage of flour. The survival to the present day of salts and salt-boxes in consid-
247/248 erable numbers nevertheless indicates an extensive production. Salt-con-
tainers were popular as marriage gifts in every country and did not entirely
fall out of fashion even during the 19th century.

Saffron tablets open blockages of the liver and the spleen, disperse wind and flatulence, resist putrefaction of the body fluids and strengthen the heart.

Pharmacology, 1752.

Whereas salt-boxes intended for hanging on the wall were therefore provided with a semi-circular or other opening for a hook there was a further

range of box-like containers which had small feet or stood directly on their bases. The most varied commodities were kept in these free-standing boxes, for example, spices, string, dried fruit, millet, rice and the like. Until well into the last century pewter *dinkel*-boxes were to be found, especially in Southwest Germany. *Dinkel* (spelt) is an age-old cereal which was harvested before it was completely ripe, dried and then used as an additive for soups and stored accordingly; now and again unleavened loaves were baked with it. In France and Holland the housewife kept flour or sugar
249 needed in the kitchen in large boxes with handles on both sides and a securely closing cover. So that a variety of substances could be put into a single box, some of them were made with several compartments; they were
245/246 popular mostly for spices and some had a sliding cover.

Pots, screw-cans and casks

Pots were used even more than bowls on the cooking stove. Because pewter melts at about 230°C (445°F) it is astonishing to read every now and again of the use of pewter for boiling and stewing. Although a housewife might take great care to keep sufficient liquid in bowls and pots, the heat of the fire was often so great that one or another vessel was damaged. That pewter stewing- and baking-pans predominated for such a long time in the kitchen despite such mishaps was due to easy and cheap facilities for having pewterware repaired by soldering or to exchange it. Because material cost primarily determined the price of utilitarian pewterware, new pieces were always available providing that material in the form of a damaged item was supplied. It was, moreover, hardly a hardship to receive in return the latest fashion.

The all-embracing description pots and pans for kitchenware (German *häfen*) had already been quoted. In a narrower sense this means the pots which either stood upon an iron trivet or hung from a pivoted arm over the stove. "Two soups simmer in one pot" was an often used figure of speech in the 18th century to emphasize the most popular function of the pot. In Scandinavia and northern Germany, when a soup was being prepared the house-
250 wife used a *hangelpott* or *seeltopf* which in northeastern Europe was called a *schwengkessel* (swinging pot). This container had a cover and a drop-handle and was not only a cooking-vessel but also a storage container for water and milk as well as for carrying. Hot food, prepared in the kitchen, was taken to field-workers in "hanging-pots" and "swing-kettles" out of which they ate directly. For this particular purpose, pewterers now and again made double pots which had a common handle; related containers were also produced in Hungary, but in ceramics. In Austria, southern and central Germany pewter carrying-pots were made from the 17th century which are considerably slimmer than hanging-pots, slightly concave close to the bottom
251/254 and with either fixed or pivoting handles. The pewter trade consequently adopted a form which already existed in Roman-Germanic times in the

He must first be instructed to make a large bowl, afterwards a wine jug to hold an entire pot or four quarts, then a well-finished hanging-kettle; if, however, he is seeking master's rights within the boundaries of an incorporated town, apart from the prescribed bowl, of the last two pieces, the wine jug or cooling-kettle, one piece shall be free for him to choose and so that sufficient manufacturing time is allotted for these pieces, 4 weeks shall be granted.

Article of the Glogau (Glogów) pewter guild, 1771.

shape of bronze situla and which was a forerunner of a pewter vessel which enjoyed great popularity in rural circles until into the mid-19th century. In the kitchen carrying-pots were frequently used as storage containers for milk but solid commodities were also kept in them. Pewter pails were rarely to be found in the kitchen because more durable ones of wood were preferred.
253 Pewter pails have fixed soldered carrying-handles but were, in fact, used almost exclusively as storage vessels.

In the year 1762 a pewterer from Mainz, Sebastian Faerber was permitted to make a bouillon-pot with cover and underlay dish as his masterpiece.
252 This may well have meant an ordinary soup-pot, which resembles the carrying-pot in appearance, but is smaller and has its handle at the side; Faerber
255/256 actually made a tureen following a fashion which he had learnt in Karlsbad (Karlovy Vary). The frequently removable cover of these pots made it easier to spoon-out the soup or bouillon which could readily be kept warm in this small vessel. Food was perhaps kept hot in it ready for the father or son of the family upon return from work; on the other hand it could always be taken to
356 their place of work. Yeast-cans were among the equipment of many kitchens which have handles like soup-pots and are drawn-in at the base but are provided with a lip for pouring. More will be written later about the yeast which was generated in them and its use for medicinal purposes.

259 Screw-top canisters were greatly treasured storage containers. They had their place not only in the kitchen but also held food and drink upon journeys and during field work. Their esteem is evidenced by the fact that particularly in central and southern Europe pewterers always held an impressive stock ready for immediate delivery whereas many other utilitarian pewter articles
23/257 were only made to order. Their flat sides were a positive inducement for engraving. This was gladly exploited when a screw-top can was to be a wedding gift. In Switzerland and Austria the engraving on these cans is sometimes so fine as to have to appear to have been intended for display alone. This is misleading because there, as elsewhere, they were used for a variety of purposes. In Austria mead was brought home in them, drink was carried out into the fields and even unrisen dough was stored in them. The screw-
273 top opening which is sometimes very small indicates that these cans were also used directly to drink from. In Switzerland wine and also cereals and foodstuffs were kept in the same kind of screw-closure cans which made not only in prismatic but, above all in northern Switzerland, bell-shaped profiles. At the beginning of the 18th century pewterers diesigned screw-closure cans with encircling bands which were particularly attractive. These types of container involved craftsmen in a great deal of extra time for their production and were, as "bent work", expensive whilst over against simple round or multi-sided cans they had no enhanced usefulness. Various masters tried their luck with these containers but never achieved production in quantity. This has come about only in our own time whereby pewter sheet is shaped,

To you always the best
The flagon at the feast
Be always full of wine
Remember constantly mine.

Inscription on a screwed flask.

211 Olden kitchen
with ware of pewter, brass and pottery.
Goethehaus,
Frankfurt-on-Main

Following pages:

212 Cast funnel;
length 15 cm ($5^7/_8''$), *c.* 1800.
Museum Weissenfels

213 Funnels made up from sheet; length 8–14 cm ($3^1/_4''$–$5^1/_2''$), *c.* 1860.
In private ownership

214 Strainer with cover;
height 32 cm ($12^1/_2''$),
dated 1814.
Traditionsstätte Erzbergbau Aue

215 Strainer; height 21 cm ($8^1/_4''$), dated 1845.
Schlossmuseum Altenburg

216 Strainer on feet;
height 21 cm ($8^1/_4''$), *c.* 1800.
Vogtländisches Kreismuseum Plauen

212

213

214

215

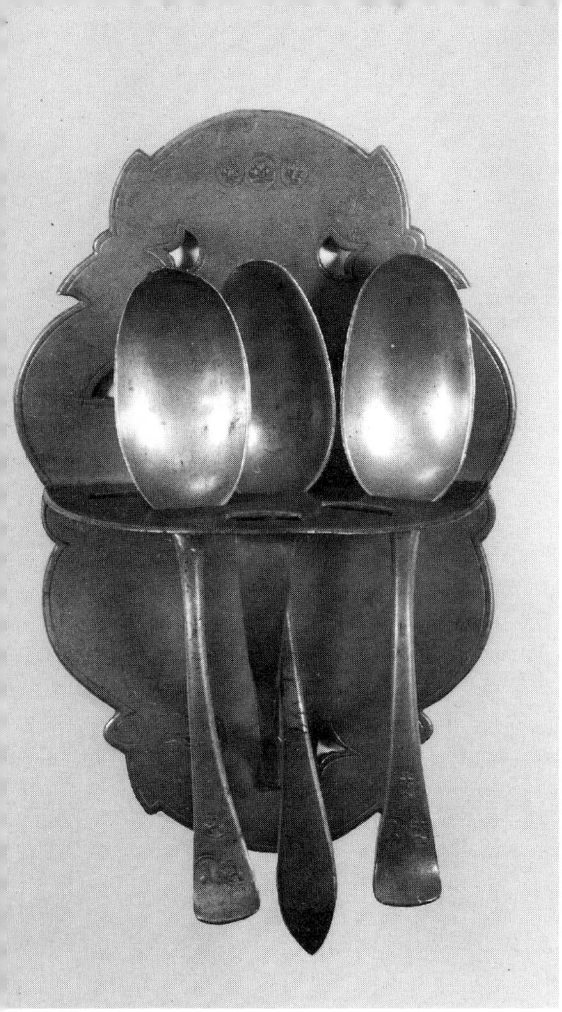

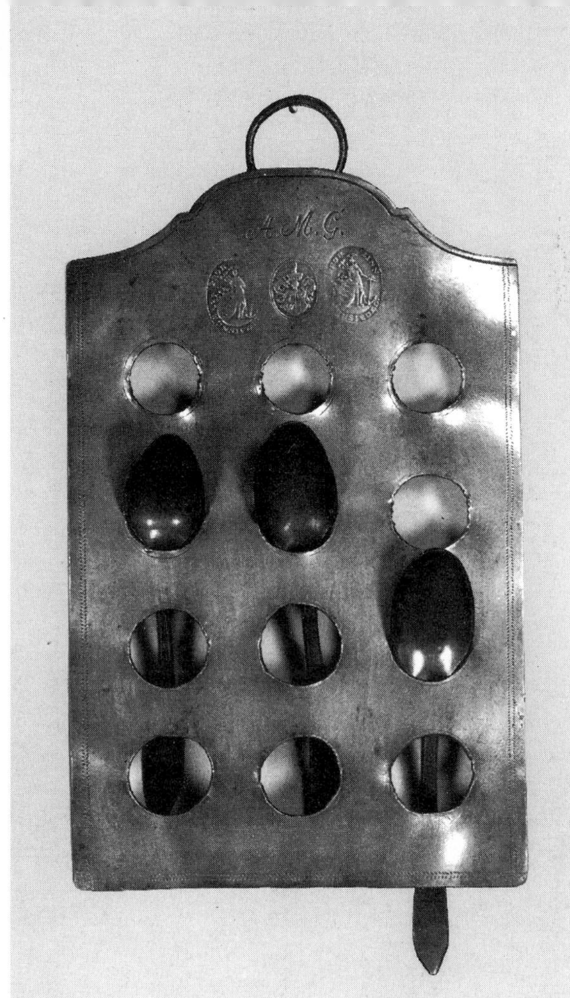
A.M.G.

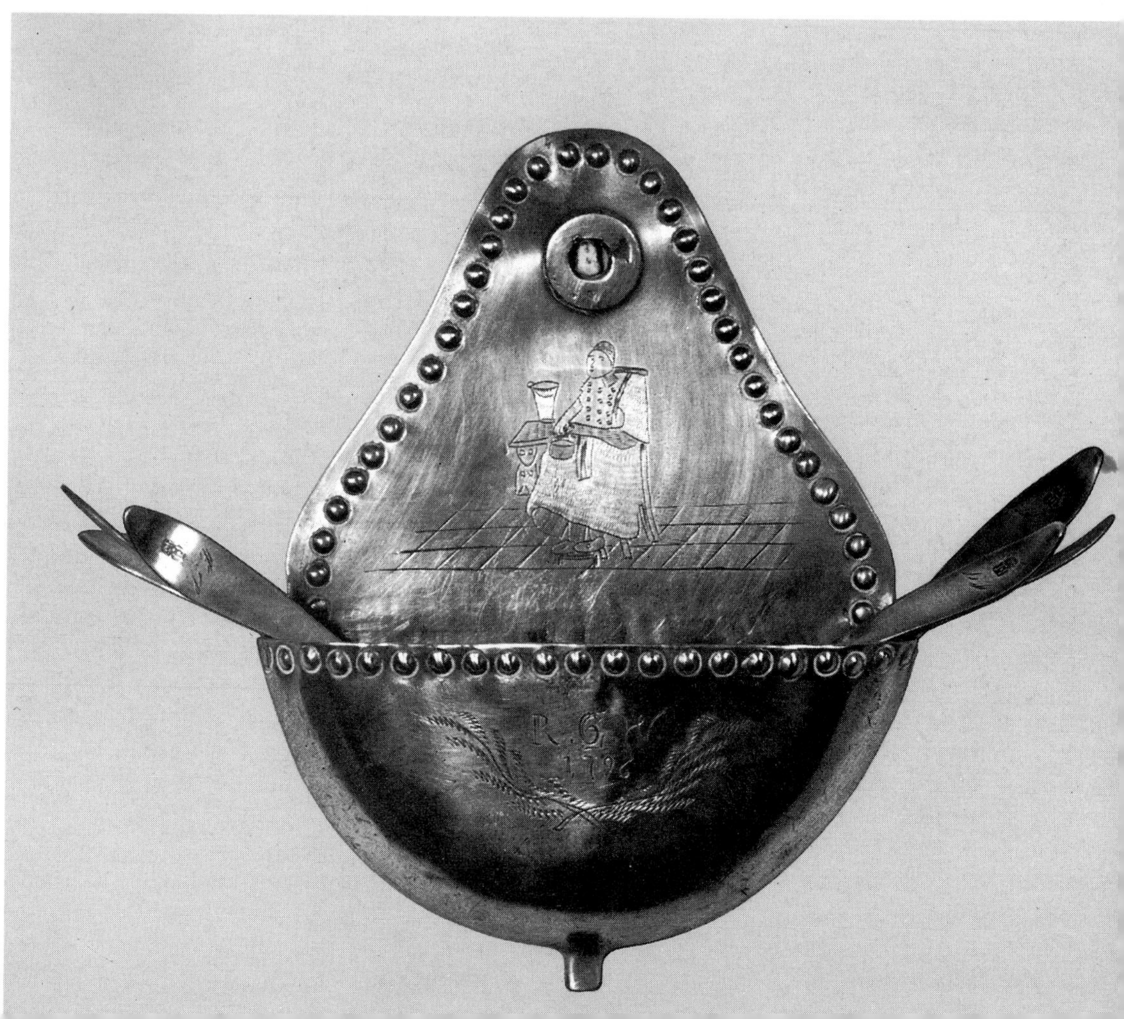

217 Spoon-holder; height 25 cm (10″), *c.* 1830.
Kulturhistorisches Museum Rostock

218 Spoon-holder; height 27 cm ($10^5/_8$″), *c.* 1840.
Vogtländisches Kreismuseum Plauen

219 Spoon-bag; length 28 cm (11″), dated 1850.
The long spoons with twisted stems which it contains were used for serving food.
In private ownership

220 Spoon-holder; height 34 cm ($13^3/_8$″), dated 1801.
Traditionsstätte Erzbergbau, Aue

221 Spoon-bag and spoons; height 27 cm ($10^5/_8$″), dated 1796.
In private ownership

222 Spoon-holder; length 22 cm ($8^5/_8$″), dated 1578.
Traditionsstätte Erzbergbau, Aue

222

223

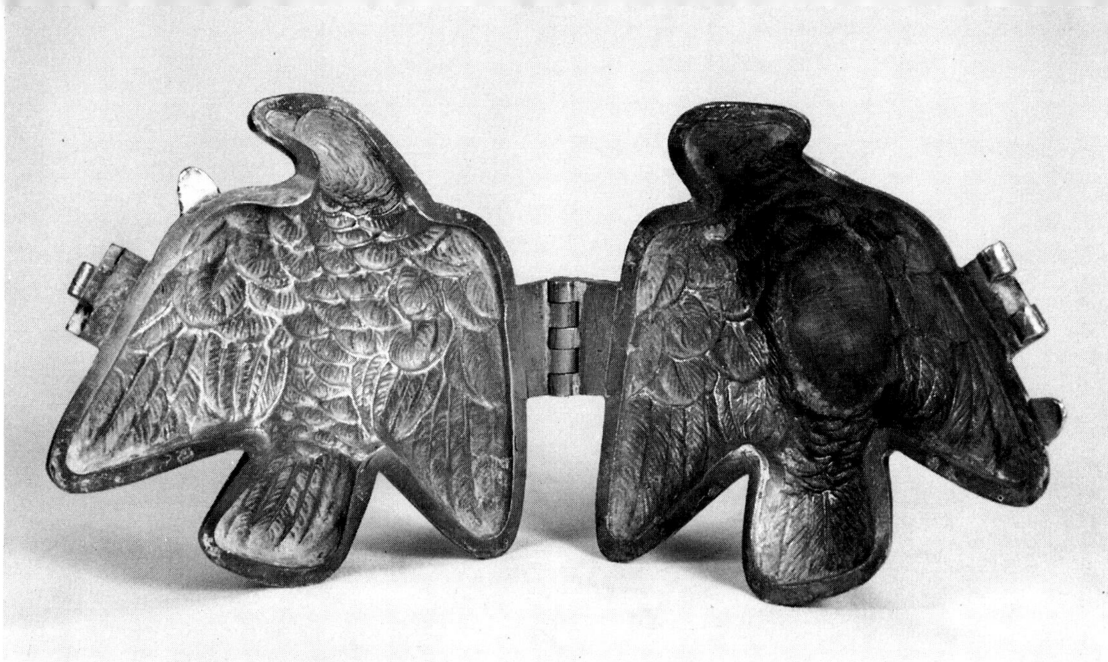

224

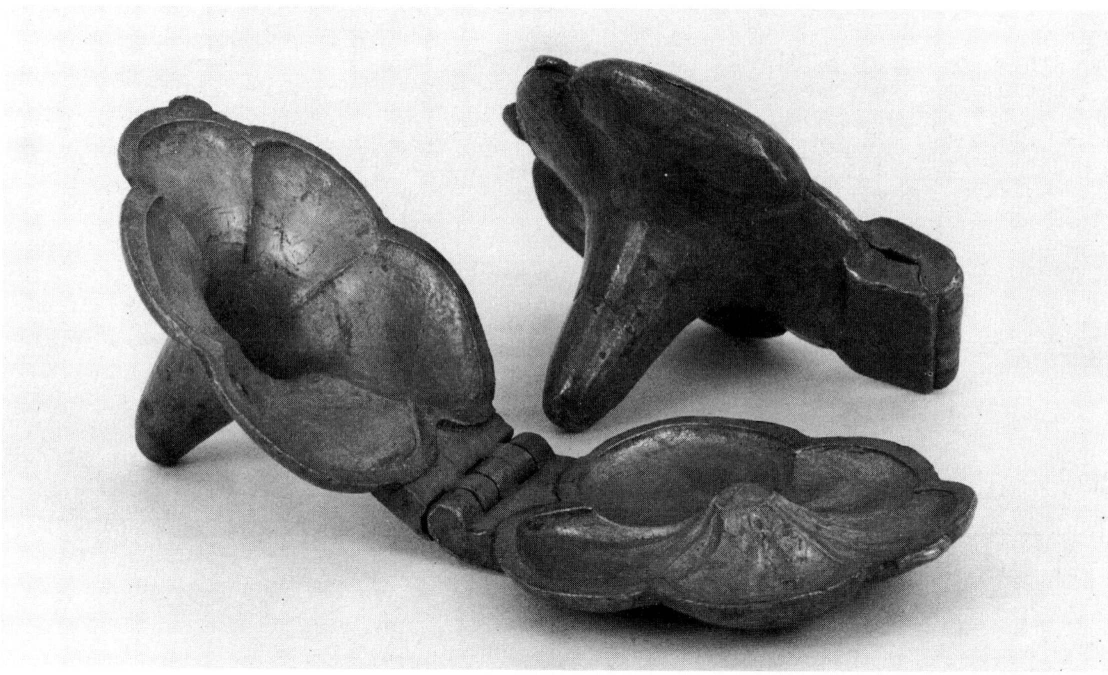

225

223 Full mould in the shape of a bird, open; height 11 cm ($4^3/_8$"), *c.* 1800. In private ownership

224 Two full moulds (flowers); diameter 8.5 cm ($3^3/_8$"), 2nd half of the 18th century. Heimatmuseum Mühlhausen/Thuringia

225 Two full moulds (fishes); length 9.5 and 13 cm ($3^3/_4$" and $5^1/_8$"), 2nd half of the 18th century. Heimatmuseum Mühlhausen/Thuringia

226 Half-mould "The Creation of Eve"; diameter 14 cm ($5^1/_2$"), 1st half of the 17th century. Städtisches Museum Schwäbisch Gmünd

227 Half-mould "Autumn"; diameter 15 cm ($5^7/_8$"), 1st half of the 17th century. Städtisches Museum Schwäbisch Gmünd

228 Half-mould "The Resurrection"; diameter 14 cm ($5^1/_2$"), 1st half of the 17th century. Städtisches Museum Schwäbisch Gmünd

229 Half-mould; diameter 9 cm ($3^1/_2$"), 17th century. Städtisches Museum Schwäbisch Gmünd

230 Half-mould in the shape of a pine cone; length 9 cm ($3^1/_2$″), 2nd half of the 18th century.
In private ownership

231 Mould for a small basket, opened-out.

232 Mould for a small basket, closed-up; length 18.8 cm ($7^3/_8$″), *c.* 1800.
In private ownership

233 Full mould in the shape of a snowman; height 30 cm ($11^3/_4$″), 19th century.
Kulturhistorisches Museum Rostock

234 Narrow-rimmed kitchen-bowls without handles; diameter 16.5–30 cm ($6^1/_2$″–$11^3/_4$″), late 18th/early 19th centuries.
In private ownership

235 Kitchen-bowl with deep basin, with handles; diameter 27.8 cm (11″), 19th century.
Kulturhistorisches Museum Rostock

233

236 Deep bowl with handles; diameter 27 cm ($10^5/_8''$), dated 1765.
Städtisches Museum Halberstadt

237 Hanging-bowls; diameter 16 and 24 cm ($6^1/_4''$ and $9^1/_2''$), dated 1827.
Kreisheimatmuseum Grimma

237

238 Ice-canister with bayonet-locking closure; height 37 cm ($14^{1}/_{2}$″), 19th century. Kulturhistorisches Museum Rostock

239 Wide-based tea-caddy; height 16 cm (6$^{1}/_{4}$″), dated 1807.
Museum "Schloss Moritzburg", Zeitz

240 Cooking fat-tub, with knob-handles soldered on; height 21.5 cm (8$^{1}/_{2}$″), dated 1725.
Kreisheimatmuseum Grimma

241 Storage pot with carrying handles; height 30.2 cm (11$^{7}/_{8}$″), *c.* 1810.
Kulturhistorisches Museum Rostock

242 Multi-purpose box; diameter 13.5 cm (5$^{3}/_{8}$″), dated 1759.
In private ownership

243 Spice-boxes for cloves, saffron and cinnamon; height 15 cm (5$^{7}/_{8}$″), *c.* 1820.
Museum "Schloss Moritzburg", Zeitz

244 Tea-caddies, one with a hinged cover; diameter 8.5 cm (3$^{3}/_{8}$″), *c.* 1815.
Museum "Schloss Moritzburg", Zeitz

245 Spice-box with sliding-cover; height 9.5 cm (1$^{3}/_{4}$″), *c.* 1800.
Vogtländisches Kreismuseum Plauen

245

246 Spice-box with hinged cover; height 4.6 cm ($3^{3}/_{4}$″), dated 1772. Vogtländisches Kreismuseum Plauen

247 Box for storing salt or flour; height 25.5 cm (10″), dated 1797. Vogtländisches Kreismuseum Plauen

248 Box; height 23 cm (9″), dated 1824. In private ownership

249 Box with handles, loose cover and ball-feet; height 34 cm ($13^{3}/_{8}$″), *c.* 1830. Städtisches Museum Halberstadt

247

248

250

251

250 North German covered pots with pivoting handles, known as *hangelpott* (hanging pots); height 21 and 23 cm ($8^1/_4$″ and 9″), 18th and 19th centuries.
Kulturhistorisches Museum Rostock

251 Carrying-pots; height 23 cm (9″), dated 1845 and 1865.
Schlossmuseum Altenburg

252 Small soup-pot with loose cover; height 18 cm (7″), dated 1852.
Vogtländisches Kreismuseum Plauen

253 Tub with shell-shaped grips; height 19 cm ($7^1/_2$″), c. 1790
Kulturhistorisches Museum Rostock

254 Carrying-pot with fixed cast handle; height 28 cm (11″), 19th century.
Vogtländisches Kreismuseum Plauen.

254

252
253

255 Small soup-pot with hinged cover; height 22.5 cm ($8^7/_8''$), *c.* 1800.
In private ownership

256 Small soup-pot with loose cover; height 17.5 cm ($6^7/_8''$), dated 1866.
In private ownership

257 Square screw-top flask with integrally cast carrying-ring; height 20.2 cm (8″), dated 1843.
Vogtländisches Kreismuseum Plauen

258 Cylindrical flask with screw-closure; height 21 cm ($8^1/_4''$), 1st half of the 18th century.
Städtisches Museum Halberstadt

259 Screw-closure flasks, octagonal and hexagonal; height 23 and 17 cm (9″ and $6^3/_4''$), 1750 and 1708.
In private ownership

260 Flat oil-bottle with screw-closure; height 13 cm ($5^1/_8''$), 2nd half of the 18th century.
The Henry Francis du Pont Winterthur Museum, Winterthur, Delaware

261 Screw-closure flasks with reinforced bases; height 22 and 18 cm ($8^5/_8''$ and 7″), 18th century.
Staatliches Heimat- und Schlossmuseum Burgk/Saale and in private ownership

262 Flat oil-bottle, closed with a cork; height 13 cm ($5^1/_8''$), *c.* 1850.
Museum "Schloss Moritzburg", Zeitz

263 Cylindrical screw-closure flask; height 21.5 cm ($8^1/_2''$), *c.* 1750. When the exterior cover is screwed tight the interior cover is pressed down firmly so that the container protects its contents especially well against ingress of air.
In private ownership

264 Screw-closure tub on small feet; height 12 cm ($4^3/_4''$), 18th century.
Schlossmuseum Altenburg

259
260

261
262

263
264

265 Typical water-can with beaker; height 37 and 10 cm ($14^{1}/_{2}$″ and 4″), dated 1821. The numerous engraved names seem to indicate a use foreign to its intended purpose, namely for serving wine in a guild.
Städtisches Museum Halberstadt

266 Small oil-jug; height 13 cm ($5^{1}/_{8}$″), 16th century.
Museum Boymans-van Beuningen, Rotterdam

267 Small oil-can with flap-cover and stop for refilling on its outlet; height 13 cm ($5^{1}/_{8}$″), dated 1839.
Schlossmuseum Altenburg

268 Oil-jug; height 24.5 cm ($9^{5}/_{8}$″), dated 1704.
Gedenkstätte Crimmitschauer Textilarbeiterstreik 1903/04, Crimmitschau

269 Oil-can with stay; height 25.5 cm (10″), *c.* 1835.
Städtisches Museum Halberstadt

270 Pottery jars with pewter screw-closures; height 23, 23.5 and 28 cm (9″, $9^{1}/_{4}$″ and 11″), 17th century.
In private ownership

271 Pear-shaped tankards; height 25 cm ($9^{7}/_{8}$"), 1st half of the 19th century. In private ownership

272 Water-jug on raised foot; height 33.7 cm ($13^{1}/_{4}$"), 15th century. Museum des Kunsthandwerks Leipzig

273 Swaged screw-closure flask; height 30 cm ($11^{3}/_{4}$"), 18th century. Museum des Kunsthandwerks Leipzig

274 Serving-jug; height 9 cm ($3^{1}/_{2}$"), 1st half of the 19th century. In private ownership

275 Serving-jug; height 9.5 cm ($3^{3}/_{4}$"), dated 1860. Schlossmuseum Altenburg

276 North German urn (dripping minnie); height 32 cm ($12^{1}/_{2}$"), 19th century. Museum "Schloss Moritzburg", Zeitz

277 American coffee-urn; height 35 cm ($13^{3}/_{4}$"), mid-19th century. Brooklyn Museum, Brooklyn, New York

Following page:

278 North German urn (dripping minnie); height 24 cm ($9^{1}/_{2}$"), 18th century. Museum "Schloss Moritzburg", Zeitz

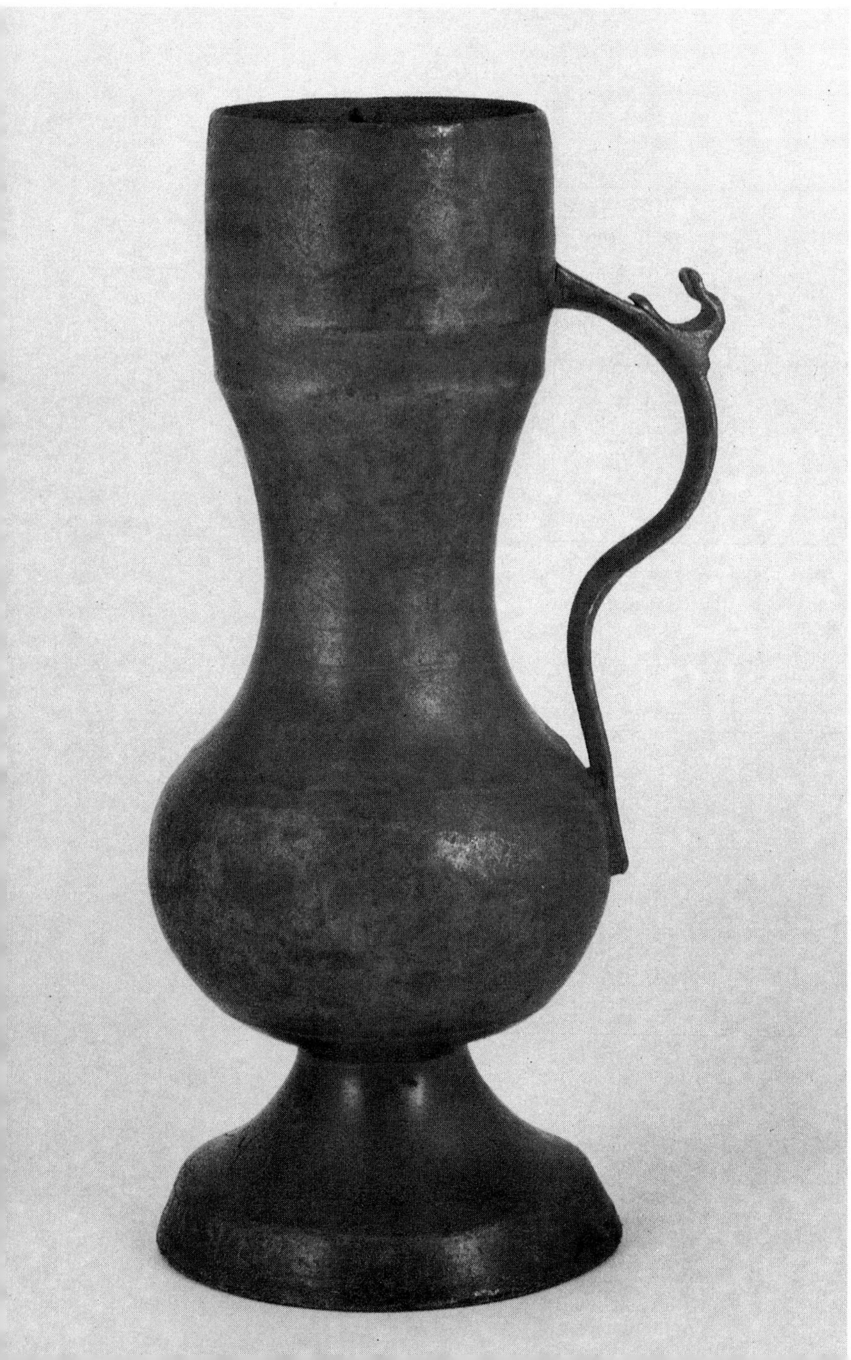

273

261/263 cut-out and soldered together, the screw-closure mostly originating from a
258 hot-water-bottle. Simple round screw-closed flasks were made by pewterers comparatively rarely in contrast to the multi-sided ones but have nevertheless been assiduously copied in our own day and appropriately chastised, i. e. with whips to whose cords are tied hard substances. Thus there is no lack of spurious dents and blemishes of old age.

Polygonal screw-closure cans were for centuries associated with the work of Italian pewterers. As early as 1552 native casters of pewter cans and Italian sheet casters were mentioned in a police ordinance regarding conditions in Alsace. This distinction discloses the fact that the itinerant Italians preferred to make screw-closed flasks constructed from pewter sheet which they had cast themselves. Resident masters did the same but because they did not work anonymously and illegally they were able to mark their goods in conformity with the regulations. This possibility was denied to the Italians working without permission from the authorities so that their wares remained unmarked. Many such screw-cans are to be found today which are of solid handmade workmanship although there are no town or masters' marks. The itinerant pewterers' preference for screw-can production was determined by the very limited equipment required. The mould for the screw-tops was easy to carry. In addition, two rectangular slabs of sandstone were necessary. (In German these were called *blechersteine* and *blättersteine*, freely translated respectively as sheet and leaf stones.) The pewterer laid a sheet of paper on one of them and then put thin strips of wood round three edges. These were covered with another sheet of paper and the second stone placed on top. The mould thus created was firmly clamped in a wooden frame. Molten pewter was poured into the side where there was no wooden strip. To assist this the projecting papers were held apart to serve as a funnel. Sandstones about three feet long and two feet wide produced about 20 pounds of heavy pewter sheet, which was then cut up into the sizes required for subsequent putting together to form a vessel. The pewterer soldered the screw-closure on as a final operation.

Otherwise, the journeyman who desires to make a masterpiece shall prepare 2 stone moulds, one for a bowl and the other for a jug as he may wish including the two boards belonging to the stone slabs, but the two stones must not be prepared in advance but only as they come from the quarry.

Instruction relating to masterpieces by the Council of the town of Augsburg, 1589.

Although the screw-tops were fairly tight, both resident and itinerant pewterers provided the vessels with an interior lid which was pressed firmly against the neck of the canister when the exterior cover was screwed-down. The result was that screwed cans could be used for the transport of liquids without loss. Smaller flasks were carried on the belt which was drawn through the pivoting handle of the screw-closure. For larger containers and longer journeys an affluent citizen would use a *flaschenkeller* or *feldkeller* (flask- or field-cellar). This means of protecting and keeping flasks hot was mentioned in Austrian and Hungarian documents as early as the 16th century. For instance, the Viennese pewterer Thomas Oettinger supplied a maple container with pewter flasks to the municipal hospital in 1551 and received written acknowledgement. These protective containers were in fact more common for glass but in about 1750 it was reported in connection with mounting complaints about the condition of the roads, that even pewter flasks must be conveyed in containers. A few stages were known far and wide as "tip-over" stretches and even for example 50 strokes of the cane administered to the postillion ordained in Prussia in 1772 for over-turning hardly changed the situation because there was a corresponding constraint under threat of punishment to maintain running times. It was gratifying when a pewter flask in its cloth-lined wooden container survived an overturning without damage and a strong draught of bouillon might be taken from it to counteract shock. Many accounts go on to say that unfortunately the foot-warmer was damaged; more will be written later about pewter hot-water-bottles when travelling.

In some places a cask for victuals (German *speisefass*) of several pounds weight was included in the stipulated masterpiece already in the 16th century. It is, however, clear that this usually meant a container for food-stuffs which was not necessarily in the shape of a cask. The German word *fass* (cask, barrel, tub) often simply means any one of a large variety of wooden containers. An example is provided by *spiegelfass* (mirror tub) which in old colloquial speech is a shallow vessel with a completely flat bottom. Pewter wares resembling a barrel in shape and which were closed with
264 a screwed cover appeared only at a later date. These screw-top casks also usually had an additional internal cover. Screw-top casks do not seem to have been made in large numbers and they are all of relatively small size. Their principal use in the household was the storage of spices for the kitchen. Included among storage containers were screw-top pottery casks (German *schraubkruken* = screwed crocks), larger in size, with a pewter
270 closure together with *lechelen*—small barrels made of wooden stays with pewter bands and pewter screw-tops which (as on casks entirely of pewter) had "an ample ring for easy closing and carrying". Although small wooden pots had no handles they were also used as drinking-vessels.

Oil- and water-cans and urns

Amongst storage containers frequently found in households were those used for oil. From early times they were usually sold by pewterers under the name of "sweet oil jars". These were primarily intended for the keeping of olive-oil, known as "tree-oil". They were also used later for linseed and
266 rape-seed oils which were required as fuel for lamps. Early oil-cans resemble biberons in appearance but with hinged covers. But because they were not designed for sucking from, there was no need for the spout to be set right down at the base of the can. At the beginning of the 18th century those with a
268/269 screw-cover and spout with a flap or screwed closure came onto the market in increasing numbers. The Swiss bell-shaped cans which have previously been mentioned were also used to keep oil. It is clear that this happened sufficiently frequently over a period that Swiss pewterers in the 18th century felt

encouraged to leave the spout off entirely, i. e. to make bell-shaped cans with a screw-closure. Similar polygonal flasks were also made for this purpose. Anyone who wished to keep quite a large domestic reserve of olive-oil would order a suitable cask from a pewterer and its manufacture seems not to have been without complications. As an example, when in 1750 a journeyman from Brieg (now Brzeg), Johann Friedrich Bischoff, was allotted the task of producing as a masterpiece a hand-cask in the shape of a melon, a pear-shaped jug, a four-quart flask and a six-pound dish, he asked the magistrate for these to be reduced to two pieces. He justified his request by stating that he intended to marry the widow of a master and in particular because he had already made an olive oil-cask of $91^1/_2$ pounds weight which more than sufficiently proved his skill. Large containers were probably only seldom made. In the 19th century they were entirely displaced by containers of tinned sheet-iron. In contrast, production until about 1850 of small oil-cans and oil-
267 bottles in every European country with a pewter trade and also in America, was extensive. Many of them were so frugally made that they were closed
260/262 only with a cork instead of a pewter cap.

Due to oxidization, particularly thorough cleaning of oil storage containers was a frequent demand on the housewife. This involved considerable trouble because sometimes the openings in the containers were very small and the interior of bellied vessels could not be reached everywhere with a brush. From generation to generation a practical domestic expedient to solve this problem was to shake up pulverized egg-shells; in obstinate cases even lead shot of varying sizes (shot for hares and shot for fowl) was used. Shaking with egg-shells or lead shot was also a domestic recipe for cleaning jugs
271 into which milk for the preparation of curds had been allowed to trickle. Slightly swelled, slim containers were favoured for this purpose. Jugs were obviously eminently suitable because they were still used until well into the second half of the 19th century. Finally, this homely remedy was also used to remove calcium deposits from jugs and tankards.

Pewterers manufactured special containers for storing water for washing and for pouring it into wash-bowls, about which more will be written later. Water needed in the kitchen for the preparation of food was kept in wooden
265 casks, internally tinned copper tubs or large pewter cans and jugs. The
272 shapely curved jugs on small feet, known from the 15th century, may well have been intended for drinking-water and probably other drinks. Whilst the containers ancillary to the water cans, from which washing-water was actually dispensed were common household equipment, these large vessels are very rarely found in pewter. The use of coopered casks and tubs was cheap-
274/275 er, simpler and more practical. A pewter dipper was nevertheless used, especially as this served a variety of purposes. The dipper is a small mug, with a curved handle and no cover, the lip of the rim formed with a shallow pouring outlet, and it was used for ladling water from heavy storage containers into

Tree-oil flagon

It is a long and deep container of pewter or sheet-iron, with a cover, in which tree-oil is kept in kitchens and larders.

Frauenzimmerlexikon, Leipzig, 1715.

pots and bowls. When needful, the slim soup-pots with removable covers were also used.

276–278 In America, Denmark and northern Germany a storage container came into being in the 18th century which was simultaneously a serving vessel—the urn. Often three urns were even provided so that all who were gathered at table could conveniently help themselves. Coffee, previously brewed in the kitchen, was contained in urns. The German housewife decanted it into a *dröppelminna* (dripping Minnie) or poured it in through a sieve. The popular expression *dröppelminna* for an urn derived from the fact that their taps were mostly not entirely tight and therefore dripped. As has already been mentioned, a careful housewife therefore liked to stand a salt-cellar under the tap. In spite of these small irritations urns were very popular. In northern Germany an active export trade to all other districts of Germany developed and Danish pewterers supplied the Scandinavian countries. Their popularity increased when "coffee-lamps" were supplied with them to keep the coffee warm or to re-heat it. Although the Russian brass samovar which originated at the same period was considerably more practical in use it was not even able to displace the pewter urn when from 1825 Ivan Grigoryevitch Batashov of Tula produced samovars in a factory for the first time and thereby offered much lower prices.

Coffee-urn

The urn performs the same duty as the coffee-pot except that generally more coffee can be served in it than from a pot and it is a vessel formed from silver, brass, copper or pewter or even mere sheet-iron, standing on three high feet and with one, two or three small taps and two handles.

Explanatory definition, 1752.

Coffee-lamp

A small round container of brass, pewter or sheet-iron, provided with a wick, to be filled with spirits of wine and placed under the coffee-urn after having been lighted, to keep it hot for a time or even to let it boil up over it.

Explanatory definition, 1752.

Preceding page:

279 Depiction of a pewter beaker (amongst other pewterware) on a tapestry "Garden of Love"; *c.* 1450. Historisches Museum, Basle

280 Gauge; height 14.5 cm ($5^3/_4$"), dated 1771.
The measure is for checking one *nösel*
(just short of half-a-litre).
In private ownership

weil der Storch
bracht
wiees der
mel fügt

282 Cylindrical tankards with inscriptions and pictorial engraving, Saxony; height 25 and 26.5 cm (10″ and 10⁷/₈″), dated 1794 and 1797. In private ownership

283 Oil-can with screw-closure for the spout; height 27.5 cm (10³/₄″), end of the 18th century. In private ownership

285 Brass candle-snuffer on a simple, heavily patinated pewter plate together with a candlestick; diameter of plate 16.5 cm ($6^1/_2''$), *c.* 1800.
In private ownership

Following page:

286 Body-warmer, known as coaching-bottle; diameter 20.5 cm (8″), 2nd half of the 18th century.
In private ownership

Measures

The use of measuring vessels is closely bound up with inn-keeping, culinary practices and trade. Inn-keepers used them for measuring wine, beer, small beer, brandy, mead und must. Containers in the form of jugs and tankards were very practical for this, which were gauged as of a specific volume. Housewives also recognized the merit of being able to use pewter jugs and drinking-vessels in the kitchen as well to measure milk, olive-oil and other fluids. Whilst, however, it sufficed them to include a few gauged measures among their possessions, inn-keepers and, to an even greater extent, shop-keepers and traders concerned with foodstuffs, spices, lamp-oil and other goods acquired complete sets of measuring containers of which some were beaker-shaped and specially intended for measuring. Brass and copper measures were generally preferred for dry goods but besides these there were always still some of pewter.

Local measures were used for the distribution of liquids and dry goods which were established by many urban authorities for themselves, sometimes for centuries, uninfluenced by efforts at centralized direction. On the other hand, precise centralized regulations were lacking for a long time. There was, for example, a general decree in Norway for as early as 1302 that beer was to be sold only in gauged barrels but until into the 19th century the gauged measure might be variably determined from place to place. A popular epigram of the time says in German that there is much cheating in a beer barrel, a reference to the problems of accurate measurement of volume. These problems stemmed not only from fraudulent marking of pewter vessels but also from local variations in the volume of the same units of measure which were considerable from region to region in all countries. For the pewter trade the varying regulations had the effect that gauged pewter measures could only be sold in a restricted territory. This became significant at the earliest from the 18th century when trade in pewterware was able to expand far beyond the bounds of its town of origin. On the domestic market gauged vessels had a greater utility and therefore better sales potential than those which were not gauged. Because of this pewterers had endeavoured since the late Middle Ages to attain the right themselves to be recognized as gaugers (in German *eicher, iker, visierer, wroger, sinner, fächter*). This right was often granted to them for pewterware made in their own workshops. For the purpose of gauging the guild was provided with a master measure by the municipal authorities which was carefully safe-guarded in the guild's Chest. From about the 17th century an individual master could then borrow it for a short time to make his own master measure. Previously, the procedure had been generally much more strict when, in fact, each individual vessel had to be compared with the master measure. To do this the pewterer involved had to go to the senior master of the guild (who looked after the master measure) and gauging took place in the presence of a further master. Half the fee went to the senior master and half to the guild's Chest.

Any new piece made by a pewterer himself, he must gauge himself with the measure provided by the Chamber for the purpose and afterwards strike the gauge mark on it together with the other marks, as previously notified.

Communal instruction of the Munich pewterers, potters and rope-makers, 1531.

Sometimes a particular individual pewterer underwent the dignity of being installed as gauger for the entire town. He then had to carry out visitations into every workshop, including those of brass founders and coppersmiths, and record the outcome. The considerable amount of work was only meagrely rewarded and the master concerned therefore exerted a special kind of authority. The in-
280 spection measure used for visitations had a small hole in its body below which was soldered a little tongue. The volume to be checked was poured into the inspection measure and if it was correct a droplet had to overflow onto the tongue. The master and control measures were always of particularly pleasing shape and they were often decorated with attractive engraving. One may suppose that a certain dignity was striven for in the case of official measures and perhaps also to influence the development of shapes of vessels.

The gauger had to visit pewterers working in rural areas only once a year. Mounted constables and the rural militia were, however, therefore directed always to carry out checks when they were out in villages—particularly of beer containers.

289
290

291
292

293 Gauge mark in the form of a town coat-of-arms on the body of a tankard; 1st half of the 18th century.
In private ownership

294 Swiss jugs *(stitzen)*; height 19 and 20 cm ($7^1/_2$″ and $7^7/_8$″), dated 1780.
In private ownership

295 Flagons *(pitschen)* from Eger (Cheb) in Bohemia; height 26 cm ($10^1/_4$″), *c.* 1850.
Kreisheimatmuseum Grimma and in private ownership

Following pages:

296 Swiss jugs *(stitzen)*; height 16 and 27 cm ($6^1/_4$″ and $10^5/_8$″), 1st half of the 18th century.
In private ownership

297 South German measuring tankard; height 24 cm ($9^1/_2$″), dated 1753.
In private ownership

298 Measuring tankards, tapered and flared towards the base, known as *spitz* (point) tankards; height 30 and 24 cm ($11^7/_8$″ and $7^1/_2$″), 18th and 19th century.
This type of tankard is typical for the Vogtland.
In private ownership

299 Open-topped viewing-jug; height 25 cm ($9^7/_8$″), *c.* 1790.
Heimatmuseum Mühlhausen, Thuringia

300 North German measuring tankards; height 26 and 29.5 cm ($10^1/_4$″ and $11^5/_8$″), *c.* 1815.
In private ownership

301 French double-litre measure; height 28 cm (11″), 19th century. In private ownership

302 Tapered measuring tankard; height 24 cm ($9^1/_2$″), *c.* 1800. Gedenkstätte Crimmitschauer Textilarbeiterstreik 1903/04, Crimmitschau

303 Measuring tankard, northeastern Europe; height 27 cm ($10^5/_8$″), dated 1638. Kulturhistorisches Museum Rostock

301

302

Measuring jugs

In every country there was a great number of the most varying ways in which a jug might be gauged but the most numerous and also the most confusing were in Germany. There not only were differing measures in a town valid only for individual trades, but sometimes it was also necessary to take care whether a measure was for wine or beer. For example, in many North German towns two quarters of beer were 1.86 litres, two quarters of wine only 1.82 litres. Although the difference was only minimal it was nevertheless likely to sour pewterers' work. Whilst two quarters of beer were called a
299 *kanne*, two quarters of wine were referred to as a *halbstübchen*—a liquid
290 measure. If anyone ordered a container for beer to hold one *kanne* the pewterer had to make sure that this did not mean the *kanne* which was current in Dresden in the Electorate of Saxony, which only held 0.94 of a litre; a view *kanne*, on the other hand, contained 1.40 litres. Half a Dresden *kanne* of beer or wine was called a *plank* in northern Germany. Jugs gauged for one *plank* are often intended for brandy. Because the authorities in towns and other officials enacted alterations at short notice, pewterers had to exercise diligent care that they did not supply containers gauged for out-of-date measures. If something of this sort was discovered they had to reckon with drastic financial penalties.

In other countries accustomed measures mostly had more continuity, as for example the Esthonian *stoof*, the Russian *vidrov* and the Hungarian *icce*.
295 The *pitschen* which have already been mentioned produced in Eger (now Cheb) in Bohemia are often gauged on the basis of one of these units but also of the *nösel* which was current in various German regions. This indicates that many of the attractive *pitschen* from Eger were exported without being gauged and that the purchaser then had them gauged in accordance with the locally current measure of volume. *Pitschen* were made in great numbers in the 19th century at a time indeed when good communications existed between large towns and when, moreover, trade channels to many small towns and parishes were already established.

Until the revolutionary year 1791, the *pot* and the *quart* (approx. 1.90 litres) were, in France, the most frequently used liquid measures. Then, however, pewterers and other craftsmen as well as the shop-keepers were obligated by a decree of the 18th Germinal in the year III to support the introduction of the decimal system of measurement. This obligation entailed considerable difficulties for the pewter trade. Trusting in the relative continuity of the *quart* and respectively the *pot*, they had prepared accurate moulds which would cast vessels of exactly the required volume. Now, they were supposed to alter these measures which held a precise amount and, moreover, to do away with measuring beakers completely! Because there was scarcely a master who could afford to do this, workshops kept the old moulds in use. As regards jugs (and tankards) the expedient was sometimes adopted of gauging them in litres after manufacture in case anyone wanted to buy a

The pewterer shall make a jug of three-and-one-half stoups with a hollow foot and a bowl three-quarters of an ell wide, a flask of three stoups capacity, of sheet.

Pewter regulation, Wormditt (Orneta), 1552.

combined serving and measuring container. This situation did not alter for a long time so far as measuring vessels were concerned—only the identifying mark of the workshop was prudently forgotten. At first, trade in the old measures flourished as in the past because the new system met with obstructive popular and often uncomprehending opposition. Measures based on the litre nevertheless gradually took over which many an older pewterer viewed with dismay. Their colleagues in the trade in England did not have this kind of problem. There the most widespread generally used measure, the pint, endured; it was also adopted by various pewterers working in America.

The newly introduced system of measures in France is a matter of the utmost importance not only for the new republic but for urban communities, for art, science and trade generally.

Journal for factories, manufactories, etc., Berlin, February 1798.

Whilst in French-speaking Switzerland the *pot* (about 1.13–1.5 litres there), originating from France, recurs, in the German-speaking districts preference was given to one of the more frequently used measures in Germany, namely the *mass* (about 1.80 litres, almost exactly a pint). Certainly here there was not a further variety of other confusing measures, but the *mass* was the only definitive basic unit. Many of the splendid Swiss utilitarian containers conform to this measure. For instance, the pewterers of Chur
287 produced in large quantities a polygonal pouring vessel, called a *quartkanne* (quart-can) with a screw-closure and a rigid upright ring upon the lid, a deco-
294/296 rated escutcheon on the side which is typical of the work of Chur. The *stitzen* could hold up to three *mass*, the smallest containing little more than one-hundredth *mass*. A relatively large number of progressive measures, namely five, is also found for Swedish *stitzen (stop, halvstop, kvater, tväjumfru, jumfru)*. Many Swiss bell-jugs *(glockenkanne)* accept up to three *mass* of liquid. Such large pouring vessels, as also the small ones—the bell-cans which hold only a quarter of a *mass*—are not very common. The most popu-
288 lar seem to have been those of one *mass*, equivalent to a quart. A small flap-
291 cover on the spout opened when pouring and at other times shielded the wine or other liquid from impurities when the jug was used as a storage container. Swiss pewterers were fond of punching their mark upon the flap-lid, which was found not only on the spouts of bell-jugs.

Gauged jugs were also produced in Austria, the Netherlands and Scandinavia from the 16th century. In 1617 the Emperor Matthias decreed that in "Austria below the Enns" the masterpiece must include, amongst other items, a bellied jug which must contain two *ächtering*. As in the Netherlands and Scandinavia, tankards which held a specified measure seem here to have been more plentiful than jugs.

Measuring tankards

As against measuring jugs, gauged tankards frequently exhibit a special characteristic; they bear in their interior not just one, but several gauge marks. The separate marks indicated the share due to each person when the tankard was handed round. Many considered it flattering to enjoy the reputation of being able to drink their exact share during a round and to perform this at a single draught.

Preceding page:

287 Swiss quart-can; height 36 cm ($14^1/_8$"), dated 1820. In private ownership

288 Single-measure Basle bell-can; height 35 cm ($14^1/_8$"), dated 1789. In private ownership

289 Netherlandish baluster measuring jug; height 20.6 cm ($8^1/_8$"), 16th century. Stedelijk Museum "De Lakenhal", Leyden

290 Small measuring tankard, gauged for one *plank*; height 16 cm ($6^1/_4$"), *c.* 1700. Heimatmuseum Mühlhausen/Thuringia

291 Detail of Fig. 288: The polygonal spout is closed with a flap-cover which opens when pouring.

292 Gauging plug in the interior of a jug, mid-18th century.
The recess in the ring under the cover, which was originally exactly fitted to the plug has clearly become enlarged with the passage of time.
In private ownership

304

305

304 French water tankard (aiguière), gauged; height 12.7 cm (5″), 1st half of the 19th century.
Museum des Kunsthandwerks Leipzig

305 Baluster-shaped measuring beaker, with handle; height 7.5 cm (3″), 17th century.
Stedelijk Museum "De Lakenhal", Leyden

306 Measuring beaker with insert to fit, Swiss workmanship; height 21.8 cm ($8^1/_2$″), 2nd half of the 17th century.
Schweizerisches Landesmuseum Zurich

307 Measuring beaker, probably Swiss; height 16.3 cm ($6^1/_2$″), 1st half of the 18th century.
Schweizerisches Landesmuseum Zurich

306

307

308 Measuring beakers in the litre system; height 5.2–11 cm (2″–4$^3/_8$″), 19th century. Kreisheimatmuseum Grimma and in private ownership

309 Measuring beaker, probably Swiss; height 12.1 cm (4$^3/_4$″), c. 1800. Schweizerisches Landesmuseum Zurich

310 Gauge marks on the rims of litre-system measuring beakers; 2nd half of the 19th century. In private ownership

Following page:

311 Measuring vessel for rum, Danish; height 16.5 cm (6$^1/_2$″), dated 1834. Used aboard ship, the measure can be hung securely by its heavy cast hook. Det Danske Kunstindustrimuseum, Copenhagen

308

309

310

Tankards and jugs were gauged in accordance with the measures of volume in general use at a given time in trades connected with liquids. The most
292 frequent gauge mark in all regions was a little soldered plug ("gauging nail") which might also have a hemispherical shape. Its use was already prescribed in guild regulations from the second half of the 15th century. Another method of marking was to file two square apertures in at a level corresponding to the appropriate volume of liquid. This form of gauging was simple to carry out in every period but was nevertheless not common. It is possible that there was apprehension that this method of gauging would damage a vessel after it had once been made. Furthermore, it did not allow the popular practice of indicating more than one measure in a tankard. This also applies to the provision of a small hole as gauge mark, which was occasionally done
289 by Netherlandish pewterers. The baluster wine measures produced there in the late Gothic period are certainly among the most attractive creations of everyday pewterware. The volume of the few surviving examples conforms with the *mass*. Sometimes orders for a number of sets of beer tankards which held a given measure were fulfilled at the behest of beer-house keepers. It is permissible to make a general assumption that this kind of work had to be specially approved in many places. Thus, for example, in 1561 a pewterer from Nördlingen, Leonhardt Vinck, had to answer for the fact that he had produced measures which held beer to the value of one pfennig without being authorized to do so.

Whenever beer measures and jugs such as are used in beer-houses are ordered from a pewterer, he shall not make them larger or smaller than the test measure available at the Town Hall nor let them pass to anyone else or sell them unless they have previously been gauged by a member of the police or other authorized person and marked accordingly.

Charter of privileges of the Königsberg (Kaliningrad) pewterers, 1745.

In Switzerland there was a gauging procedure known as *pfächten*. This was to swage one or more grooves round the body of the container. These grooves not only mark specific measures of volume but are also an external indication that the piece has been gauged. External gauging marks likewise appear with a variety of differences: mostly they are official confirmation of the correctness of the plug, slot or hole which had been applied. When in 1547 in Breslau (now Wrocław) the pewterer Andres Schwartz was sworn in officially to apply gauging plugs to the measuring vessels of wine-merchants, he was at the same time committed to distinguish those measuring vessels with a crowned letter "W" (as symbol of Wratislavia). This provided formal confirmation of gauging by the authorities. In general, the coat-of-
293 arms of the town was the preferred gauge mark but many individual details taken from them were also punched as inspection marks. Measuring tank-
300/303 ards from Brandenburg often bear an eagle as gauge mark, which sometimes also appears on northern German tankards. The mark for gauged wares in use in Lübeck during the 16th and 17th centuries is extremely unusual. The pewterer in fact punched a master's mark which incorporated either the figures "79" or "33". This indicated gauging in accordance with the official regulations for 1579 or 1633 respectively. In the second half of the 19th century it became the general practice only to strike numerals after official gauging or after the capacity check which was carried out from time to time.

Master pewterers shall in future be obliged to carry out marking themselves and not leave it to journeymen.

Council order, Chur (Switzerland), 21st May, 1772.

Positioning of the gauge mark upon tankards is usually prescribed by order. When the tankard was made in such a way that its total volume contained a current liquid measure, the gauge marks were applied to the edge of the lip, on the lid or on the handle. Many Scandinavian and French tankards, in particular the *pichets*, provide examples of this. In Germany, the statutes of many guilds established why the handle was the only place where the mark might be put: both townspeople and farm workers had to be able quickly to recognize whether a tankard conformed with the town-measure and to make this possible, pewterers had to apply, or cause the mark to be applied, in an easily visible position. In the district round Hanover a tankard was normally gauged as a *krug*—in Hanoverian measure one *krug* made four *ort* or sixteen *viertelort* (quarter *ort*), totalling 1.385 litres. The volume of a container frequently exceeded the town-measure in force at any particular time. The gauge mark was then commonly struck where the first gauging stud was positioned. The authorities often stipulated that the tankard must hold a further
298 "thumb's breadth" above the gauging stud, for instance for the tapered tankards which were a speciality of German pewterers who were resident in Vogtland.

Pewterers, potters and rope-makers.

Your revised regulations have been given as follows: item, henceforward for pewter gauging, one of the community, who is not himself of the craft, shall be authorized to view the gauging also. Item, the gauging stud shall be one thumb's breadth under the lip of the jug.

Combined ordinance of the Munich pewterers, potters and rope-makers, 1480.

The name of these tankards, made principally in the 18th century, stems from the small tapered point which continues the conical shape of the body and is found at the centre of the lid and is a sure indication of Vogtland work.
297/302 Measuring tankards of this type with flat smooth covers are otherwise widespread in southern German districts.

In northern Europe, cylindrical measuring tankards predominated. Their wide diversity of sizes indicates the multiplicity of measures which also in this region determined the final shapes to be produced by pewterers. For example, in Münster (Westphalia) during the 16th and 17th centuries there was a type of tankard designed to hold one *quart* being a measure of volume in Münster (*c.* 1.25 litres). Because another generally used measure there was the *mengel* (four *mengels* = one *quart*) many tankards were not only gauged for the quart but also with three further studs which were destined for the *mengels*.

Measuring beakers

It has already been mentioned that measuring beakers were specially intended for measuring liquids and only rarely for dry goods. Whereas jugs and tankards which held a specific measure of volume could also be used as serving-and drinking-vessels if there was a change in the system of measurement this was not the case with measuring beakers. Because they were also of little decorative value, housewives would readily part with them to hawkers or to pewterers for melting and they then bought up-to-date ones to replace them. Thus not many measuring beakers have survived from the past although they were for centuries part of the household and likewise had a continuous practical function in trade.

Early measuring beakers already testify to the diligence with which vol-
305 umes were checked. In the multitude of inspection marks struck upon the rim of a beaker there is such a diversity to be seen that is explicable not only by changes in regulations but also by the appointment of different inspectors *(consolibus)*. The shapes of early measuring vessels were not chosen at random since there was an endeavour to indicate the substance intended to be measured in them in the first place by their appearance. Thus, for exam-
307/309 ple, two measuring beakers which may possibly have been made in Weinfelden, Switzerland, have the same capacity (0.31 litres) but differ in appearance.

A measure likewise made in Switzerland in the second half of the 17th
306 century is extremely rare and is provided with a beaker-shaped insert. The insert has a volume of about a fifth of the full measure (1.37 litres); it may therefore have been intended for sharing the total contents.

Until the 19th century measuring beakers with handles and feet were plentiful in America and England: they may well also have served for drinking from. Wine-merchants in France sometimes used measuring beakers as well as *pichets* to measure and dispense wine. An 18th century chronicler alleged that pewter wine-beakers were good for very little because they contained much lead. In Paris particularly, wine for the common people was young and weak and therefore very apt to become sour. Since, however, lead absorbed acid and converted it into a salt, wine-merchants strove to acquire these poor-quality measures. It would seem that this refers to the
304 gauged cylindrical measuring beakers without lids which were used for commercial distribution and could also be used for water (in French called *aiguières*).

For measuring alcoholic drinks, many German pewterers not only had to provide for different gauging for wine and beer jugs but the drink for which they were intended was also critical for measuring beakers. Thus, for example, in some districts the beer *nösel* contained 0.451 litre against 0.496 litre for the brandy *nösel*. The muddle only ended with the introduction of the litre system of measurement—1868 in Prussia and 1872 for the entire German Empire. By this time, pewterers had long been in decline yet measures in the litre system were so much in demand that individual workshops specialized in them and were to some extent able to exist by producing them. Cylindrical
308 beakers were made with and without lips and handles, also similar tapered ones which are more rare. Although no longer sold by weight, measuring beakers were thick-walled to make them insusceptible to mechanical damage which would entail a falsification of volume. Continued rigorous control of their measuring capacity is shown by the many inspection marks, which
310 are usually applied to the rim.

After the revolution of 1789–1793, the most frequently produced litre
301 measure in France was the *double litre*. It took the place of the *pot* as a mea-

Champagne cream

Take one and a half small measures of cream, cook it with nutmeg and blossom until a quarter of it has boiled away; afterwards stir it until it becomes cold so that the cream remains on the surface, sweeten it with lump sugar, pour four or five spoonfuls of good Spanish wine or champagne into it, then stir it a little and pour it into a bowl; when it has stood for half a day one can eat thereof.

Cookery recipe, 1772.

sure of greater volume; the half-decalitre was introduced in place of the
broc. French double litre measures are provided with a cover, which is otherwise extremely rare on measuring beakers. Scandinavian ships' beakers
were nevertheless sometimes furnished with a cover. Containers gauged
311 for a *pot* in Norway and Denmark were a necessary part of ships' equipment
until the 19th century. Only then were iron water-tanks introduced instead of
wooden barrels, so that drinking-water no longer fouled so quickly. Previously rum or brandy had to be available, which was mixed with the water, to
make the taste more bearable. To prevent disputes and arbitrary action, this
was frequently done under the auspices of a measuring beaker.

Lighting Devices

Nobody can say when the first candles were produced and this applies likewise to pewter lighting devices in the shape of candle-holders and oil-lamps. It can be assumed as highly probable that such commodities nevertheless existed at a very early point in time because their production imposed no great demand on pewterers' lack of resources and skill. Therefore scarcely a guild regulation is known which stipulates amongst other items, a candlestick or an oil-lamp as masterpiece. In many places, for example in Germany in the Altmark, candlestick-makers did not at first belong to the guild of pewterers. Quite apart from this is that the importance of lighting devices in daily life is much less in comparison with ware for eating, serving and drinking. Daylight was of primary importance, which entered through horizontally divided doors and through windows which until the 18th century were without glass. If work was continued after dark, burning of resinous pinewood or even only the fire in the hearth had to suffice. Even after a housewife possessed pewter moulds to cast tallow candles or when cheap rape-seed oil was available, she had to use them frugally and exercise restraint in acquiring the corresponding lighting appliances. Multi-armed candle-holders, namely candelabra, or chandeliers were found only in well-to-do homes. Candlesticks, candelabra and oil-lamps are sometimes unmarked. This is usually due to the fact that lighting devices did not come into direct contact with food and drink and therefore the health-damaging admixture of lead did not have to be considered. Sometimes it was expressly conceded to pewterers by statute that they were permitted to sell items not exceeding a certain weight, unmarked. Simple candle-holders and lamps were among these items. On the other hand, these are the very articles of utilitarian pewter which most frequently display the master's name and often also the place of manufacture in relief casting. Presumably masters wished clearly to indicate that their

No piece of finished work weighing more than one pound shall be sold or exchanged if its mark is not struck upon it, under penalty of 1 reichsthaler.

Trade regulation, Liegnitz (Legnica), 1636.

name warranted good-quality material even for these items and therefore they did not forgo marking.

Other reasons for the total absence of masters' marks on utilitarian pewter are re-casting or deliveries made directly against orders from customers who did not insist that pieces should be marked. Sometimes too, marks have disappeared due to mechanically generated wear or are obscured by a patina.

Candlesticks and candelabra

Candlesticks are holders for only one candle, candelabra hold at least two. Until about the 14th century there may have been no distinction made at
312 the time of manufacture between those for sacred and those for secular purposes. During the period which followed, however, as candlesticks and also, increasingly, candelabra, became popular in domestic circles, pewterers started to produce candle-holders in two variants, namely with and without a pricket for mounting the candle. Needless to say, churches did not have to use poverty-stricken tallow candles but were able to burn the brighter but more expensive wax candles. Wax candles could simply be impaled upon a spike. This was not possible with tallow candles because of their brittleness so that a socket had to be provided to hold them. Because in the course of centuries wax candles became so expensive that even the lesser nobility was not in a position to use them all the time, candlesticks and candelabra with a pricket can usually be regarded as church furniture from the 15th century onwards. The frugality of practices connected with lighting is illustrated by *lichtschalen* which were available from pewterers. These flat, shell-shaped devices were used to put the candle in when it had burned down to its socket and thus use it to the very end. A small spout enabled molten tallow to be poured into a storage container. Home manufacture of candles benefitted by careful accumulation of these residues.

313/315 The most plentiful production of candlesticks and candelabra in most countries was during the 18th century. "Night-lights" were already in general use everywhere from the beginning of that century and were proclaimed by pewterers to be suitable for use "without worry, during the night's sleep". The trade was thus seizing upon the ever-present fear of fire damage to both house and outbuildings. It was thanks to only a slight difference in comparison with other candle-holders that night-lights were valued in town and country and generated good business. The difference was that the base of the holder was in the shape of a dish which could be filled with water. If—as
317 clearly frequently happened—a piece of burning wick fell down unnoticed, it was extinguished in the water. Another variation of the night-light is a kind of hurricane lamp. Tallow candles radiated only a very dim light in these beaker-like receptacles with glass sides so that they were not particularly in demand.

Night-lamp

It is formed of pewter or sheet-iron and must—before the night-light is put into it—be filled with water.

Frauenzimmerlexikon, Leipzig, 1715.

Taper-stands were another device, designed to be fire safe, which pewterers were unable to sell as well as they did night-lights. Originally candle-
holders of iron or brass in the form of spring-loaded scissors were put forward as a simple solution for automatic extinguishing of candles. After they
had burnt down the scissors were supposed to close under spring-pressure
and put out the flame. Because this often did not happen due to inadequate
316 spring-pressure, taper-stands came into being, in whose production pewterers took part. The box-like body of the container, made of iron, brass or
pewter, had a hole in the lid from which was pulled the taper-wick stored in
the interior. The longer the candle was intended to burn, the higher the taper
was raised. It was held by a small sheet-metal support soldered to the hole in
the lid. This also served to extinguish the flame by a lack of oxygen when the
taper had burnt down the appropriate amount. It was in any case extinguished upon reaching the hole in the lid. This design necessitated flexible
tapers, i. e. of wax. It is thus self-evident that they could not become an everyday household commodity.

Candlesticks with an arrangement for regulating the height of the candle
319 are as rare as taper-stands. They were usually made of brass. Brass candle-
holders were universally popular in town and country so that pewterers were
under constant pressure to put down this unwelcome competition. It was
therefore worthwhile to consider how to put forward lower prices. The design of moulds which could be used in a variety of ways was one expedient.
Thus, for example, the mould for a candlestick-base could also be used for
the lids of earthenware and pottery tankards. The multi-purpose function of
some moulds enabled certain masters to make them of solid brass. These
could be used to produce an almost unlimited number of castings. In contrast, cheap lead moulds permitted only about 50 castings. The increasingly
numerous cast-iron moulds of the 19th century permitted substantially more
but with these there was risk of breakage resulting from hammer-blows necessary to extract the pewter.

Many candelabra were also of a rationalized design in that the centre part
320 comprised a candlestick upon which the candle-holder arms could be
mounted. When, in the 18th century, fashion tended to the imitation of silverware, pewterers had an advantage over coppersmiths and brass-founders
because they could not only give their candle-holders the fluted shape of
silver ones but were able to achieve almost the same brilliance as silver. Independent designs originating from the pewter trade can again be looked for
at latest from the beginning of the 19th century. Amongst other things, these
included the quantity production in large numbers of baluster candlesticks,
also known as "pear"-sticks, so-called because of their shape and which
might have either a round or polygonal foot. German pewterers were fond of
mounting a round foot on top of a polygonal one; today one of this pattern is
318 sometimes called a "Berlin" candlestick. The socket insert of a baluster stick

is usually detachable so that the remnants of tallow or wax can readily be removed. Baluster candlesticks were also sometimes varnished. For instance, Anton Heilingötter, a pewterer from Karlsbad (now Karlovy Vary) exhibited some of these at a Bohemian exhibition of industry in 1829 in Prague and stimulated the interest of a wide public as had happened before in the Netherlands. Blue varnished candlesticks principally conformed with contemporary taste but also those in yellow, green and red.

Candlesticks
in a fashionable style
shining like silver or
pleasingly painted
the pair, 40 Saxon groschen.

Pewterer's advertisement, 1837.

It has already been mentioned that candlesticks and, above all, candelabra were not very plentiful in private households. When, however, there was a celebration, a great deal of festive illumination was called for. This meant the moulding of many candles and the provision of many candlesticks. Some pewterers guilds enjoyed the privilege of hiring-out candlesticks and cande-
321 labra. In Scandinavia and England multi-branched lights were an essential for the wedding table. In some districts of Germany a funeral without candlelight was unthinkable and superstitious practices played a part. There was, for example, the custom of placing three lighted candles upon the coffin in the house of mourning and then to leave them behind alight while the coffin was accompanied to the cemetery. The candles were only to be extinguished after the mourners' return. Superstition forbade that the candlesticks should ever again be used for normal purposes. This was accordingly a preference for borrowing them from pewterers. Because the privilege of hiring-out pewter candlesticks (and plates for the funeral repast as well as a pewter crucifix) was also claimed by brotherhoods of grave-followers or funeral guilds, in times of economic hardship there was often bitter strife with the pewterers over the prerequisites to be gained by lending on hire.

The festival of Christmas has been celebrated with a great display of candlelight from the *Biedermeier* period on. A few pewterers promised themselves good results from the production of Christmas-tree lights of which some were made with brass sockets. They had only modest success because the Christmas-tree and its decoration with lights was not yet a traditional accessory to the celebration.

Wall-sconces and chandeliers

"Lights which one hangs up" were already mentioned by Hans Sachs among the artistic items which the pewterer made. What exactly he meant by this in his gnomic poem can only be explained in so far that in addition to the standing candlesticks which were already well-known in the 16th century, there were also some which were hung up. The information given by Johann Gabriel Doppelmayr is not much clearer in his *Historische Nachrichten von den Nuernbergischen Mathematicis und Künstlern* (Historical Account of the Mathematicians and Artists of Nuremberg) of 1730, in which he says that Caspar Enderlein made "hanging lights". The latter may have been lanterns as well as chandeliers or the forerunners of chandeliers which were only furnished with one candle and hung from an extended hook or on a chain.

313

314
315

Preceding page:

312 Candlestick with small pricket; height 10 cm (4″), 14th century. Museum Boymans-van Beuningen, Rotterdam

313 Candlesticks, height 17–21 cm ($6^3/_4$″ – $8^1/_4$″), 18th century. Two of the candlesticks have dished bases, so that they can be filled with water. Staatliches Heimat- und Schlossmuseum Burgk/Saale and in private ownership

314 Candlestick on pedestal foot; height 16.3 cm ($6^1/_2$″), dated 1798. Kulturhistorisches Museum Rostock

315 Candlestick with broad foot; height 19.5 cm ($7^5/_8$″), 1st half of the 18th century. Städtisches Museum Halberstadt

316 Taper-stand; height 12 cm ($4^3/_4$″), 2nd half of the 18th century. Vogtländisches Kreismuseum Plauen

317 Night-light holder, with blue glass; height 10 cm (4″), 19th century. Vogtländisches Kreismuseum Plauen

318 Candlestick, of a type known as "Berlin" candlestick; height 23 cm (9″), *c.* 1800. In private ownership

319 Candlestick with a device for regulating the height of the candle; height 16.7 cm ($6^1/_2$″), dated 1841. Vogtländisches Kreismuseum Plauen

320 Candelabra; height 24 cm ($9^1/_2$″), *c.* 1800.
The candelabra can also be used as single candlesticks.
Kreisheimatmuseum Grimma

321 Candelabrum, Scandinavian work; height 41 cm ($16^3/_8$″), *c.* 1800.
Nordiska Museet, Stockholm

320

322 Three-armed wall-sconce;
height 18 cm (7″), 1st half of the 19th century.
In private ownership

323 Chandelier; height 70 cm ($27^1/_2$″),
c. 1800.
Traditionsstätte Erzbergbau, Aue

324 Chandelier; height 68 cm ($26^3/_4$″),
c. 1800.
Vogtländisches Kreismuseum Plauen

325 Chandelier; height 59.5 cm ($23^1/_2$″),
c. 1800.
Vogtländisches Kreismuseum Plauen

323
324

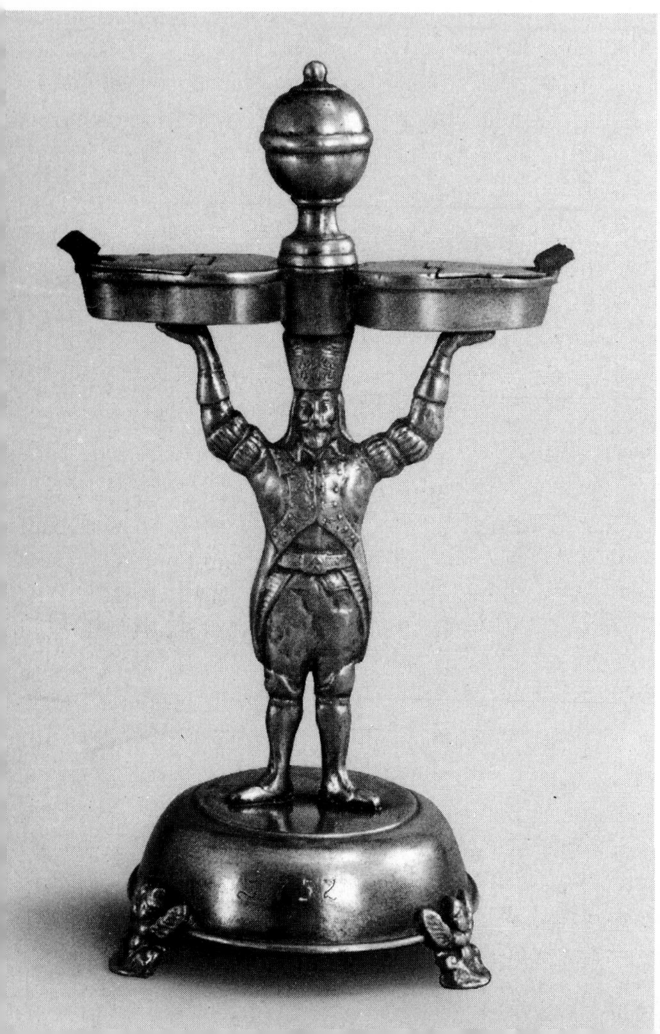

326 Oil-lamp with vertical wick-holder; height 25.5 cm (10″), dated 1757.
The dish round the column, known as the collar, was to catch escaping oil.
Heimatmuseum Mühlhausen/Thuringia

327 Oil-lamp with pewter wick-holder; height 24.5 cm ($9^5/_8$″), *c.* 1850.
Städtisches Museum Halberstadt

328 Twin oil-lamp mounted on the figure of a miner; height 29 cm ($11^3/_8$″), dated 1752.
Gedenkstätte Crimmitschauer Textilarbeiterstreik 1903/04, Crimmitschau

329 Small oil-lamp with strap-handle and copper burner-tube; height 16 cm ($6^1/_4$″), 1st half of the 19th century.
Traditionsstätte Erzbergbau, Aue

330 Oil-lamp with four burner-arms; height 14.7 cm ($5^3/_4$″), *c.* 1810.
Vogtländisches Kreismuseum Plauen

331 Oil-lamp with extinguishing cover which also confined the fumes; height 8.5 cm ($3^3/_8$″), dated 1791.
Vogtländisches Kreismuseum Plauen

332 Oil-lamps; height 21 cm ($8^1/_4$″), early 19th century.
A sheet-iron extinguisher hangs from the centre lamp.
Kreisheimatmuseum Grimma

330
331

332

333
334

335
336

337

333 Oil-lamp with no stem, known as *gakellämpel;* height 7.5 cm (3″), 19th century. Museum "Schloss Moritzburg", Zeitz

334 Oil-lamp in the form of a small spice-dish; height 4.5 cm ($1^3/_4$″), 1st half of the 19th century. Heimatmuseum Mühlhausen/Thuringia

335 Small hanging oil-lamp; height 14 cm ($5^1/_2$″), 19th century. In private ownership

336 Oil-lamp in the shape of an egg-cup; height 7 cm ($2^3/_4$″), dated 1864. Kulturhistorisches Museum Rostock

337 Funnel for a candle-mould with a centreing arm for the wick; early 19th century. In private ownership

338 Oil dish-lamps, adjustable upon a brass rod; height 56 and 64 cm (22″ and 25″), dated 1799. Gedenkstätte Crimmitschauer Textilarbeiterstreik 1903/04, Crimmitschau

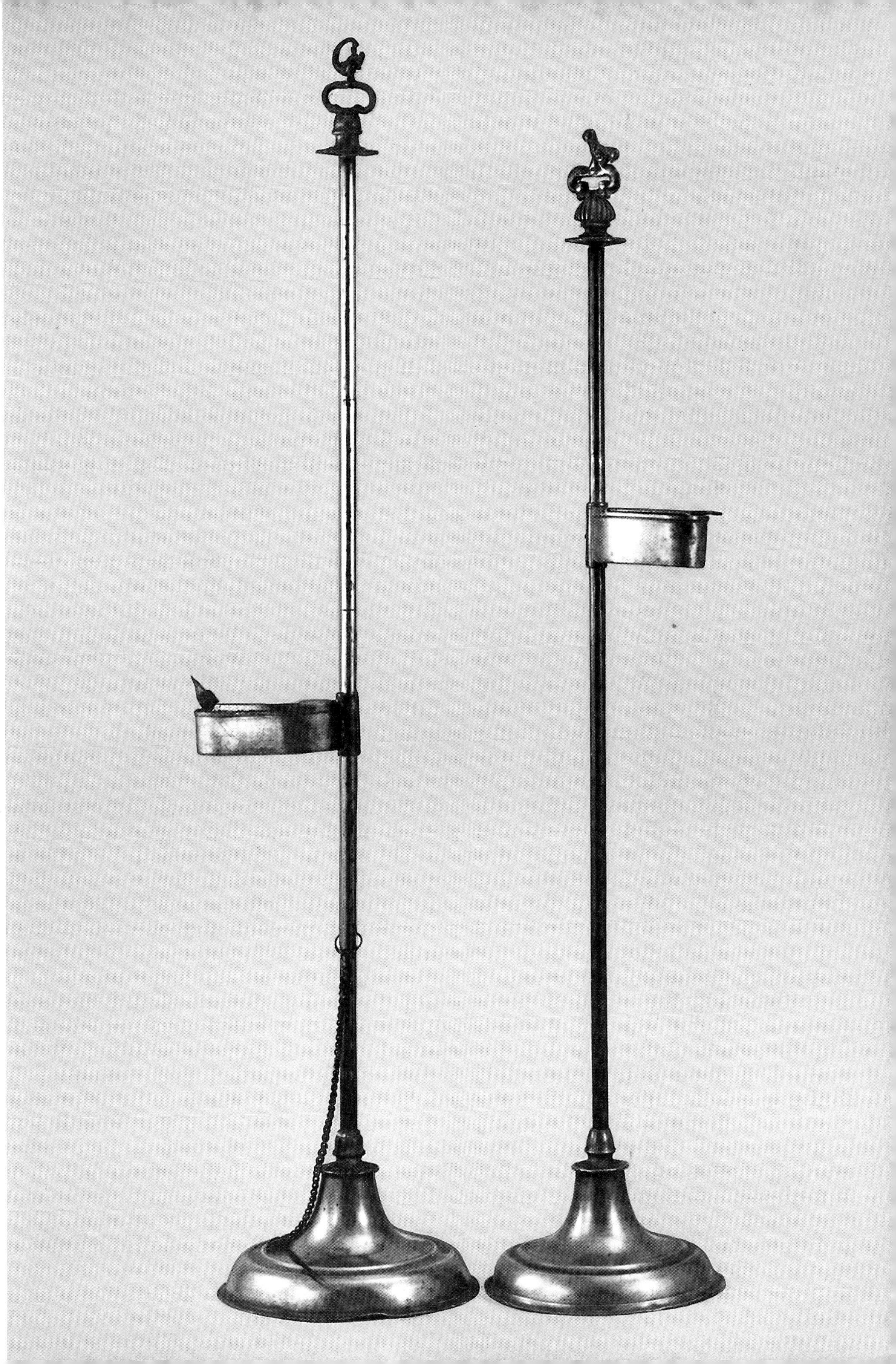

339

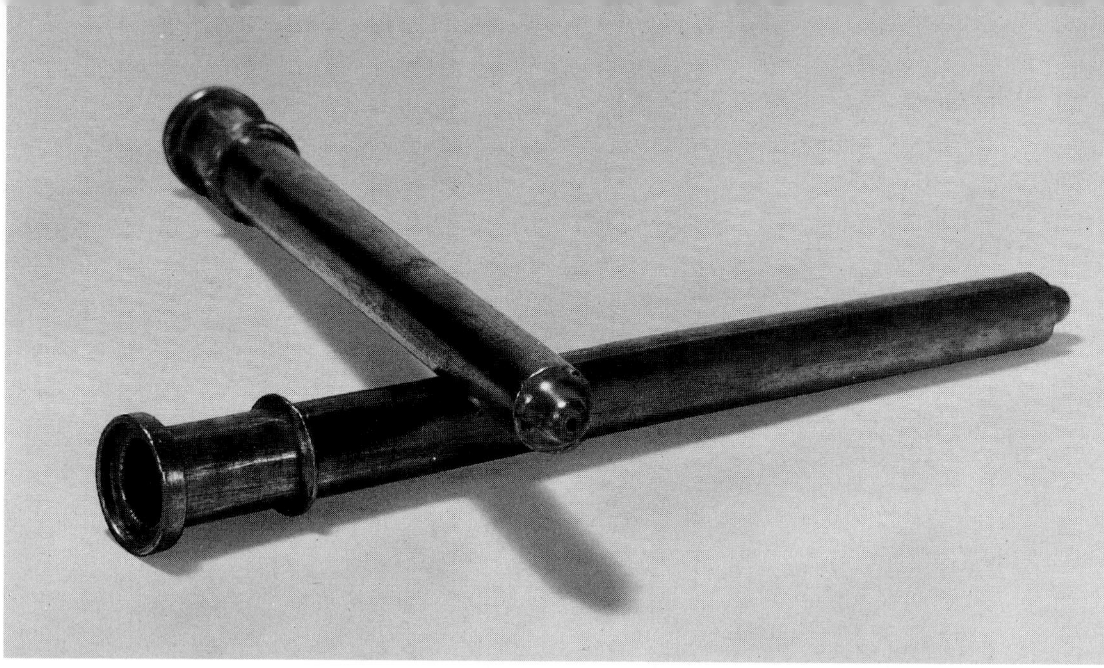

340

339 Candle-moulds; length 20 cm ($7^{7}/_{8}$″), early 19th century. Museum "Schloss Moritzburg", Zeitz

340 Pewter band on the glass reservoir of an oil-clock with the numerals IX (9 p.m.) to VII (7 a.m.); 19th century. In private ownership

341 Oil-lamps with hour-glasses, known as oil-clocks; height 36 and 40 cm ($14^{1}/_{8}$″ and $15^{3}/_{4}$″), *c.* 1810. Gedenkstätte Crimmitschauer Textilarbeiterstreik 1903/04, Crimmitschau

VI
VII
VIII
IX
X
XI
XII

342

343

342 Spill-holder; length 21 cm (8 1/4″), 18th century. Museum Weissenfels

343 Night-light gang moulds on stand; height 14 cm (5 1/2″), 2nd half of the 18th century.
The small candles were cast in halves and then pressed together in pairs round a wick.
Kulturhistorisches Museum Rostock

344 Candle-snuffer stand; length 23 cm (9″), 1st half of the 18th century.
Museum des Kunsthandwerks Leipzig

345 Candle-snuffer dish; length 21 cm (8 1/4″), *c.* 1780.
Museum Waldenburg/Saxony

346 Matchbox with roughened striking surface; length 6.2 cm (2 3/8″), 19th century.
In private ownership

347 Extinguisher cap; height 8 cm (3 1/8″), 18th century.
Vogtländisches Kreismuseum Plauen

Following page:

348 Small oil-lamp with wick-needle; height 8 cm (3″), *c.* 1820. The shell-shaped base which could be filled with water, favoured the use of this type of lamp as a night light.
In private ownership

344
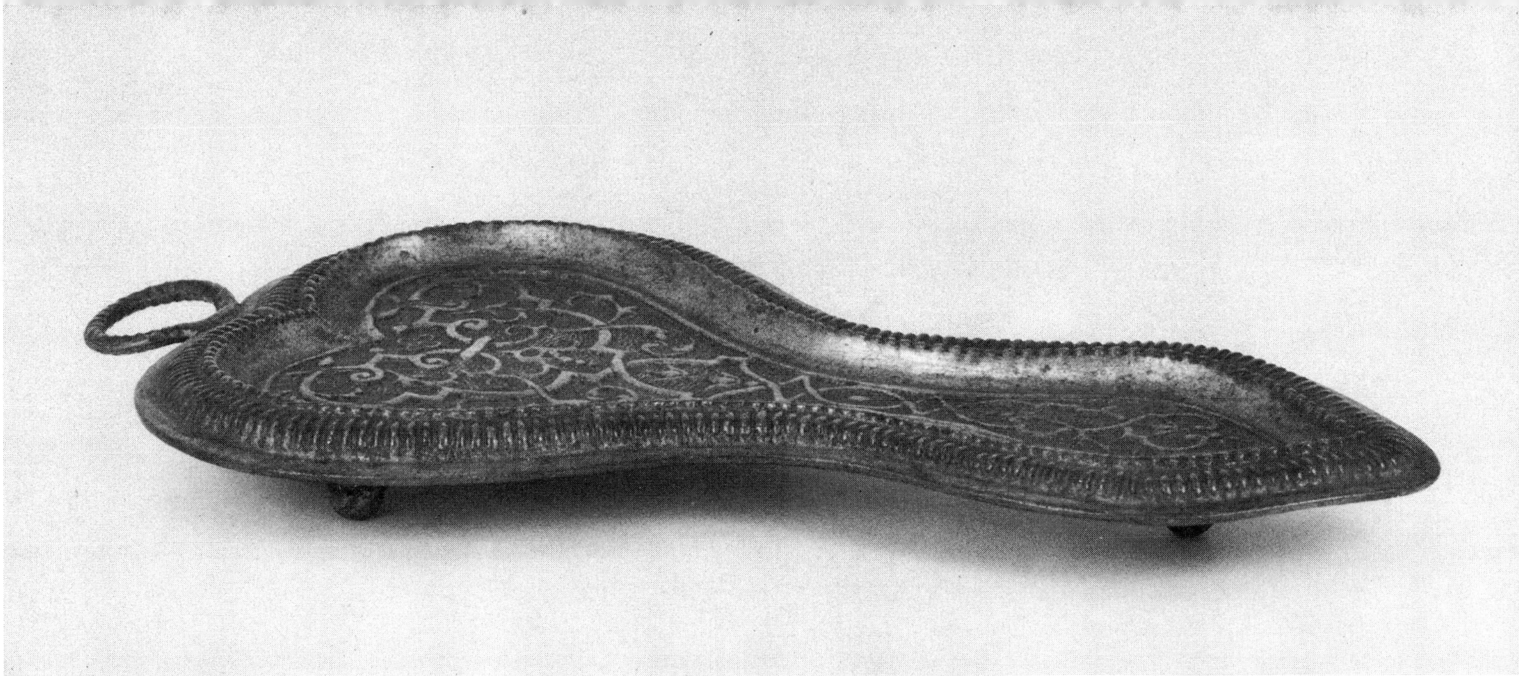
345
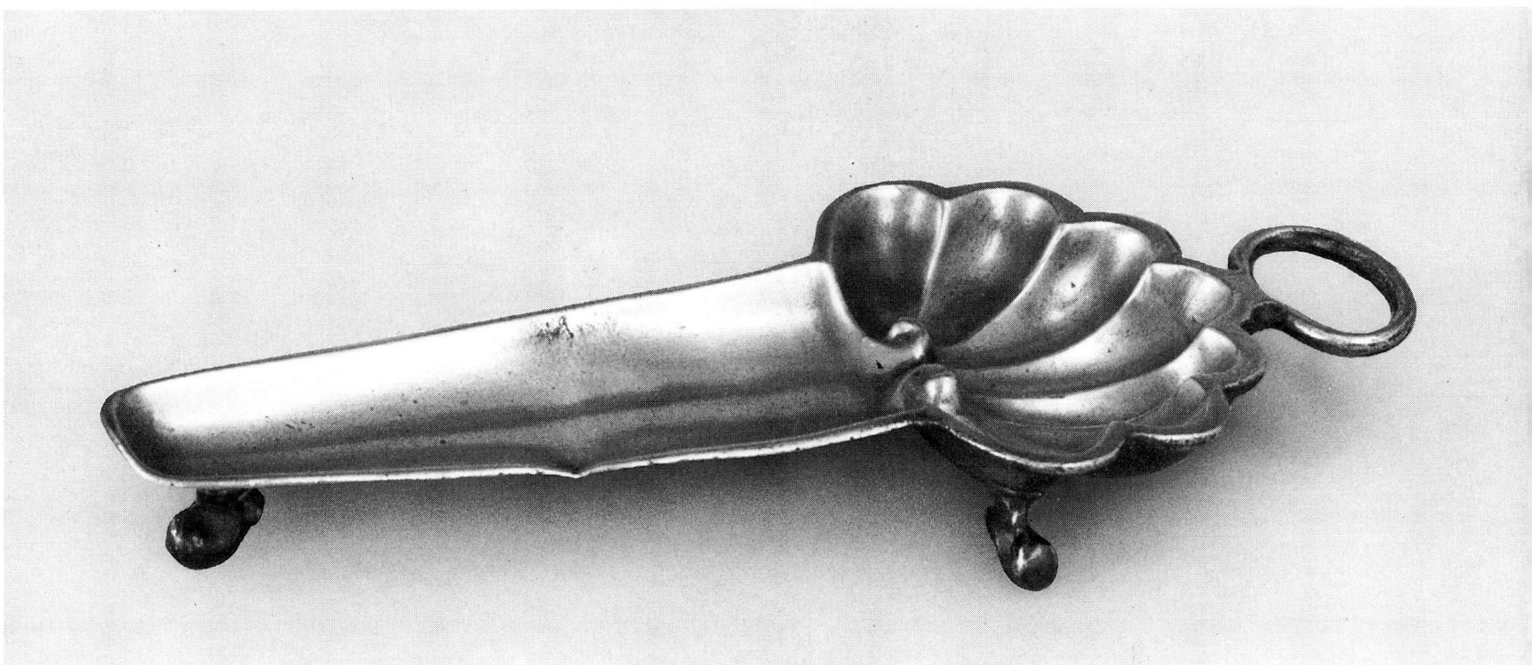
346
347

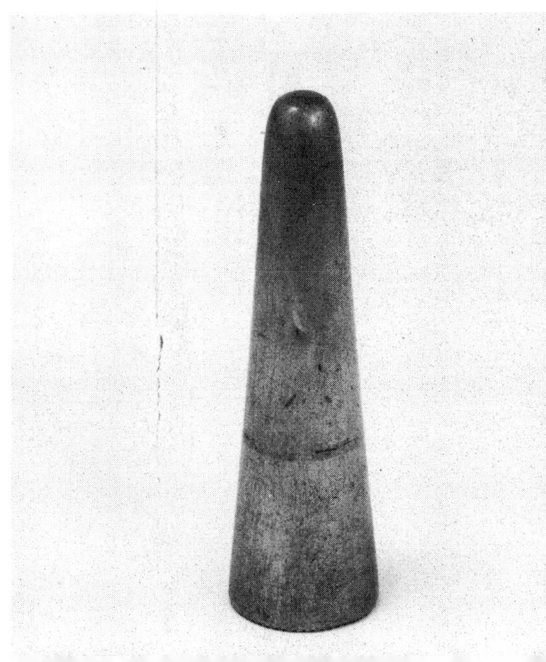

Hanging lamps
are named thus which can be hung somewhere. If they are intended to be specially bright the backplate is a mirror or very highly polished metal, which is decorated in a fashionable style and they are called "blaker".

Explanatory definition, 1787.

The term *blaker* was in former times not everywhere taken to mean the same type of lighting device. In some places it was a term for a candlestick with no stem, like a soup-plate with a socket in the centre and a knob or tongue soldered to its rim to carry it by. In the 18th century it was said that with such a light one could walk around the house without spilling tallow onto the floor or onto one's person and scholars used candlesticks of this kind so that their paper did not become soiled. In other districts, and far more frequently, *blaker* (wall-sconce) was the name for that type of candle-holder whose arms were inserted into a sheet. These were made mostly in Germany from the 16th to the 18th centuries, some in England and the Nether-
322 lands, occasionally in France. During this period, wall-sconces were available from various craftsmen in metal, among them also pewterers. The original function of the metal plate was to lessen the danger of fire and probably also as soot protection. The Low-German word *blaken* has a meaning akin to "become sooty" or smoulder and emphasizes the connection between the production of black (as in lamp-black) and the *blaker* described above. It was soon realized that a brightly polished plate ought invariably to be used as a reflector. This naturally involved considerable trouble to keep reviving the metal's brilliance. Because of this, on pewter wall-sconces over a period the primary purpose of the backplate became ornamental. It was therefore provided with decorations and also engraving which would be pleasing in both urban and rural houses, polished as well as dull. Wall-sconces were in any case not to be found in craftsmen's workshops. They used glass balls ("cobblers" balls, "condensers") which effectively concentrated the light from a simple pewter candlestick. In the Erzgebirge these balls also had a domestic purpose: this is indicated by the name "lace-balls", namely to provide light for lace-making carried out at home.

Some families were able to afford the expensive chandeliers which because of their appearance were also called "spiders". Chandeliers were of more recent development than all other lighting devices; pewterers made them principally in the second half of the 18th century. Because of the rather limited demand it was not worthwhile to manufacture special moulds. They were therefore produced from a range of individual moulds. The centrepiece, from which the arms extended was usually from the mould for the lid of a round dish. Moulds for handles sometimes provided the basis of the
323–325 arms whilst candlestick-moulds were used for casting drip-shells, stems and sockets.

Chandeliers are marked even more rarely than the general run of lighting appliances. This makes it difficult today always exactly to determine their date correctly, especially as historizing works exist from as early as the late *Biedermeier* period. Examples are the six-armed chandeliers of about 1835 in the neo-Gothic style from the workshop of the master Franz Hirsche who had been working in Brünn (now Brno) since 1824. One is inclined to judge these chandeliers to be some 50 years younger. Chandeliers were, moreover, made in the second half of the 19th century whose design incorporated the universally popular "miner's light". "Miner's lights" are candlesticks in the form of a miner holding a socket in his hand. At first they were made only by pewterers established in the German Erzgebirge. From the end of the 18th century these popular candlesticks had, however, come to be made elsewhere, as, for example, in the workshop of a pewterer of Italian origin, Johann Albert Lana in Teschen (now Cieszyn). Partiality for the miner's candlesticks was to some extent exploited to stimulate sales of expensive candelabra.

Wall-sconces and chandeliers belonged to the items in many German households designated as *ungerade*. The difference between *gerade* (direct) and *ungerade* (indirect) in many districts served to decide inheritance upon a husband's death. The items called *gerade* (to which all candlesticks belonged) remained to the widow alone, whereas agreement had to be reached with all the heirs about the items being *ungerade*. A wall-sconce or chandelier could even be claimed from other heirs when it was engraved with the widow's name.

Oil-lamps and oil-clocks

Oil-lamps in the form of round pottery bowls are known among the Greeks as early as the 7th century B.C. and among the Romans shortly post-A.D. It was not until about the end of the 16th century that they came into use north of the Alps when both those of pottery and those of pewter which were emerging at that time only came to be included among normal possessions over a long period. This was generally for two reasons: tallow lights were cheaper to burn than oil and did not create as much disagreeable smoke in use. Heavy smoke emission meant that oil-lamps could at first be used only in kitchens or workrooms. The use of these lamps only became more tolerable when small improvements led to complete combustion of the oil and less carbonization of the wick.

In early versions the wick rose vertically from the reservoir which was not
326 favourable to the combustion process. The wick frequently smouldered more than it flamed and in addition dripping oil made the lamp very unclean. In the Netherlands this earned them the name of *snotneuzen* (snotty nose). Positioning the wick at an angle helped to overcome the problem. Its carbonization was reduced when it was led through a tube. This definitely improved drawing-up of oil from the reservoir. Even after the base of the lamp had been formed like a dish and an intermediate plate positioned under the wick-tube to catch any overflowing oil, the need to refill the lamp after a short time cannot have been satisfactory. This nuisance was largely overcome by design alterations to the wick-tube in such a way that it was only closed right round where the wick emerged, the rest being exposed on one half-side. Pewterers
327/329 made these wick-holders from sheet-iron, copper and sometimes of pewter.

Wick-tongs, wick-pricker and an extinguisher were necessary equipment for the care of oil-lamps. Pewterers supplied these with the lamp, to the
handle of which they were usually secured by a slender chain. In their sim-
plest form, wick-tongs are a sort of iron clip used to pull the wick out of the
tube. The pricker was used to push the wick through the tube from the reser-
332 voir. The extinguisher was in the shape of a conical hat; it was usually of
sheet-iron and its size was suited to the wick-tube. Original small 18th century oil-lamps are, however, recorded which were extinguished by shutting
down a closely fitting lid. There were probably less fumes afterwards than
331 when an ordinary extinguisher was used because the entire combustion
area was covered.

Oil obtained from rape-seed, linseed-oil, train-oil, olive-oil, and (particularly in America) whale-oil, were the usual lamp fuels. Now and again a
housewife would go to the trouble of extracting oil from lime blossom, which
because of its pleasing aroma was burnt on special occasions. At times
many pewterers kept oil for sale and more often, wicks. French masters favoured ribbon-like wicks for their lamps, coated externally with grease, these
having been invented by their compatriot Léger in about 1780 and which enjoyed the good opinion and favourable recommendation of the famous
chemist Lavoisier. Pewterers even advised their customers about saving oil
when using lamps or how to minimize smoke and obtain a specially bright
light. It was, for example, recommended that half-an-ounce would burn for at
least seven hours instead of six if the wick were moistened with water before
being lighted. A wick which had been immersed in wine-vinegar and then
dried would smoke less and one soaked in brandy and camphor would give
forth such a bright light that one would be able to see one's reflection in the
surface of a pewter lamp. Pewterers naturally at the same time drew attention to the advantage of being able to obtain copious illumination when par-
328/330 ticularly needed, namely by the use of an oil-lamp with several burner arms
of which one, two, three or all of them could be used as required.

Regardless of style or size, oil-lamps were produced from up to six
moulds—for the font (oil-reservoir), its cover, the intermediate plate, the
stem, the foot and the handle. If a spouted lamp had to be cast, the mould for
the tubular spout through which the wick was led would also be required. After the various parts had been cast and the rough flashes removed, they
were soldered together. The base of the lamp had a hole in its centre into
which was set the hollow stem. This was so that the finished lamp could not
only stand on its base, which resembled a plate, but could also be erected on
a wooden upright. In spinning-rooms there were special carousel stands
which enabled the source of light to be positioned at the best working height.
Pewterers occasionally produced oil-lamps where the reservoir and wick
338 slid up and down on a long brass rod so that the desired height of the light
could be adjusted. A hanging-lamp without stem or foot was a frequent pur-

To make wicks for candles and tallow lamps.

Take five or several threads of tow wound together, beat them well and twist them into a cord. Coat them with tallow or wax and they will burn well.

Housekeeping book, 1724.

chase which was provided with a soldered-on pewter strip in which there was a hanging hole so that a hook or nail in the wall took the place of the brass
335 rod. Small *gakel* (flickering) lamps were without a stem or almost stemless
333/334 like hanging-lamps. These were understood to be small lamps, without an
336 intermediate dish, whose reservoir was usually shaped like a spice-contain-
348 er or egg-cup and had no cover.

Small lamps were provided with a thin wick which produced only a modest flame. The low oil consumption made it possible to use them as night-lights, that is, to burn right through the night. This was important mainly beside a sick-bed when, amongst other things, drinks were heated over the flame so that the patient did not have to take them cold. If no *gakel* lamp was available, oil-lamps of normal size were also used for this purpose. Persons who were particularly frugal acquired a pewter cap which had a small hole in the top.

Night-lamp

It is either a thick and round stock of cast wax provided internally with a delicate wick or a slender tapering cotton wick placed in a pewter dish filled with olive-oil, which is usually put into the rooms of women in child-bed or the sick during the night.

Frauenzimmerlexikon, Leipzig, 1715.

The cap was placed in a pewter dish filled with oil and had a long wick which was pulled out a little through the hole in the top. Contemporary descriptions of this simple type of night-light affirm that they would burn for three nights on only half-an-ounce of oil. In any event, the fumes were so disagreeable that preference was given to wax or tallow candles.

340/341 The first "oil clocks" (hour-lamps) appeared in the 18th century. They are oil-lamps with a glass reservoir up which runs a pewter strip with graduations to indicate the time from IX (9 p. m.) to VII (7 a. m.). When the wick was lighted at 9 p. m. the hour could be read off from the oil level at any given time. Until the invention of sulphur matches in about 1830, in towns people were dependent on the night-watchman's hourly cry if they were unable to afford a repeater-clock and wished to know the time at night. Now pewterers were making available oil-clocks which at first appeared to be something extraordinarily useful. However, it soon became clear that their practical value was much less than had been hoped. Indication of the time was far from satisfactorily reliable due to the variable consistency of the fuel oil and differences in quality of wicks which did not allow regulation of the clocks for reasonable maintained accuracy. Pewterers' endeavours to open up a fairly good earning potential by the production of hour-glasses was also fraught with problems from the start in so far as it demanded the glassworkers' co-operation. Although oil-clocks were not made in great numbers, their decorative appearance made the production of copies at the end of the 19th and beginning of the 20th centuries tempting. Old work can most surely be recognized by the way in which the glass reservoirs are made, when they usually have an uneven surface finish which looks genuine, inclusions of blowholes or a not entirely symmetrical shape.

Musy of Vienna invented night-lamps, which not only illuminate the bedroom but also show the hour on a dial and are further provided with an alarm.

Fresenius, *Gemeinnützige Kalenderlese-reyen* (Almanac of generally useful readings), 1786.

Candle-moulds and other utensils

For centuries the term "tallow light" was used to describe tallow candles. Tallow is the term generally used for the raw fat of cattle and sheep of which simple candles were made. In rural households tallow lights were made in the home; in towns they could be bought from soap-boilers and candle-makers. Pewterers made moulds intended for both domestic use and for professional candle-makers. Whereas candle-makers built up the tallow layer by layer round the wick, in the home candles were mainly made in a single pouring. Moulds were also available in sheet-iron, lead, copper, glass and wood but the best results were achieved with those of pewter. Pewterers gave an assurance that "the compounding of tin with some other metals" would make them so durable that moulds of no other material could com-
339 pete.Candle-moulds intended for domestic use were of a single piece;
337 pewterers supplied a kind of cylindrical funnel with those for commercial production. The demand for candle-moulds was sometimes so great that many pewterers specialized in their production, for example the master Vitus Popp of Wertheim (Baden) (circa 1796), Georg Michael Heide of Kulmbach (Bavaria) (active from 1815) and Johannes Reinöhl from Ulm (Wurttemberg) (circa 1860) who was also renowned as a supplier of confectionery moulds.

Butchers and such who need fire shall melt no tallow by night but make their fires by day.

Fire regulation of the town of Leipzig, issued A. D. 1596.

In those households where all candles were normally self-made, at least a dozen moulds would be available which were either own property or borrowed from the neighbourhood. The golden rule for domestic candle-moulding was, if possible, to heat the tallow only once and pour it into the moulds. Every time it was re-melted when the quantity had been misjudged and sufficient moulds were not available detracted from the quality of the candles. A valued hint for making firm and bright-burning tallow lights, with the appearance of wax, was to mix in ground oyster-shell which had previously been stirred to a paste with hydrochloric acid. Because many an inexperienced housewife did this in a pewter bowl which was attacked by the acid, her pleasure in the subsequent fine candles was sometimes clouded. In some regions, for example in Hungary and some districts of Germany, candle-moulding was a festivity accompanied by music and dancing. On these occasions, wooden stands for the moulds, usually kept in the houses, were brought out into an open meadow, the moulds were hung up, provided with wicks and next the tallow, prepared over a large fire, was poured in.
343 Close by, decorative candles for night lights were cast in halves in small pewter stands with moulding cavities, two halves after having been moulded then being pressed together round a wick. The mould was first moistened with water so that the candle-halves could be extracted easily. During the 19th century a few pewterers offered boxes of soldered sheet pewter for storing tallow lights after they had been moulded and which were supposed to preserve their flexibility for a specially long time. It is clear that demand for these boxes was only limited. Pewter moulds for casting large candles as

well as those for small ones were usually among the *ungerade* household
goods and upon a husband's death could not be claimed by a widow for her-
self alone if there were other heirs.

A necessary adjunct to lighting-devices came into being as early as the
16th century—the candle-snuffer. Whereas previously, ordinary scissors
344 had been used, these were now provided with a box-like receptacle into
which the severed part of the wick was pushed when it was cut off. ''Snuff-
ing'' could be carried out repeatedly like this without the scissors having to
be cleaned each time. None of the wax or tallow-candles gave a light in any
way satisfactory without frequent trimming and candle-snuffers only became redundant with the development of stearin or paraffin wax-candles.
They were usually made of brass and although pewterers offered them more
cheaply, no business came as a result. On the other hand, special pewter
345 plates, trays or dishes upon which the snuffers were laid after being used,
proved more popular. Although the tablecloth was protected from soot by little peg-feet on the snuffer itself, it was preferable that it should be put onto a
285 special tray for the purpose; often one of the somewhat smaller plates had to
serve. The typical shape of pewter trays for candle-snuffers was already established in the 17th century and during the Rococo period they were made
with small curved feet and a scrolled handle.

I do not know what would be better
for you to discover
than lamps
to burn without cleaning.

J. W. von Goethe (1749–1832)

Until the 18th century a spark for lighting candles and oil-lamps was obtained from a flat steel plate upon which a flint was struck. Pewterers offered
small boxes in which this equipment for generating a flame could be kept. After the invention of matches some masters went over to the manufacture of
346 similar containers incorporating a rough striking face but it is not recorded
that they achieved any success with them. Things went a bit better with the
production of pewter charcoal-pots (''fire-cups'') in the 19th century. Smok-
ers in particular used them to ignite spills for lighting their tobacco. Charcoal-
pots stood on the table for this purpose. Inventive pewterers contrived spe-
342 cial spill-holders which were usually cylindrical but also took fanciful forms.

A small cup, which was used as an extinguisher cap, is mentioned as early as in the *Hortus deliciarum* (a compilation of everything worth knowing
composed in the second half of the 12th century by the Abbess Herrad von
Landsberg) under the name *extinctoria*. It can safely be assumed that pew-
347 ter extinguishers for domestic use came into being concurrently with the development of pewter lighting-devices. Early examples have, however, not
survived. This applies also to those made of sheet-iron, brass and silver. Regardless of material, these extinguishers took the form of a hollow cone.
Those of pewter are specially thick-walled so that they can also be applied
directly to a number of flames to extinguish them one after another.

Equipment for Hygiene and the Sick-bed

8

Before water-mains were laid to town houses during the 19th century in the majority of countries, storage containers in the form of water-kegs and the many associated washing-bowls were part of virtually indispensable domestic equipment. Shaving-bowls are not nearly so well represented; they emerged principally in towns at a time when visiting a public bath-house fell out of fashion. There are grounds for inferring that pewter chamber-pots already existed in the Middle Ages. For centuries they were included in the production range of very likely every workshop involved in the manufacture of utilitarian pewter. It is similar with bed-warmers, which were particularly valued by old and ill persons as well as for travelling.

Cupping-bowls and enema-syringes for use at home were widely distributed for the treatment or prevention of illnesses. In addition to these, there was a variety of other wares whose principal purpose was not, in fact, to combat or care for illnesses but which in certain cases also played a part in this connection. Thus, for example, olive-oil was allowed to stand in a yeast-pot, normally used as a kitchen storage container, until dregs known as *amurca* had settled and could be extracted by decanting. When this was laid on the forehead in cases of headache, relief would quickly follow—a homely prescription passed down from generation to generation. Even pure tin was, in fact, recommended for the treatment of liver complaints as well as for young mothers, to be taken in the form of filings.

General purpose small spout-jugs were used as drinking-vessels for the bed-ridden. Special small pots with a cover and long spout *(canards)* were made solely in France. Finally, pewter or pewter-mounted screwed-jars in which medicinal substances were kept, must be mentioned.

A remedy for malignant nerve- and putrid-fever.

Add half an ounce of prepared tartar to half a litre of boiling cow's or goat's milk, stir the milk with a spoon until it is thoroughly curdled. The whey is filtered off through a pewter sieve.

Homely prescription, 1833.

Water-kegs and washing-bowls

Water-keg is the term most frequently encountered for the containers for washing-water which were mounted on the wall or hung from a loop. In German it is called *giessfass*. It means a container out of which one could let water run over one's hands. Washing was done in a washing or hand-basin; this stood upon a stand or hung from the wall like a water-keg. The stand was often provided with a fine white cotton or light linen cloth, sometimes other fabrics, embroidered with lace, were used.

The water-keg was included in the production range of pewterers as early as the 14th century. In Germany occasionally *hantvetere* or *handfatghetere* (those who cast the water-kegs) are mentioned specifically, distinguished from those who cast jugs. Yet sometimes a water-keg was also demanded from jug-casters as a masterpiece, for example in a guild ordinance in Brünn (Brno) of 1387 and in 1493 in the Archbishopric of Würzburg (Franconia). A water-keg of the Gothic period with a handle on the tap in the form of a cockerel has survived to the present day. It was found in 1903/4 in a wrecked ship while dredging. Guild regulations sometimes prescribe a specific volume (in Augsburg, for example, 6 *mass*) or a candidate would be given a sketch exactly in accordance with which the keg had to be shaped (e. g., 1730, in Mannheim). In many instances it was required that the keg be of sheet, i. e. pewter cast in a mould of stone slabs.

Because niches for water-kegs are now made in a variety of styles and yet are not in general use and due to this the amount which should be paid to the maker cannot readily be judged, whosoever wishes to have one of them made shall reach agreement about the cost with the pewterer as best and as near as he can.

Pewterers' regulation, Fribourg/Breisgau, 1511.

349/352 Water-kegs and washing-bowls were, in fact, very plentiful in Germany although they are also encountered in all other countries with a pewter trade. This type of ware was sometimes included in household goods even in the Far East. For example, a "washing-vessel of cheap tin" belonging to the household of the sixth Wang is mentioned at an early date in the work *Kin Ping Meh* by Wang Shi Tshong which first appeared in 1610. In Switzerland water-kegs in a wide variety of shapes were positioned in "pewter-niches" or buffets. In the pewter-niches the water-keg usually hung above a hemispherical basin which collected the water and in which was an outlet for the water to run out into a pail or other vessel standing underneath. A special pewter wash-basin was therefore not necessarily provided. When, however, one was built-in it was often of shell-shaped form. It has already been mentioned in connection with drinking-vessels that the *brunnenkesselchen* or *sugerli* was not only used as a biberon but also for replenishing the water-keg. It therefore usually hung from an iron hook or on an upright of the pewter-niche or buffet. It was, of course, also possible to let water run over one's
354 hands by tilting the *brunnenkesselchen* or to rinse out one's mouth from it but it was more convenient to use the water-keg because it had one or sometimes two outlets controlled by a tap. The dolphin—king of fishes—was the most popular shape for water-kegs. The dolphin-shaped water-keg was normally made entirely of pewter but there are instances where the eyes are inset red glass and the tail, fins and mouth inlaid with brass. The filler opening is in the tail and the small outlet tap in the mouth. Because these storage con-

tainers cast in the form of dolphins are of very decorative appearance, they
350 have repeatedly been copied in the present century and even now are still
cast from old moulds. In contrast, the simple box-like water-keg has hardly
351 ever been reproduced. This is nevertheless the type most frequently still to
be found today because it was the one which was produced in the greatest
numbers. The melon, pomegranate and the acorn are other shapes adopted
for water-kegs and some were on pedestals.

Wash-basins were predominantly of plain appearance; those which
359 were carried to and from a stand were equipped with two folding grips so that
they could be lifted and emptied easily. It was not until the 19th century that it
became the normal practice to solder a high pewter sheet vertically to the rim
of the basin which was also joined to it with a handle at each end. This pewter
sheet was originally intended to prevent the wall being splashed but later
357 served rather as a vehicle for decorative engraving or embossing. Numerous inscriptions testify to the fact that these wash-basins were popular gifts
at weddings and christenings. Bowls were no longer usually used in conjunction with a water-keg but were more frequently filled from a ewer. According to contemporary accounts from the first half of the 18th century ew-
358 ers were supposed in principle to have no cover but it can safely be assumed
that no such theoretical distinction was made in the everyday life of the people. Special water cans seem to have been differentiated only in France
where they appeared at the end of the 16th century, shaped like helmets of
antiquity and disappeared again in about 1750.

361 Soap required for washing was obtained from tallow and lye derived from
lime and ashes. This rather harsh substance was kept in larger or smaller
363 troughs and in little bowls or dishes which were designed to be hung up
—small soap-tubs.

364 Many of the wall-mounted soap-dishes had a stubby draining outlet, as did spoon-holders. Those which are shaped like this make it specially clear that a part of the spoon-holder mould was also used for the manufacture of soap-dishes. In about 1830 a few pewterers started to make boxes for soap but did not stimulate much interest in them from customers.

Soap-keg

It is a small box formed from pewter or sheet-iron, without a cover, in which rests soap for the hands and which is generally hung on the stand for the water-keg.

Frauenzimmerlexikon, Leipzig, 1715.

Shaving-basins and chamber-pots

It is not known when the first pewter shaving-basins (''beard dishes'') were made. There is nevertheless a fixed starting point inasmuch as the use of soap for shaving only became general after the Thirty Years' War. Previously the beard had been softened by a sweating treatment taken at the barber's. Early shaving-basins were probably made in faience. Examples of this type have, for instance, survived from the German manufactories of Erfurt and Durlach. Because it was the general practice in time of war for barbers to take the field as army surgeons responsible for the care of the wounded and for trimming beards, a more robust material was required for shaving-basins than fragile pottery—pewter was available accordingly. By and by, shaving-basins were next brought into the household where they became most numerously represented at the beginning of the 19th century.

The characteristic feature of shaving-basins is a cut-out section which was held against the throat while the beard was being soaped. Early examples sometimes have two opposed recesses together with two loop-like openings through which a strap may have been passed so that the bowl
355 could be worn hanging. This may also be a pointer to the fact that these basins served a principally military purpose. Later there is only one loose ring by which the basin could be hung up instead of the two looped openings. There was usually no decoration except for inscriptions relating to ownership which are of interest in themselves. In exceptional cases basins are found which are splendidly engraved with foliage or other subjects and even with
360 embossed decoration.

The basic shape of shaving-basins is almost invariably oval. The round bowls, usually of brass, which even today can occasionally still be found hanging above the entrance to barbers' saloons, have nothing to do with the preparation of lather but are symbolic of a different tradition. Once a bath-house proprietor had heated his bath-house it was necessary that his customers should arrive as soon as possible. An apprentice therefore ran through the streets banging two metal bowls together with a great deal of noise. The two bowls were then hung up outside the bath-house door for as long as the water was still hot enough for bathing. The round pewter barbers' basins which appeared towards the middle of the 19th century are a result of pewterers' economizing: their basis was the mould for a small bowl. After they were cast a semi-circular piece was cut out of the rim when someone
362 asked for a shaving-basin. The small round bowls were incidentally also put on sale as spitoons for all. In French hospitals they hung at the head of the sick-bed and were sometimes provided with a handle.

In the houses mainly of townspeople were always several examples of chamber-pots (bed-pots, night-pots, night-basins, chamber-basins) to be found. In Berlin in the 18th century the authorities saw themselves obliged to regulate the emptying of these. This was permitted at three specific points in the town, after 11 p.m. from April until August but after 10 p.m. during the rest of the year. Pots had to be equipped with a loose cover for transport. The pewter trade reacted promptly to such regulations and made available chamber-pots with lids which had no hinges but which closed tightly. Cov-
366 ered cans were used as night-pots as early as the late Middle Ages. In the Netherlands especially, the shape of these *kamerpotjes* was reminiscent of
368/369 the Hansa jugs. The characteristic shape of chamber-pots developed from about the 17th century and did not change again with the passage of time. One occasionally encounters examples with two handles, which according to a contemporary report ought "to be in general use in certain situations" although people usually managed with a single handle. Whilst pottery

Good shaving-soap

Take one and a half pounds of powdered Venetian soap or if this is lacking, only good household soap, add to it seven or eight knife-points of ground orris root and two to three drams of lavender-oil, so that one can smell it well, knead it all well together in a pewter bowl and then add to it: cinnamon- and rosewood-oil, of each four to five drops, oils of cloves, lemon and orange, of each four drops, two grains of musk, stir it well together with an iron spatula or knife and make it into balls.

Recipe book, 1743.

chamber-pots were available at very favourable prices during the 19th century, those of pewter were very popular far and wide. A chamber-pot, including prior calculation of the quantity of material it would require, was frequent-
376 ly a masterpiece for journeymen in the pewter trade.

In many places strict customs were connected with chamber-pots at marriages. Thus, for example, the wedded pair might have to scour the dulled pot together on the morning after the wedding until it was bright again. A maiden drink of brandy and raisins was also brought in a chamber-pot to the couple in their marriage bed. After they had taken a few mouthfuls the wedding party finished off the remainder.

For us Germans, drinking-vessels cannot only not be made large enough, but also not beautiful and rare enough. One drinks out of monkeys and parsons, monks and nuns, lions and bears, ostriches and cats and out of the Devil himself: I will and can say nothing about the filthy wine-topers who drink to each other out of mugs, bowls, pots, hats, boots, hand-basins and in a totally sybaritic way from matulis and urine pots.

Sermon against wine drinking, 1589.

Bed- and foot-warmers

What motivated the City Council of Bremen in 1557 to arrange to be supplied with several bed-warmers by a local pewterer will now never be explained but one learns from documents relating to this and other orders that hot-water-bottles were already being made in considerable numbers at a very early date. The German poet and dramatist Andreas Gryphius (1616–1664) repeatedly mentions pewter bed-warmers in his works. At about the time he was writing night-garments were coming into use, that is the fashion of putting on lighter clothes before the night's sleep. This necessarily led to a strengthened desire to warm the bed before retiring for the night. At first, bed-warmers in the form of embossed brass or copper pans with pierced covers were the usual expedient. Glowing coals were put into the pan and it was moved to and fro under the bedclothes by a long handle immediately before going to bed. Various pewterers copied this long-handled design for which the source of heat had to be hot water and the pans are therefore
371 closed with a screw-cap. The filler-hole is usually in the centre of the pan. In Switzerland examples occasionally appear which have no handle and are provided with a filler-hole at the side.

Body-warmers are rarer than bed-warmers. These body-fitting hollow containers were easier to make from brass or copper-sheet although pewterers also tried to do so. Whilst they were, of course, also very welcome in a cold bed, they were principally in demand for those who had to travel the country in winter. That body-warmers—which were held against the torso by straps—do not come to light very often is largely attributable to the fact that travelling was not a mass activity. To travel by mail coach was something that the bulk of the people could almost never afford. For example, in about 1820 the cost of a place in the "ordinary" post from Kassel to Frankfurt-on-Main was 6–7 thalers which was nearly half-a-year's wages for a servant-girl. When a journeyman had to undertake the extravagance of travel, a box-like
372 foot-warmer went with him in the cold season. Naturally only short journeys were involved, perhaps to the seat of the local landowner or a regional guild meeting. Pewterers offered special "foot-bottles" for the use of gentlemen for the 12-day journey from Paris to Leipzig in about 1700. These were large

hot-water-bottles with two tunnels in the body into which the feet could be inserted while travelling. In the second half of the 18th century pewterers in America made foot-warmer bottles which were flat on the base and one side but otherwise sharply curved and no longer with an opening for the feet, which could be rested on the curve. So that foot-bottles remained stable even on bad roads, they were filled with hot sand. Although this type of foot-warmer was also known in the Netherlands—there is one in a painting by the artist Jan Luyken—they seem in total to have been made only rarely because evidence of them is difficult to find today. In America, one of these foot warmers, from the workshop of the master Henry Will, who worked from 1761 to 1793 in New York and Albany, has survived to the present day.

367 A tall hemispherically arched bed-warmer from the workshop of a Belgian pewterer has likewise survived. It is reasonable to assume that this bed-warmer had a similar function to the "heat-pots" (coal-pots) known from the Middle Ages: anyone unable to remain close to the warm hearth took a heat-pot with him. In the 18th century this was described as a two-handled round container of copper, sheet-iron or pottery which was filled with glowing charcoal. Pewter containers were, of course, filled with hot water or hot sand. They therefore did not radiate so much heat as the charcoal-pot but largely eliminated the danger of fire. In about 1245 a piece of equipment is first mentioned which later came to be found, made of pewter, in many house-
365 holds—the "warming-apple". This was used to keep the hands warm. It was probably intended mainly for churchgoing in winter. Containers in the form of
375 a book are more plentiful than warming-apples and have a screw-closure. Filled with hot water they were likewise used when on the way to church and during the service.

In many German districts a metal container which housed an insert filled with glowing charcoal was known as a *gicke*. The *gicke* had evolved from a turned wooden cylinder of the Middle Ages which had a sheet-iron lining into which was put a red-hot iron-billet. They could nevertheless not be used as bed-warmers because of the fire hazard. The pewter trade therefore put on sale slim cylindrical flasks, which sometimes have a tapered portion becoming conical towards the top. A hot steel-rod was put into these when in use and they were jestingly called "demoiselles". However, cylindrical bottles which could be filled with hot water and therefore had a screw-closure forming a tight seal were more successful. They are known from Reval (now Tallinn) from as early as the beginning of the 16th century and were described as "maidens" in municipal exchequer accounts from 1463 to 1507: "Maidens of pewter for prisoners so that they can warm their feet in winter." There is moreover a surviving bill from the same period from a doctor who had to amputate prisoners' hands and feet because they had become frozen. In
370 northern Germany cylindrical hot-water bottles were called *bettjuffern* (bed-maidens). Their screw-top took the form of a ball or a clenched fist.

Stomach-quilt

It is a small quilt copiously stuffed with down which womenfolk and also small children are in the habit of tying on their fronts at night.

Frauenzimmerlexikon, Leipzig, 1715.

350

351

352

353

Preceding page:

349 Water-keg; height 26.5 cm ($10^1/_2$"), 15th century. Kulturhistorisches Museum Rostock

350 Chamber water-keg; height 32 cm ($12^5/_8$"), late 18th century. Museum des Kunsthandwerks Leipzig

351 Water-keg (water-bladder); diameter 12.5 cm (5"), 18th century (cover is missing). Museum des Kunsthandwerks Leipzig

352 Detail of Fig. 349: The finger-piece of the tap is in the shape of a cockerel.

353 Detail of Fig. 349: Relief decoration. The plain areas have suffered from delamination, one of the "tin pests".

354 Pewter-niche with water-keg and *brunnen-kesselchen*; height of the water-keg 30 cm ($11^3/_4$"), 2nd half of the 17th century. Schweizerisches Landesmuseum Zurich

355 Shaving-basin; length 40 cm ($15^3/_4$"), dated 1709.
Victoria & Albert Museum, London

356 Bellied can, known as yeast-can; height 24 cm ($9^1/_2$"), 1st half of the 18th century.
Kunstgewerbemuseum Cologne

357 Wash-basin with splash-back; diameter 30 cm ($11^3/_4$"), dated 1842.
Schlossmuseum Altenburg

358 Netherlandish water-jug; height 20.5 cm (8"), 17th century.
Stedelijk Museum "De Lakenhal", Leyden

359 Washing-bowl engraved with its owner's name; length 23 cm (9"), dated 1741.
Museum "Schloss Moritzburg", Zeitz

355

CARL·CHRISTIAN·MÜLLER

1832

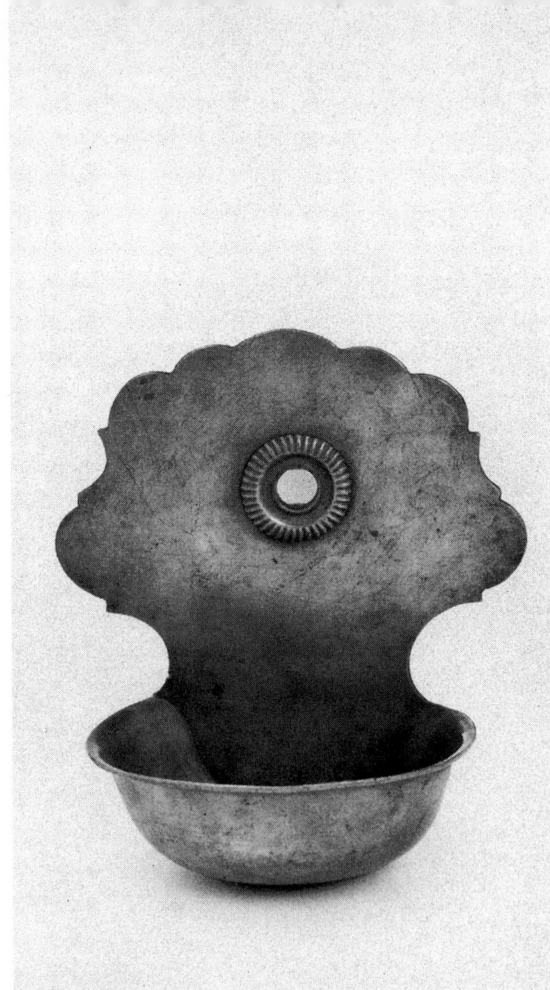

1822

360 Shaving-basin, decorated with engraved and embossed floral designs; length 20.5 cm (8″), dated 1822. In private ownership

361 Wall-mounted soap-box; height 13 cm ($5^1/_8$″), *c.* 1800. Vogtländisches Kreismuseum Plauen

362 Shaving-basin, cast from a bowl-mould; diameter 16 cm ($6^1/_4$″), dated 1832. Traditionsstätte Erzbergbau, Aue

363 Soap-trough, length 24.5 cm ($9^5/_8$″), 2nd half of the 18th century. Kulturhistorisches Museum Rostock

364 Wall-mounted soap-dish; height 18 cm (7″), dated 1822. Vogtländisches Kreismuseum Plauen

365 Hot-water bottle ("warming-ball"); height 15.9 cm ($6^1/_4$″), 1st half of the 19th century. Schweizerisches Landesmuseum Zurich

366 Chamber-pot with broad rim and cover; height 17 cm ($6^5/_8$″), 1st half of the 19th century. Bergisches Museum Schloss Burg/Wupper

367 Bed-warmer; height 20 cm ($7^7/_8$″), 18th century. Musée Taxandria, Turnhout

368 Night-pot; height 12.5 cm (5″), *c.* 1850. Vogtländisches Kreismuseum Plauen

369 Night-pot; height 14.5 cm ($5^3/_4$″), 1st half of the 19th century. Staatliches Heimat- und Schlossmuseum Burgk/Saale

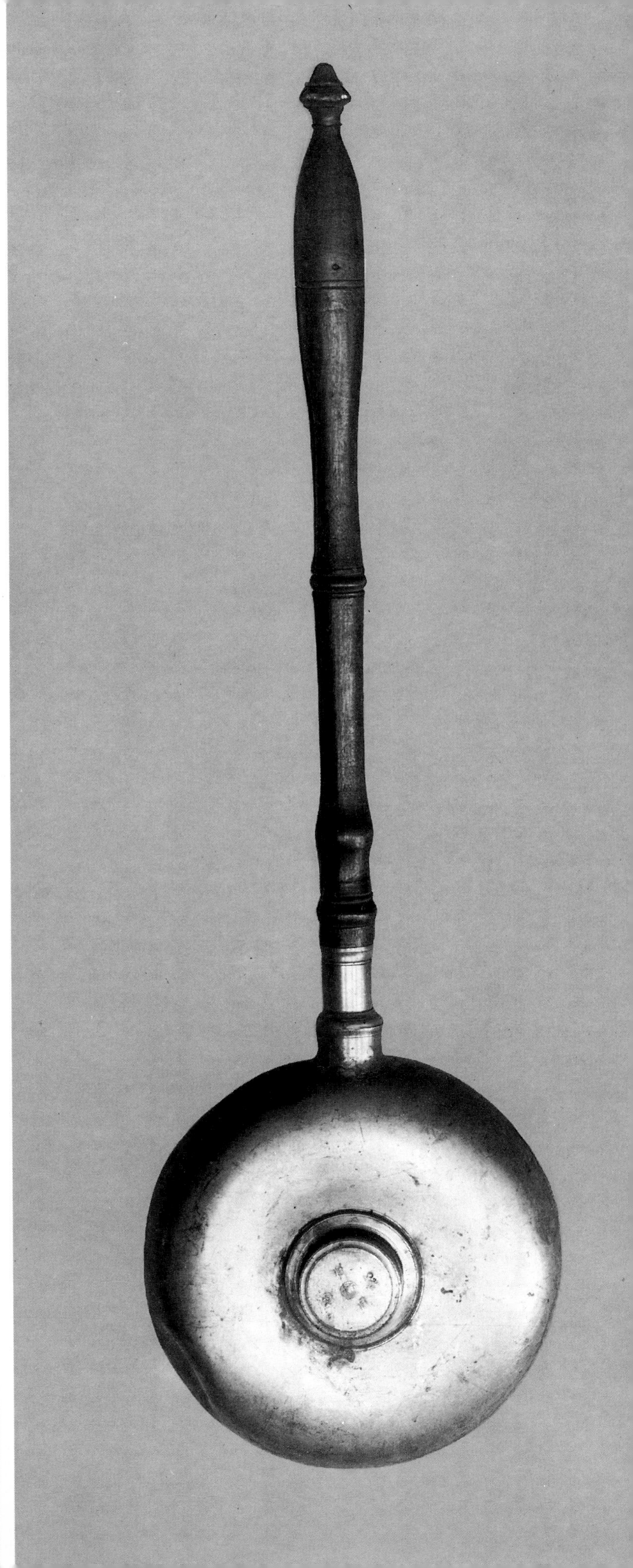

370 North German hot-water bottle, known as "bed-maiden"; height 34 cm ($13\frac{1}{4}$″), 2nd half of the 18th century.
Museum des Kunsthandwerks Leipzig

371 Warming-pan with wooden handle; early 19th century.
Nordiska Museet, Stockholm

372 Box-shaped hot-water bottle; length 30 cm ($11\frac{3}{4}$″), dated 1775.
These hot-water bottles were popular as foot-warmers.
Vogtländisches Kreismuseum Plauen

373 Hot-water bottle with recess for a child's feeding-bottle; 2nd half of the 18th century.
Rätisches Museum, Chur

374 Hot-water bottle; length 28 cm (11″), dated 1876.
Heimatmuseum Geyer/Erzgebirge

373

374

375 Hand-warmer bottle in book-shape with a dedication; height 21.5 cm ($8\frac{1}{2}$″), dated 1765. Gedenkstätte Crimmitschauer Textilarbeiterstreik 1903/04, Crimmitschau

376 Master's examination certificate, drawings and account for material for the production of a jug and a night-pot as a masterpiece; 1866. Municipal archives, Eilenburg

377 Bed-warmer with recesses for three feeding-bottles; diameter 27 cm ($10\frac{5}{8}$″), dated 1826. Kulturhistorisches Museum Rostock

378 Cupping-bowl; diameter 16.5 cm ($6\frac{1}{2}$″), dated 1836. In private ownership

Following page:

379 Travelling apothecary's chest with pewter boxes and glass bottles with pewter screw-closures; 16×16.5 cm ($6\frac{1}{4}$″×$6\frac{1}{2}$″), 1st half of the 19th century. In private ownership

380 Enema-syringes; length 10.5–34 cm ($4\frac{1}{8}$″–$13\frac{3}{8}$″), 19th century. Kreisheimatmuseum Grimma

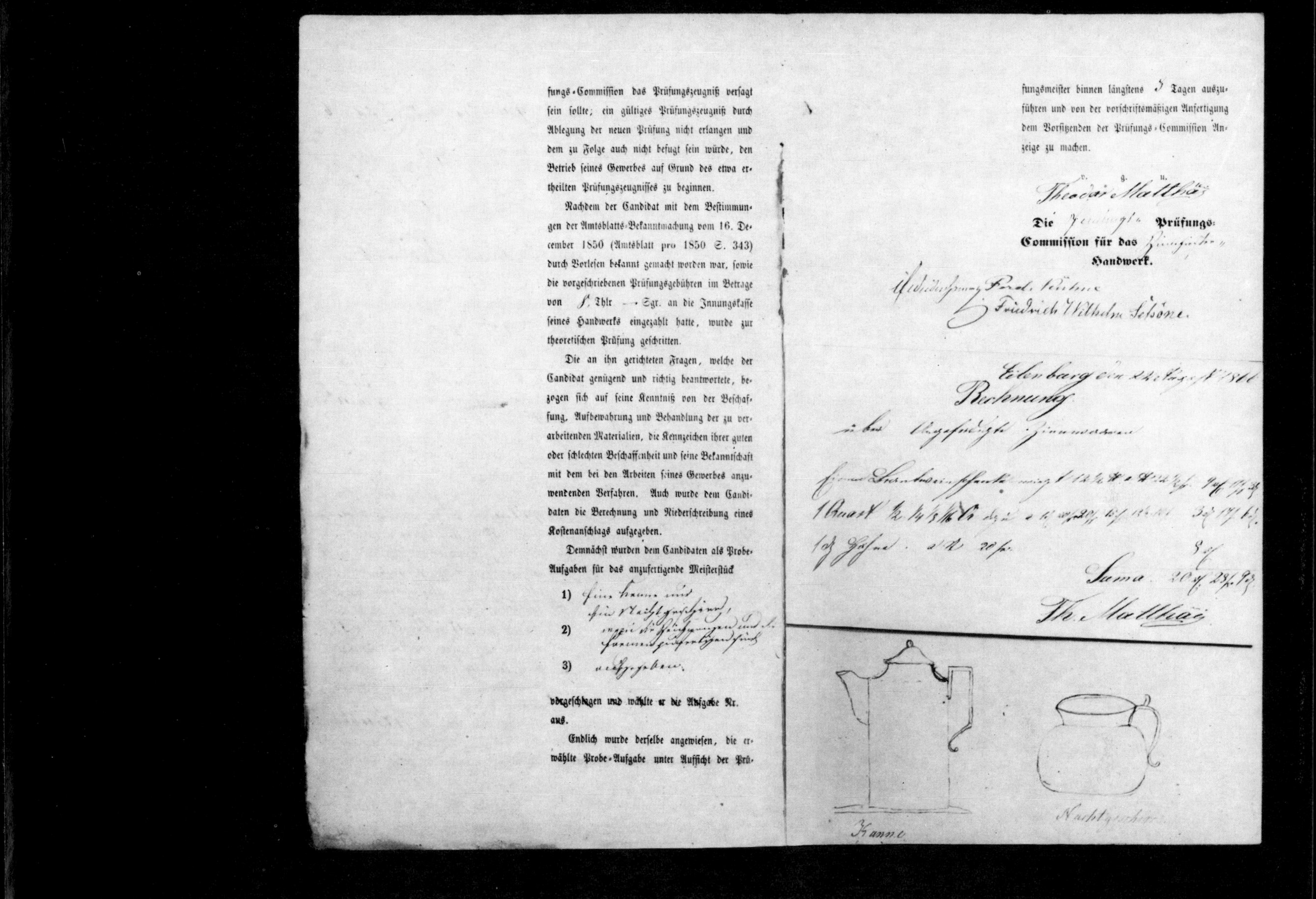

fungs-Commission das Prüfungszeugniß versagt sein sollte; ein gültiges Prüfungszeugniß durch Ablegung der neuen Prüfung nicht erlangen und dem zu Folge auch nicht befugt sein würde, den Betrieb seines Gewerbes auf Grund des etwa ertheilten Prüfungszeugnisses zu beginnen.

Nachdem der Candidat mit dem Bestimmungen der Amtsblatts-Bekanntmachung vom 16. December 1850 (Amtsblatt pro 1850 S. 343) durch Verlesen bekannt gemacht worden war, sowie die vorgeschriebenen Prüfungsgebühren im Betrage von 5 Thlr — Sgr. an die Innungskasse seines Handwerks eingezahlt hatte, wurde zur theoretischen Prüfung geschritten.

Die an ihn gerichteten Fragen, welche der Candidat genügend und richtig beantwortete, bezogen sich auf seine Kenntniß von der Beschaffung, Aufbewahrung und Behandlung der zu verarbeitenden Materialien, die Kennzeichen ihrer guten oder schlechten Beschaffenheit und seine Bekanntschaft mit dem bei den Arbeiten seines Gewerbes anzuwendenden Verfahren. Auch wurde dem Candidaten die Berechnung und Niederschreibung eines Kostenanschlags aufgegeben.

Demnächst wurden dem Candidaten als Probe-Aufgaben für das anzufertigende Meisterstück

1)

2)

3)

vorgeschlagen und wählte er die Aufgabe Nr. aus.

Endlich wurde derselbe angewiesen, die erwählte Probe-Aufgabe unter Aufsicht der Prüfungsmeister binnen längstens 5 Tagen auszuführen und von der vorschriftsmäßigen Anfertigung dem Vorsitzenden der Prüfungs-Commission Anzeige zu machen.

v. g. u.

Theodor Matthäi

Die Prüfungs-Commission für das Handwerk.

Friedrich Wilhelm

Rechnung

Th. Matthäi

Kanne

Nachtgeschirr

377

378

379

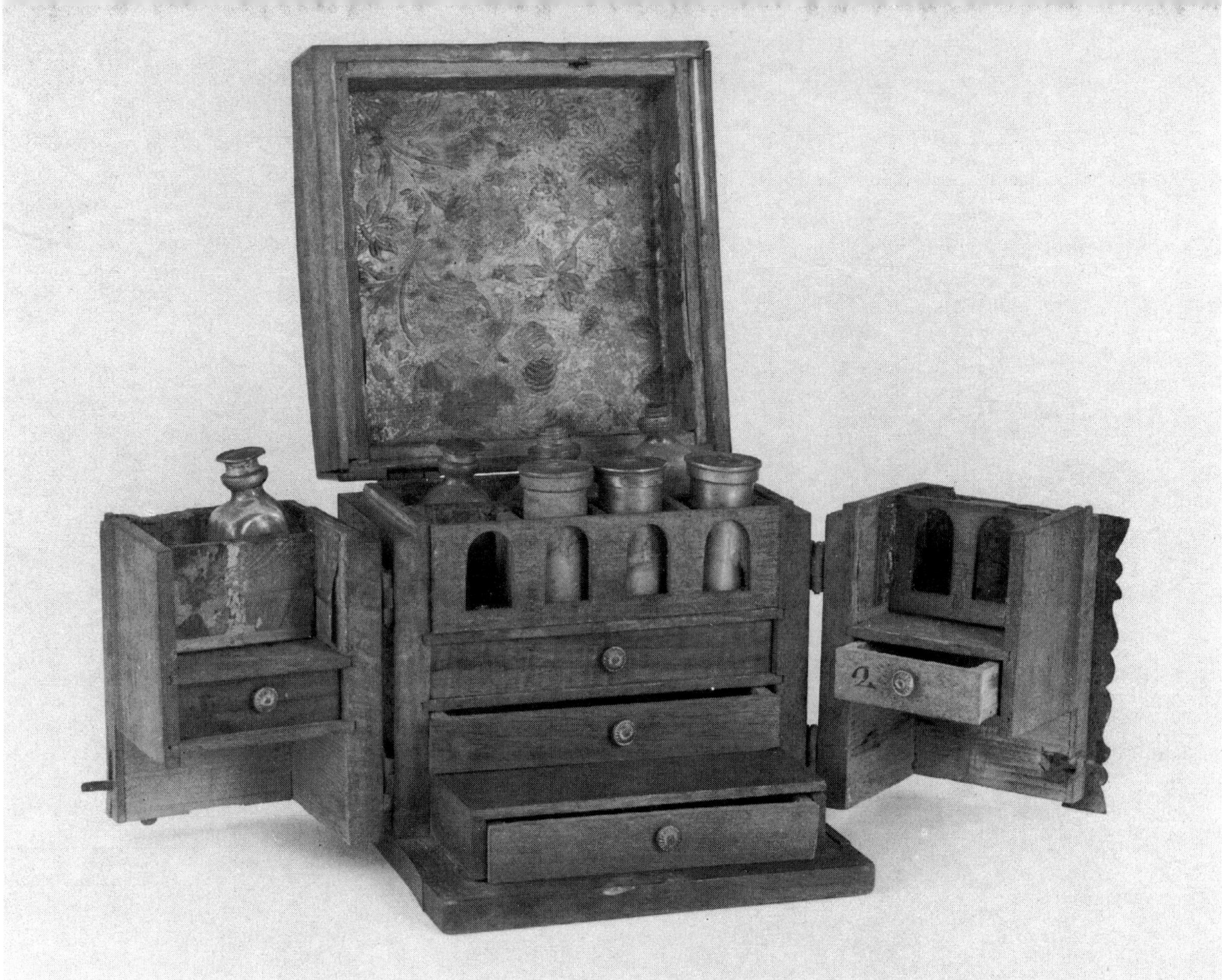

380

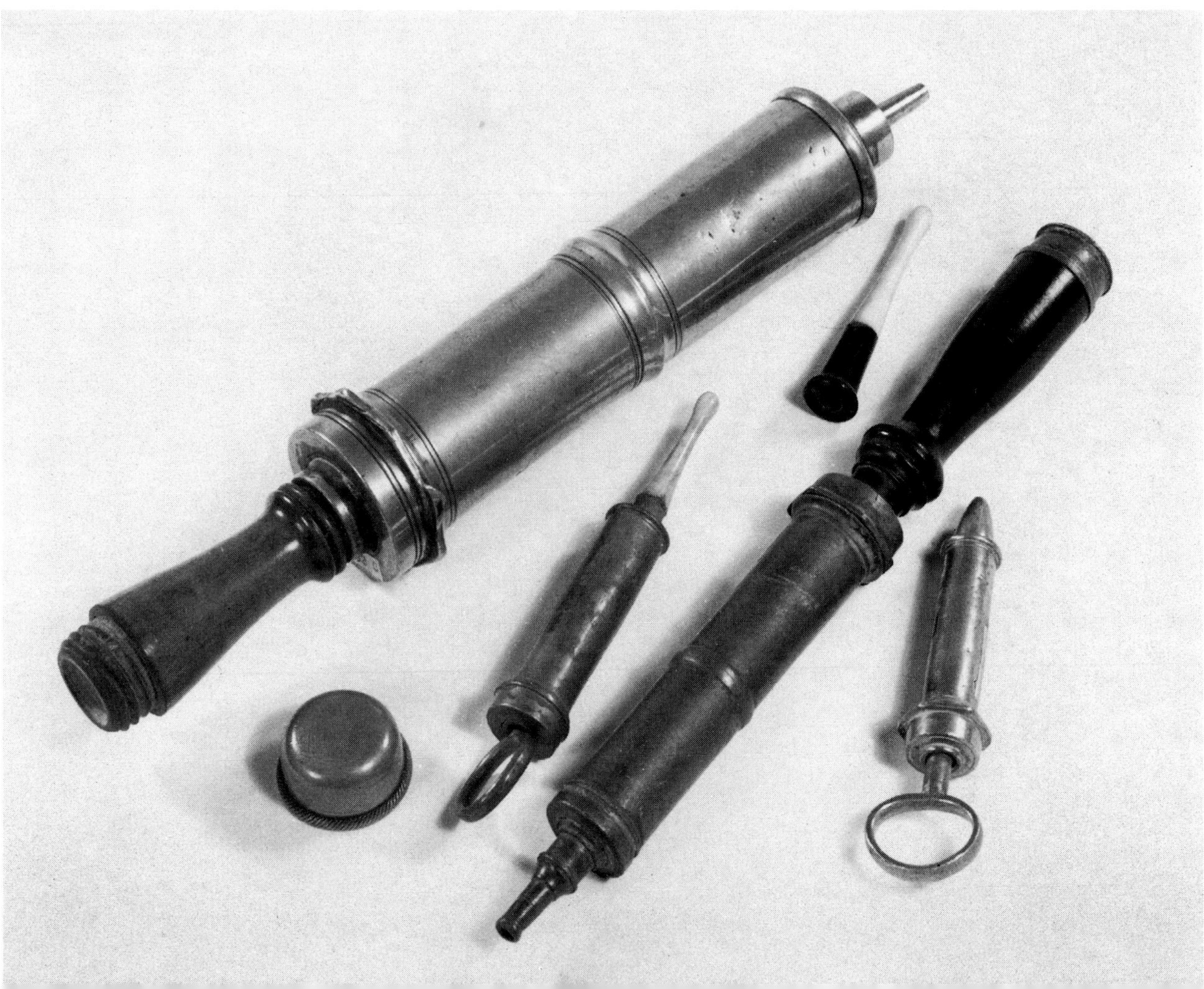

The appearance of hot-water-bottles as we generally know them today
374 evolved in the 19th century. The notion of inventive pewterers to enable mothers to keep feeding-bottles warm for small children by providing recesses in hot-water-bottles has already been mentioned. It is not surprising that for the large families which were common at that time many hot-water
373/377 bottles have not just one but up to four places for feeding-bottles. The characteristics of pewter as a material led to hot-water-bottles still being popular when public taste and the trend of prices had already favoured other materials for a considerable time. For this reason it was still worthwhile in 1850 for the trade to procure the necessary moulds of costly brass from specialized mould-makers or to make them themselves. One could, for example, obtain them from "Pewterer & Mould-maker August Grünberger" of Weissenburg am Sand. Sometimes a mould made by a candidate was accepted as a masterpiece (e.g. Carl Clemens Borchers in Wismar in 1846). The upper and lower sections were rationally cast in one and the same mould, which had a circular opening in the centre. When the bottom half was being cast this opening was closed with a disc, whilst when the top half was being cast a second mould to form the screw-closure was inserted. Even in the 18th century a clay mould was often still used for the lower half and a stone mould for the upper. In addition, the screw-closure, inner lid and swivelling-handle had to be made. When the lid and handle were cast in one operation a slender cardboard tube inserted into the mould ensured that the handle was moveable.

Cupping-bowls and enema-syringes

If credence can be given to the account of the German chronicler Johann Heinrich Zedler, cupping (bleeding or blood-letting) was practised in every country but particularly in France. There, children of only six weeks old were subjected to the treatment whilst in Germany, on the contrary, it was almost never performed on persons under 15 and over 50 years of age. Howsoever this may be—cupping was considered one of the everyday and effective means for the restoration and promotion of health.

Pewterers responded to the general trend of having cupping adminis-
378 tered at home by "skilled practitioners" by recommending small handy bowls as especially practical. Normally five or six ounces were let and bleeding was started with a lancet or fleam. In France cupping-bowls had a flat grip soldered to the rim like porringers. Bowls with graduated measures in relief appear infrequently.

Two other items connected with cupping which were likewise made only in small numbers were cupping-heads and leech-balls. Cupping-heads were heated and placed upon the skin previously roughened with a lancet; the lancet could also be used during the same operation as a cupping-iron. Leech-balls consisted of two bayonet-locking components, the upper one pierced with air-holes. They were used for transporting leeches.

Well-to-do and educated middle-class citizens provided themselves
379 with an apothecary's chest which could be conveniently taken with them when travelling. In them homeopathic medicines which were largely assembled by their owners themselves were housed in little pewter boxes. From the 18th century onwards an enema-syringe was often included in the equipment of an apothecary's chest but another was nevertheless also kept separately at home. Many pewterers specialized in the manufacture of syringes as, for example, the master Gottlieb Carl Israel Weber from Grimma in the Electorate of Saxony who in 1782 offered 27 different types. At the neighbouring Leipzig fairs he paved the way for introducing his products in every district of Germany and beyond. Weber manufactured his syringes on machines which he claimed to have developed himself and which he kept rigorously hidden from the world at large. Thanks to his rationalized manufacturing processes he was able to put his syringes on sale at such favourable prices that for a long time he had no competitors. The workshop of the Potsdam pewterer Meyerheine, supplying mainly ear-syringes, became prominent from about 1850. Non-medical uses for pewter syringes were, amongst other things, the filling of sausage skins.

The principal domestic use for syringes was to administer enemas to
380 man and beast. Their size accordingly varied from a few centimetres to half-
284 a-metre. Enemas were regarded as a treatment of the utmost importance, particularly in children's illnesses and their "timely administration was often able to circumvent the most vehement and apparently dangerous conditions". Housewives who were not able to maintain a good nurse or midwife were recommended to familiarize themselves with the easily mastered procedure for performing an enema. The rigid or flexible horn nozzle on the pewter syringe was to be eight to twelve inches long.

There were remedies for constipation as well as diarrhoea and in writings on the subject—which proliferated especially during the 19th century—it was recommended that no household ought to be without an enema-syringe. These syringes are, in fact, plentifully represented everywhere. They almost always have a wooden handle which can be screwed on or off and which in itself accommodates the screw-on pewter nozzle or the one of horn. Although the angled nozzles of French syringes did not permit this, the handles were still made hollow and accessible through a screwed cover for the storage of ointment and cotton wool. At the beginning of the 19th century in America and somewhat later in England enemas of tobacco smoke were introduced in addition to those normally administered. A few pewterers took part in the production of "appliances for tobacco smoke enemas" which comprised a combination of brass, pewter and leather. Needless to say, these were not a profitable venture.

For constipation (if the patient is an adult) give a decoction of half an ounce of senna leaves and plums. Then give an enema of about one handful of camomile, boiled in water and after straining the decoction through a cloth, add two spoonfuls of oil or butter and one spoonful of salt to it. If diarrhoea is present, give copious enemas of milk or meat broth with egg yolk or a little oil.

Noth- und Hilfsbuch für von Ärzten entlegen wohnende Familienväter, Hausmütter und Auswanderer (A book for cases of emergency and of assistance to heads of families, mothers and emigrants living remote from a doctor), Blumenau, 1838.

Miscellaneous Articles for Persons and Households

9

The range of utilitarian items made of pewter includes a multiplicity of articles which, in contrast to most of the goods which have been mentioned up to now, were made only for a very limited period or only seldom and whose function was then taken over by goods of other materials. Among these are, for instance, roof-tiles and gutters, hunting horns and sundials (particularly among American
391 pewterers) as well as chess-boards and pieces. From the late Middle Ages pewter toys were plentiful generally: almost all full-size pewter products had their counterparts in miniature.

Even though pewter buttons, buckles, fittings and window and door-bolts were available from a variety of trades over centuries in wide assortment, comparatively few have survived to the present day. The situation is similar regarding numerals for clock faces or spurs for riding-boots as well as the workmen's tokens used particularly in the 17th century and duty seals. In Riga, workers on wall and lock or sluice construction were given tokens corresponding to inspection of their work; in Thuringian towns bottles intended for the export of beer were provided with duty seals. These seals were occasionally moulded by glassworkers. An Austrian pewterer produced beggars' badges for the Vienna hospital in the 16th century. Similar ones exist from Fribourg where salt tokens were, moreover, also produced before 1600. Whilst all these tokens were used in a variety of ways to enable checks to be made that various instructions and regulations were being carried out,
384 hanging-signs served to advertise inns and workshops. Their subject was usually a representation of objects associated with the consumption of drink or of typical trade tools.

Sand-dredgers, ink-wells, snuff- and tobacco-boxes are items more frequently to be found today than those which have hitherto been mentioned although they were contemporaneously much less common in everyday-life than, say, buttons or buckles.

Buttons, buckles and mounts

Although in Denmark pewter buttons have been excavated from graves dating from as early as the Bronze Age, they were not yet items of everyday use at that period. Clothes were fastened with animal bones until about the 13th century when materials like wood, copper, precious metals, mother of pearl, leather and, of course, pewter, came to be used. In most countries pewter buttons were made by specialized pewterers. They were often described as "button-casters" or "casters of pewter and buttons" and it was important not to be known simply as a "button-maker". The latter were workers in wool, yarn or silk and wire and in part formed their own guild. From time to time many button-casters styled themselves as "white"-button-casters to draw attention to the fact that they supplied wares of particular brilliance. To achieve this, best-quality pewter had to be used which made for very soft products. Experience soon revealed that by adding antimony to the melt a harder material was obtained. Later Britannia metal, the tin/antimony alloy which has already been mentioned developed from this.

At every period there was an extraordinary number of disputes and competitive strife among those who were involved with the production of buttons. In Königsberg (now Kaliningrad) in 1678 it was necessary to formulate an agreement whereby with immediate effect no master had the right to accept, much less to fulfil, an order for their manufacture exceeding nine dozen. Naturally, jealous watch was maintained that the military authorities, with their great demand, did not favour particular individual craftsmen. In Lüneburg in 1767 and again two years later there was conflict with the belt-makers because the latter were making pewter buttons for the military. It was a cause of great aggravation to pewterers that in many districts and towns—for instance in the Mark of Brandenburg and in Breslau (Wrocław)—belt-makers were privileged to make buttons and sell them wholesale and retail; they were prohibited only from buying from pewterers and button-makers for onward resale. Finally, as a last example of these multifarious disputes, the grievances of the Berlin manufactory, the "Englische Zinnknopfmacher" (English pewter-button makers) will be cited: they reproached the pewterers of Prenzlau in 1784 because they were providing the regiments of Landsberg, Ruppin, Spandau and Stettin (now Szczecin) with buttons. The masters of Prenzlau countered that in comparison with those from the factory, buttons from their workshops were larger, not bright and above all, not provided with a wire eye but cast entirely of pewter—the bickering terminated with an agreement.

Jeremias Guillaume Michaut, button-founder in composite metal, which entirely resembles silver and will find favour with the esteemed public; orders taken and delivered on approbation.

Advertisement, about 1800.

Pewterers specializing in the production of buttons generally used three types of brass moulds in their work. The most frequently used moulds were probably those for the pewter button-plates (scales) which were afterwards secured to a usually wooden matrix. A different mould was used for button-scales of which one each of two were soldered together. The third mould served for buttons which were to be silvered and then pressed together.

A large workshop would be able to make not one but several varieties, for example *spund*, screw, *burg*, shell and others. Individual types were sold by
388 the dozen fastened to stiff paper. Not infrequently, tailors' thimbles, plain thimbles and often also seamstress clamps—a type of jaw to hold material when sewing—were included in their production. The brass moulds could
385 be used not only for casting buttons for clothing but equally for screw-knobs for windows, drawers, cupboard doors and so on. In 1656 a master in Stollberg (Saxony) invoiced one thaler and ten groschen "for pewter knobs on the windows". The Berne pewterer Adam Lienhart produced pewter window-hooks as early as the 16th century.

383 Buckles for footware, belts and clothing were generally made by pewterers as a sideline. From the end of the 18th century development of the shoe and textile industries led, however, to the specialization of many masters in the production of buckles. Some workshops achieved a significant increase in turnover by specialization of this kind and even progressed to exploitation of markets beyond state frontiers. From about 1790 the pewterer Anton Caspar Plagemann of Lübeck, like Peter Arrenberg of Ellerfeld in the 19th century, became widely known. Arrenberg carried on a regular export trade abroad and also included spurs in his sales programme. The success of many workshops stands in contrast to the failures. As an example, in 1810 Johann Christian Preil, who came from Eilenburg (Saxony) asked the Leipzig guild to admit him as a member and humbly promised "to make and sell as a member nothing more than these three articles, namely buckles, spoons and boxes and other than this not in any way to cause any harm or disadvantage to the meritorious Leipzig guild of pewterers". This request was granted to the master, who conducted himself honestly but nevertheless became impoverished and died in penury.

Since the Mayor and Councillor has made a convenient arrangement for both residents and non-residents to display their wares for public sale at the annual public market in the old town hall, pewterer Holstein will accordingly show the following finished pewterwork at the afore-said annual market in the old town hall:
. . . new types of eyebaths and pipe-stems, fine English shoe- and knee-buckles . . .

Advertisement: *Osnabrückische Intelligenzblätter* (Osnabrück information pages), 1781.

Pewter mounts are known from the late Middle Ages; in Estonia they have been found together with pewter rings, chains, beads and eyes. Belts adorned with pewter rivets stem from the 17th century in Austria. Figures of lions, stags, stars and flowers, among other subjects, are depicted in pewter studs—the motif was predominantly decorative. It is similar with coffin furniture, of which some was also cast by joiners, thereby provoking complaints from pewterers. Lastly, the pewter embellishments for pipe bowls and stems had a principally ornamental function. In contrast, fitness for purpose was the first consideration for the mounts which the pewter trade supplied for leather trunks. These were made for sale as early as the 18th century.

Tobacco-boxes, ink-stands and other goods

Seamen were already bringing tobacco back to Europe at the beginning of the 16th century although a long time had yet to elapse before the habit of smoking had developed to the extent that the pewter trade was also able to profit from it. In many countries smoking on the street was stringently prohibited until about the middle of the 19th century. The novel form of plea-

sure was enjoyed at home and from about the beginning of the *Biedermeier* period specially cheap accessories for it were on offer from pewterers. To-
396 bacco-jars were, of course, already in existence but now there came real mass production because smoking had become an everyday part of the life of the people.

Pewter containers are outstandingly suitable for the keeping of tobacco. This material does not develop verdigris like copper nor rust like iron, thus spoiling the tobacco by impairing its fragrance. It moreover conserves the moisture necessary for the full enjoyment of pipe smoking. Similar qualities were, in fact, offered by containers of ivory, silver and gold although these were substantially more expensive and unattainable for the great majority. In former times "tobacco-box" or *tabatière* was generally understood to mean not only a receptacle for tobacco for smoking but also a snuff-box. In the first half of the 18th century Augsburg pewterers developed considerable skill in "tobacco-boxes fashioned like silver". Later these boxes were decorated with arabesques and even painted or gilded. For the storage of tobacco at home, in Holland there was a preference for round canisters which had a tightly fitting detached cover. As for other purposes, these canisters sometimes had a further cover inside which was often of lead and kept the tobacco pressed down. A knob which was sometimes in the shape of an animal was
390 soldered on for lifting out the cover. The outer cover sometimes bore animal reliefs. These were not only decorative but also useful to make the cover seat more firmly.

Snuff-boxes which could conveniently be carried in jacket or trouser pockets were included in the normal production range of many English and American pewterers of the 18th and 19th centuries. Needless to say, these could not achieve the elegant appearance of those made of precious metals
394/395 but attractive results were obtained by careful decoration and best-quality
392 material. In England, North and Northeast Europe, there was an abundance of ash-trays which were used for knocking out and cleaning out the pipe. A figure against which the pipe could be tapped was positioned in the centre of the ash-tray. Usually an iron scraper fastened to a chain was also provided to loosen burnt-on tobacco. Pipe stoppers were also sometimes cast in pewter but clearly did not prove themselves in use.

It is also permitted for every guild master to work in lead and to make lead piping, tobacco-boxes, shot, ink-wells and whatever else can be named which can be made of lead.

Outline for a guild regulation, Rostock, 1773.

Ink-stands were already being made to special order in the 16th century. In 1562 the master Georg Schiernprant supplied twelve pewter ink-wells for the new writing-tables for the City Council of Vienna. It can be assumed that the master used good-quality pewter for the execution of this important order although in many places it was permitted to use lead alone for the casting of ink-wells, pipes and later, tobacco-boxes also. In 1589, for example, two ink-wells of lead were included in a delivery by the pewterer Peter Tschiepo of Fribourg. Ink-wells of lead, like those of pewter, were in any case only increasingly included in normal domestic wares from the second

half of the 18th century and even then were not acquired by many households because they were ignorant of writing. Pewterers liked making those
398 ink-stands which comprised an ink-well, pounce-box (sand dredger) and pen-rest. Fine sand sprinkled upon what had just been penned, then shaken-off and dusted-away hastened drying of the ink.
381 Ink-stands in the form of a box often have a supplementary container for sand or a compartment for sealing-wax. It was always possible to buy separate ink-wells or—before the
389 introduction of blotting-paper—pounce-boxes.

Even after 1850 many workshops still existed due to some extent, among other things, to specialization in the production of ink-wells for schools. Only cheap glass ink-holders put an end to this business. This applies likewise to ink-stands for domestic use. Attempts to increase their usefulness by a variety of additional features were also of no avail, for instance by soldering-on a candle-socket nor that there was striving for rationalization. Ink-stands thus emerged which made use of a form of base which was suitable for a range of applications. The column of a candlestick was soldered to the base as the pen-holder. Pewter paper-weights in the form of a skull were by way of a response to a current fashion.

In addition to the items mentioned up to now, there were many others designed for use in house and home which were not, in fact, typical products of the pewter trade but which nevertheless merit notice. When in 1700 two princesses from East Frisia placed an order with the pewterer Menso Hoyer of Amsterdam for two coffins of the finest English pewter, they asked the
401 master for a sample. This was to be a flower-vase which would prove the flawless high quality of the pewter which would be used. Vessels intended for flowers were usually only in the form of altar-vases; vases and flower-pots intended for secular use are rare—the Amsterdam pewterer nevertheless produced such a convincing flower-vase that he secured his order. The
386 containers which were attached to a spinning-wheel for moistening the fin-
387 gers are more plentiful—the distaff-bowl and wetting-beaker. The distaff-
399 bowl was fixed upon the distaff whilst the wetting-beaker was positioned close to the spindle. Even these apparently insignificant containers, only a few centimetres in diameter, were carefully guarded from loss. Various inscriptions connected with ownership indicate that wetting-beakers were also used by children, who all too often at the age of only six or seven had to help to safeguard the family's needy existence. Many an industrious housewife may well also have had a needle-holder at hand, which pewterers
397 sometimes made in the shape of a cradle. Even pewter smelling-bottles appeared in the 19th century. Last to be mentioned are powder-flasks with a threaded neck and screw-closure which were made in Austria in the 16th century.

Needle-case

An elongated round container with a screw-closure, in which needles and sewing-needles are kept, made of pewter, ivory, brass, silver or wood.

Explanatory definition, 1715.

Pipes and roofing-tiles

In early documents it is often recorded that certain masters were pewter and bell-founders who therefore had to be competent in the working of both pewter and bronze. Whilst bell-metal is usually free from lead, for other articles, for example knobs, bolts and buckles bronze of a good one-third lead was produced. The manufacture of goods entirely of lead was therefore closely related to pewter and bell-founding. Products of this kind are indeed recorded and foremost among them are pipes of which one learns as early as the 15th century. Like pipes, flutes were soldered together from two halves and a pea was introduced to make the trilling sound.

It is remarkable that the tinning of pipes was understood at a very early date; a pewterer, Adam, from Biel is named in the municipal accounts of 1557 in connection with this kind of work. At this early period orders emanated almost exclusively from institutions and from the nobility, later to be joined by prosperous citizens. In the 17th century each house did not yet have its own water supply; in many districts, e.g. Mecklenburg, there was one well for about every three farmsteads. As development progressed pewterers were in demand from time to time to produce piping. Apart from private persons, brewers and distillers, in addition to spa-keepers in watering places, were among new clients. Inn-keepers attached particular value to pewter beer-pipes from barrel to counter because of the beer's taste.
400 They were accordingly good customers to the pewter trade. Pewter taps cast in various sizes were on offer to inn-keepers and could be used equally for water systems. Peripheral items which should be mentioned are the pewter fountains which were supplied to order for the enjoyment of a few privileged persons.

The pewterer Engelhard Leiber recommends himself to the brewers and brandy distillers of this place and elsewhere for the supply of pewter pipes, 54 kreuzer the pound.

Advertisement, Gmünd, 1836.

Among the products already in evidence in the late Middle Ages, in addition to piping, are finials and tiles for church spires, towers and gateways. A church in Rostov on the Don is reputed to have been roofed with pewter tiles as early as 1262. The use of leaden tiles for roofing work is definitely verifiable in the 15th century, for example by Heinz Bamberger the Younger, master in Würzburg (Franconia), who clad the tower of the Marienkapelle in his home town with lead in 1480. If the tales of the knight, Rozmital, are to be believed then the use of pewter for roofing was commonplace in England at that time. In Switzerland a credible record exists from the 16th century for the use of pewter tiles—in the year 1585 Melchior Harläb supplied some for the town hall in Aarau. As late as 1701 a pewterer in Lucerne was commissioned to re-cast some sheets on the town hall. It is evident that at no period were individual citizens or farmers able to afford the luxury of pewter roof covering nor probably also the associated gutters and downpipes which were cast with heads of tasteful artistry. Cabinet-makers were regular customers for pewter sheet which they inlaid in tables and the drop fronts of secretaires; likewise artists, as palettes for oil colours. Even pewter picture frames with ornamentation in relief were made occasionally.

Du bist mir Herrmann Moritz Albert
Hermsdorfen z. u. Hartmannsdorf. am Tage
meiner Heil. Taufe den 5 Julii 1802 von
meinen Pathen geschenckt worden

382

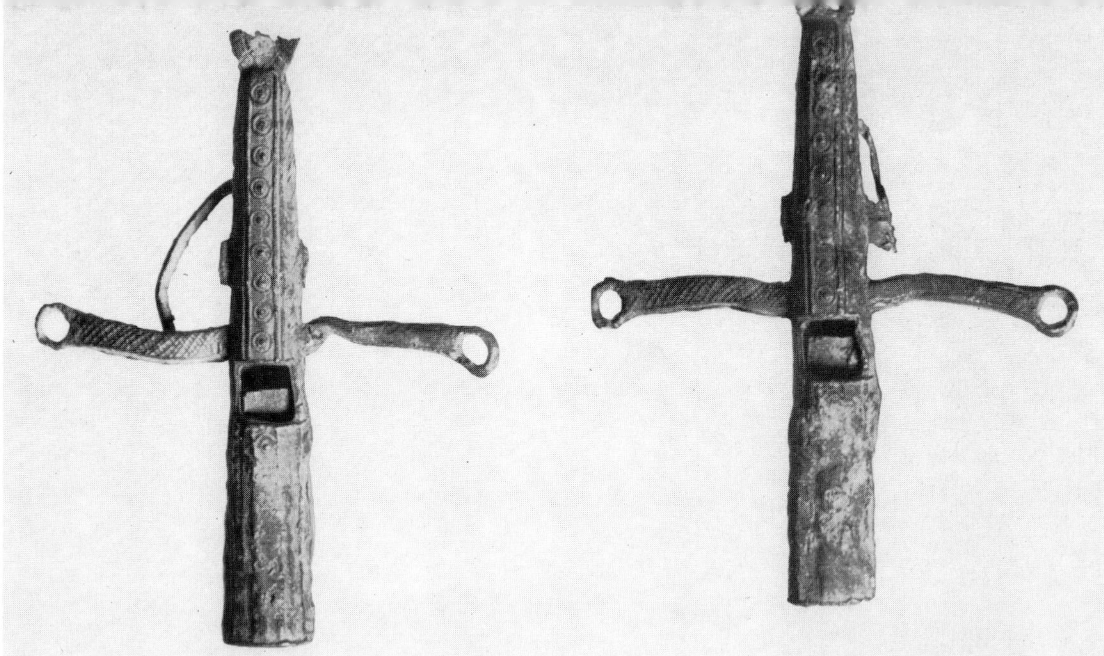

383

384
385

Preceding page:

381 Ink-stand in the form of a chest; width 17 cm ($6^5/_8''$), dated 1802. Museum Waldenburg/Saxony

382 Bird-calls; length 4.7 cm ($1^7/_8''$), *c.* 1400. Kunstgewerbemuseum Cologne

383 Buckles; width 5–7 cm ($2''$–$2^3/_4''$), 2nd half of the 18th century. Museum Weissenfels

384 Hanging-sign in the shape of a chimney-sweep's scraper; length 23 cm (9″), dated 1819. Kulturhistorisches Museum Rostock

385 Screw-knob; length 4 cm ($1^1/_2''$), *c.* 1850. In private ownership

386 Distaff-cup; diameter 8.3 cm ($3^1/_4''$), dated 1866. Heimatmuseum Mühlhausen/Thuringia

387 Distaff-cup; diameter 7.5 cm (3″). Heimatmuseum Mühlhausen/Thuringia

388 Seamstress's clamp; height 20 cm ($7^7/_8''$), 1st half of the 19th century. Schlossmuseum Altenburg

389 Sand-shaker; height 7.5 cm (3″), *c.* 1810. Kulturhistorisches Museum Rostock

390 Tobacco-box; height 13 cm ($5^1/_8''$), *c.* 1820. Museum "Schloss Moritzburg", Zeitz

386
387

388
389

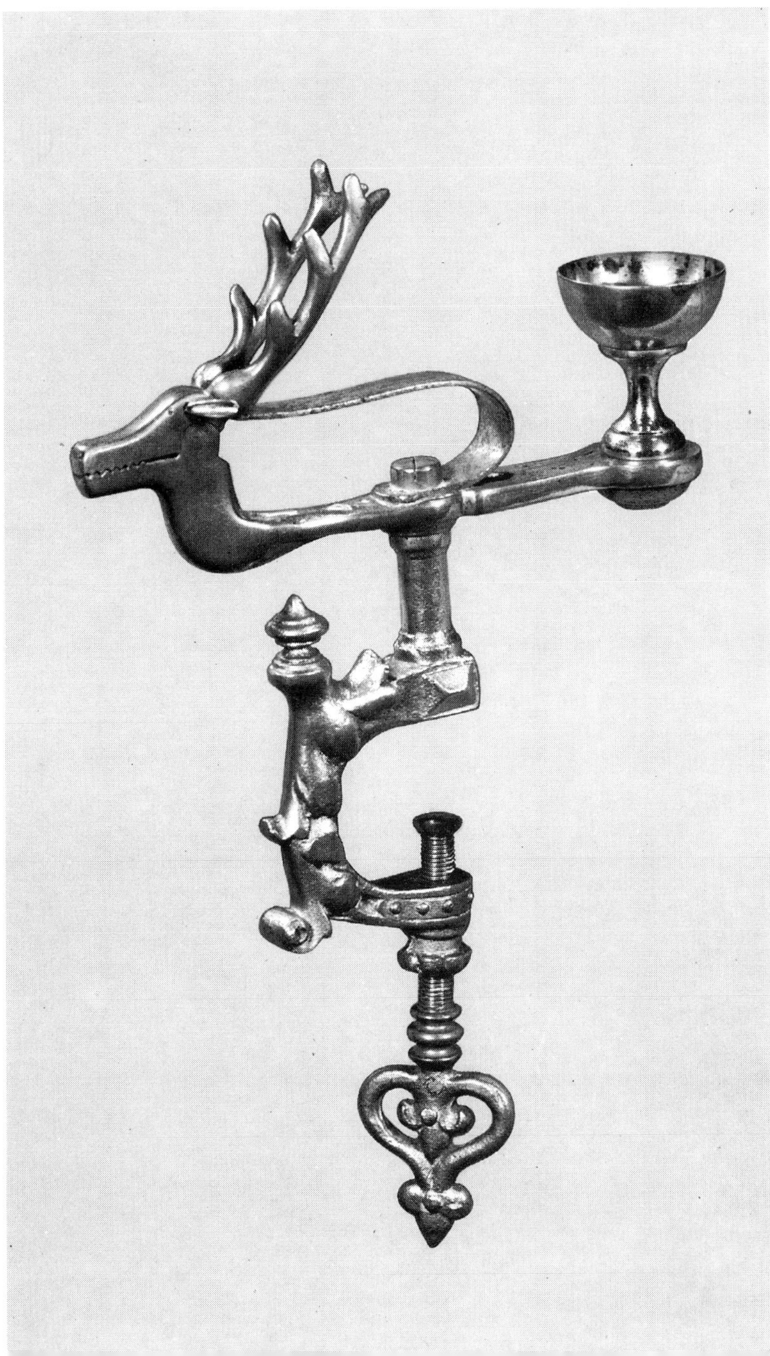

390

391 Chess-pieces and board; length 30 cm (12"), 18th century.
Vogtländisches Kreismuseum Plauen

392 Tobacco-box; length 6.6 cm ($2^1/_4$"), *c.* 1810.
Museum des Kunsthandwerks Leipzig

393 Needle-container; length 10.3 cm (4"), dated 1806.
Vogtländisches Kreismuseum Plauen

394 Snuff-box; length 8.2 cm ($3^1/_4$"), *c.* 1840.
The light-coloured patches to the right and on the front are caused by delamination.
Vogtländisches Kreismuseum Plauen

395 Tobacco-box; length 6.8 cm ($2^5/_8$"), *c.* 1800.
In private ownership

396 Tobacco-boxes; height 14.6 and 14.3 cm ($5^3/_4$" and $5^5/_8$"), 2nd half of the 18th century.
The engraving on the left-hand box depicts a smoking club.
Victoria & Albert Museum, London

397 Smelling-bottle; height 8.5 cm ($3^3/_8$"), *c.* 1810.
The bottle is decorated in relief on its other face.
Museum "Schloss Moritzburg", Zeitz

391

392
393

394
395

396
397

398 Ink-stand with containers for ink, sand and pens; height 16.2 cm ($6^3/_8$"), 2nd half of the 18th century. Schweizerisches Landesmuseum Zurich

399 Wetting-beakers; height 4.7–7.2 cm ($1^7/_8$"–$2^7/_8$"), 1st half of the 19th century. Vogtländisches Kreismuseum Plauen

400 Barrel-tap with its sleeve; length 16.5 cm ($6^1/_2$"), 19th century. Vogtländisches Kreismuseum Plauen

Following page:

401 Flower-vases; height 24 and 13.5 cm ($9^1/_2$" and $5^3/_8$"), dated 1797. Kulturhistorisches Museum Rostock

399

400

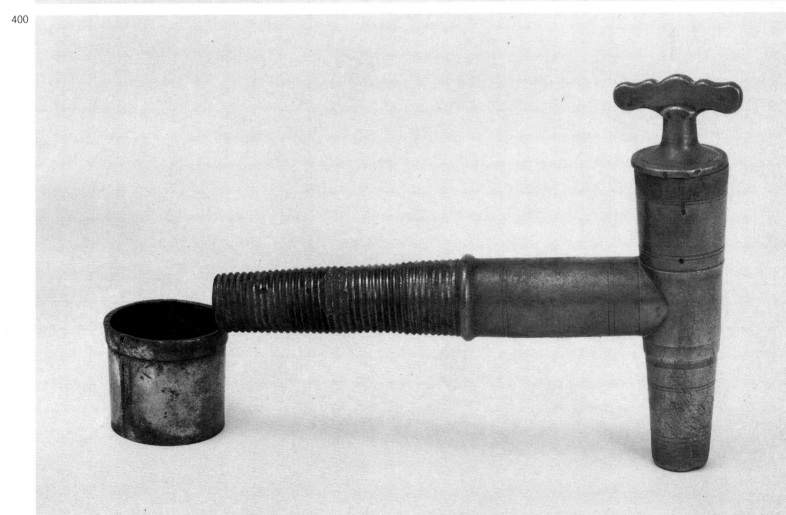

Table of Marks

The town marks are in alphabetical order, all other marks according to their subject.

Place names conform with historical nomenclature, today's names are in brackets. National designations in accordance with frontiers at the present day are—with the exception of principal towns—identified by the use of internationally accepted designations.

Town marks

1

2

3

4

5

1 Alessandria (I)
2 Altenburg (DDR)
3 Apolda (DDR)
4 Beeskow (DDR)
5 Berlin

6

7

8

9

10

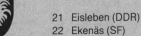

6 Brunswick (D)
7 Bremen (D)
8 Buxtehude (D)
9 Cambrai (F)
10 Casale (I)

11

12

13

14

15

11 Celle (D)
12 Coburg (D)
13 Coswig (Anhalt) (DDR)
14 Cottbus (DDR)
15 Crossen (DDR)

16

17

18

19

20

16 Delitzsch (DDR)
17 Dortmund (D)
18 Düben (DDR)
19 Düren (D)
20 Eilenburg (DDR)

21

22

23

24

25

26

21 Eisleben (DDR)
22 Ekenäs (SF)
23 Erfurt (DDR)
24 Falun (S)
25 Frankenhausen (DDR)
26 Frankfort on the Oder (DDR)

27

28

29

30

31

32

27 Fulda (D)
28 Gardelegen (DDR)
29 Gera (DDR)
30 Göteborg (S)
31 Greiz (DDR)
32 Guben (DDR)

33

34

35

36

37

38

33 Halberstadt (DDR)
34 Hall (A)
35 Halle/Saale (DDR)
36 Hamm (D)
37 Hedemora (S)
38 Helmstedt (D)

39

40

41

42

43

44

39 Helsinki
40 Jena (DDR)
41 Jönköping (S)
42 Jüterbog (DDR)
43 Kassel (D)
44 Kristianstad (S)

45

46

47

48

49

50

45 Kristinehamn (S)
46 Landskrona (S)
47 Langres (F)
48 Linköping (S)
49 Linköping (S)
50 Lobenstein (DDR)

51

52

53

54

55

56

51 Lovisa (SF)
52 Lovisa (SF)
53 Luckau (DDR)
54 Lüneburg (D)
55 Lüneburg (D)
56 Magdeburg (DDR)

57

58

59

60

61

62

57 Malmö (S)
58 Merano (I)
59 Merseburg (DDR)
60 Mühlhausen (Thuringia) (DDR)
61 Nancy (F)
62 Naumburg (DDR)

63

64

65

66

67

63 Neustadt/Orla (DDR)
64 Neustadt/Orla (DDR)
65 Östhammar (S)
66 Olbernhau (DDR)
67 Olbernhau (DDR)

68

69

70

71

72

73

68 Peine (D)
69 Pössneck (DDR)
70 Potsdam (DDR)
71 Rauma (SF)
72 Ronneburg (DDR)
73 Rotterdam (NL)

74

75

76

77

78

74 Rouen (F)
75 Rudolstadt (DDR)
76 Rudolstadt (DDR)
77 Saalfeld (DDR)
78 Saalfeld (DDR)

79

80

81

82

83

79 Salzwedel (DDR)
80 Salzwedel (DDR)
81 Sangerhausen (DDR)
82 Schleiz (DDR)
83 Sedan (F)

84

85

86

87

88

84 Seesen (D)
85 Soest (D)
86 Spandau (West Berlin)
87 Stendal (DDR)
88 Stockholm

89

90

91

92

93

89 Stockholm
90 Strängnäs (S)
91 Suhl (DDR)
92 Tonder (DK)
93 Torgau (DDR)

94

95

96

97

98

94 Turin (I)
95 Turku (SF)
96 Uddevalla (S)
97 Uppsala (S)
98 Uppsala (S)

99

100

101

102

103

99 Vänersborg (S)
100 Västerås (S)
101 Västervik (S)
102 Växjö (S)
103 Varberg (S)

104

105

106

107

108

104 Vesoul (F)
105 Vimmerby (S)
106 Visby (S)
107 Weida (DDR)
108 Weissenfels (DDR)

109

110

111

112

109 Wernigerode (DDR)
110 Wolfenbüttel (D)
111 Zeitz (DDR)
112 Zeulenroda (DDR)

Combined town and masters' marks

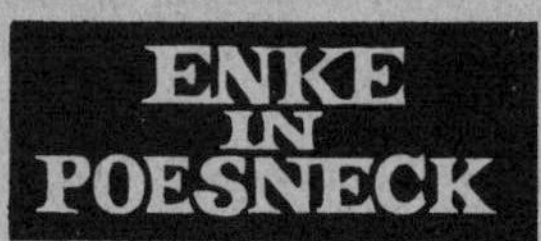

113

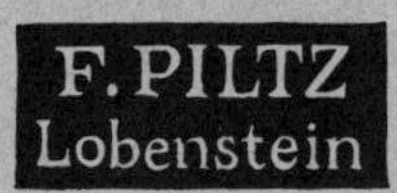

114

115

116

113 Karl Friedrich Andreas Enke, Pössneck (DDR), widow mark, 1844–*c.* 61
114 Heinrich Anton Franz Piltz, Lobenstein (DDR), 1868–1918
115 Eduard Kannegiesser, Weissenfels (DDR), master, *c.* 1851
116 John Shaw, Newcastle (GB), 1760–78

117

118

119

120

117 Johann Friedrich Fischer, Gera (DDR), 1794–1861
118 Hermann Paul Fischer, Gera (DDR), 1840–1902
119 Gustav Hermann Jahr, Gera (DDR), 1816–89
120 J. P. Baumgärtner, Altenburg (DDR), *c.* 1803

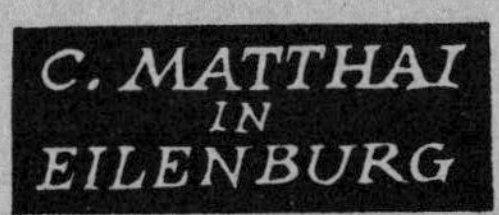

121

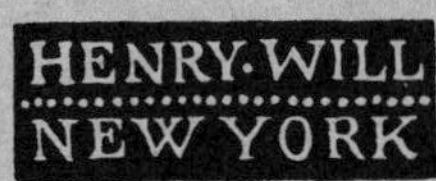

122

123

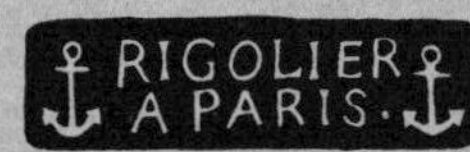

124

121 Carl Theodor Matthaei, Eilenburg (DDR), master 1866
122 Henry Will, New York and Albany (USA), 1761–93
123 Pierre Malmouche, Le Mans (F), *c.* 1747
124 Rigolier, Paris, 1825–30

125

126

127

125 Carl Heinrich August Büchner, Rudolstadt (DDR), born 1833
126 Samuel Green, Boston (USA), 1779–1828
127 Carl Ludwig Klemm, Gera (DDR), 1841–91

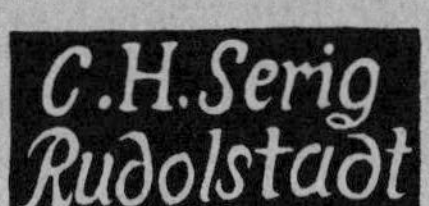

128

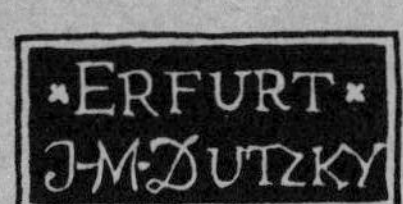

129

130

131

128 Christoph Heinrich Seerig, Rudolstadt (DDR), *c.* 1794–1824
129 Martin Dutzki, Erfurt (DDR), last third of 18th century
130 Amandus Daniel Meise, Saalfeld (DDR), 1798, *c.* 1816
131 Andreas Jakob Köhler, Erfurt (DDR), 2nd half of 18th century

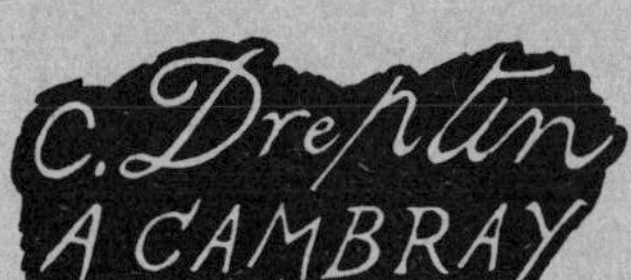

132

133

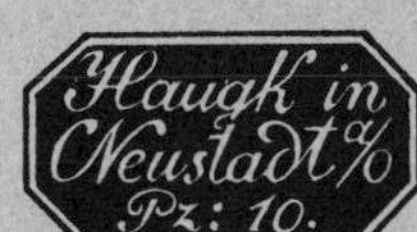

134

135

132 Catherina Dreptin, Cambrai (F), 1830–40
133 Andrew Thompson, Albany (USA), 1811–17
134 Carl Theodor Haugk, Neustadt/Orla (DDR), 1823–88
135 Johann Peter Hess, Gera (DDR), 1780–1844

136

137

138

139

140

136 Friedrich August Wirth, Gera (DDR), 1757–1813
137 Johann Meyer, Bremen (D), master *c.* 1763
138 Brüning Hayen, Bremen (D), master *c.* 1729
139 Jacob Cassebohm, Bremen (D), *c.* 1695
140 Nicolaus von Hunteln the Elder, Bremen (D), master 1737

141

142

143

144

145

141 Alexander Conrad Kräfft the Younger, Bremen (D), master *c.* 1752
142 Johan Jürgen Flörcken, Bremen (D), master *c.* 1763
143 Henrich Wilms, Soest (D), 1st half of 18th century
144 Georg Wilhelm Schütt, Bremen (D), master *c.* 1861
145 René Parain, Paris, master 1741

146

147

148

149

150

151

146 Edme-Oliver de Cesne, Triel (F), master 1736
147 Jean Pironneau, Paris, *c.* 1726
148 Claude Couroyé, Paris, *c.* 1689
149 Niclas Boicervoise, Paris, master 1771
150 Louis Pelletier, Paris, *c.* 1720
151 Jean Jacques Prévost, Paris, *c.* 1732

152

153

154

155

156

152 François Vandry, Paris, *c.* 1778
153 Friedrich Sonnekalb, Rudolstadt (DDR), 1850–68
154 George Hayter, Bristol (GB), 2nd half of 18th century
155 Carl Otto Albert Wilke, Düben (DDR), master 1864
156 Jakob Ondol, Düben (DDR), master 1807

157

158

159

160

161

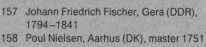

157 Johann Friedrich Fischer, Gera (DDR), 1794–1841
158 Poul Nielsen, Aarhus (DK), master 1751
159 Carl Peter, Mühlhausen (Thuringia) (DDR), *c.* 1835
160 Johann Gottlieb Holberg, Potsdam (DDR), master 1781
161 Christian Bitter-Thier, Dortmund (D), from 1763

162

163

164

165

166

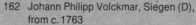

162 Johann Philipp Volckmar, Siegen (D), from *c.* 1763
163 Peder Hansen, Copenhagen, *c.* 1656
164 Carl Heidenreich, Suhl (DDR), *c.* 1835
165 Martin Extel, Prague/Old Town, master 1802
166 Carl Marchionini, Ödenburg (Sopron/H), 19th century

167

168

169

170

167 Samuel Friedrich Schultz, Prague/Old Town, master 1738
168 Joseph Mitterbacher, Prague/Old Town, master 1760
169 Thomas J. Haintsch, Prague/Malá Strana, 1st half of 18th century
170 Johann Christian Bayer, Raab (Györ/H), 1734–50

171

172

173

174

175

171 Johann Michael Friedrich, Pressburg (Bratislava/ČS), 18th/19th century
172 Johann Christoph Materna, Pressburg (Bratislava/ČS), 1st half of 18th century
173 Samuel Lederer, Raab (Györ/H), *c.* 1774
174 Mauritzius Behr, Pressburg (Bratislava/ČS), *c.* 1752
175 Elias Stahlfot, Turku (SF), *c.* 1723

176

177

178

179

176 Johann Gottlieb Zimmermann, Debrezin (Debrecen/H), 1822–41
177 Johann Gottlieb Zimmermann, Debrezin (Debrecen/H), 1822–41
178 Wilhelm Ferdinand Fröhlich, Salzwedel (DDR), 1824–99
179 Gottlieb Friedrich, Pressburg (Bratislava/ČS), 1st half of 19th century

180

181

182

180 Christoph Fritsch, Pressburg (Bratislava/ČS), *c.* 1710
181 Casper Reich, Leutschau (Levoca/ČS), 17th/18th century
182 Paul Pelsler, Ptuj (YU), *c.* 1644

183

184

185

186

183 Joseph Redáczy, Ödenburg (Sopron/H), 18th century
184 Andreas Schrick, Ödenburg (Sopron/H), 1693–1707
185 Andreas Johannes Diebel, Prague/Malá Strana, master 1687
186 Joseph Holzienger, Prague/Old Town, master *c.* 1725

187

188

189

187 Franz Wenzel Diebel, Prague/Malá Strana, 1st half of 18th century
188 Joseph Ernst, Prague/Old Town, master 1785
189 Johann Gottlieb Bormann, Pressburg (Bratislava/ČS), 1st half of 18th century

190

191

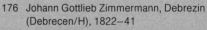

190 Gottlieb Zimmermann, Pressburg (Bratislava/ČS), late 18th century
191 Johann Justus Meuse, Saalfeld (DDR), *c.* 1778

Masters' names in full

192

193

194

195

192 W. Ondol, Torgau (DDR), *c.* 1841
193 Magnus Hertel, Stollberg (Saxony) (DDR), master 1832
194 Gustav Hermann Venus, Grimma (DDR), 1843–1920
195 Friesner, Weida (DDR), *c.* 1806

196

197

198

199

196 J. & H. Wardrop, Glasgow (GB), 1800–40
197 Friedrich Erdmann Grosse, Schleiz (DDR), 1823–94
198 Anthony Jenner, London, *c.* 1700
199 Grimes & Son, London, *c.* 1817

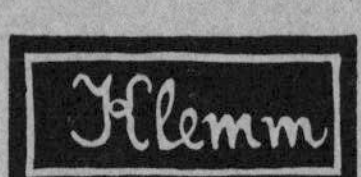

200

201

202

203

200 Carl Heinrich Klemm the Younger, Gera (DDR), 1810–90
201 Carl Rosch, Halle (DDR), *c.* 1850
202 Carl Theodor Rothe, Altenburg (DDR), *c.* 1832
203 Laurence Purcell, Dublin (IRL), *c.* 1850

204

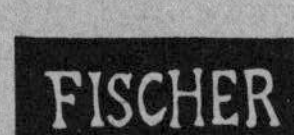

205

206

204 Gross, Gera (DDR), *c.* 1875
205 August Johann Fischer, Gera (DDR), 1835–1907
206 Lawrence Langworthy, Newport (USA), 1730–39

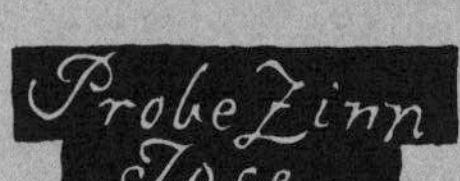

207

208

209

210

211

207 Andreas Friedrich José, Cottbus (DDR), master 1819
208 Joseph Götzl the Younger, Prague/Old Town, master 1846
209 Joseph Götzl the Elder, Prague/Old Town, master 1813
210 August Sigmund Kauffmann, Gera (DDR), *c.* 1750
211 Anton Steinlechner the Elder, Hall (A), 2nd third of 19th century

212

213

214

215

212 Silvester Savage, Dublin (IRL), 1788–1827
213 Carl Mitterbacher, Prague/Old Town, master 1823
214 Nathaniel Austin, Charleston (USA), 1763–1807
215 Johann Andreas Broelemann, Soest (D), died 1757

Initials

216

217

218

219

216 John Carruthers Crane, Bewdley (GB), 1800–38
217 Johan Frederik Werrenrath, Lund (S), 1847–1900
218 Carl de Flon, Växjö (S), 1777–1817
219 Lars Berg, Karlstad (S), 1743–66

220

221

222

223

224

220 Lars Claesson Fries, Strängnäs (S), 1760–90
221 Magnus Bergman, Malmö (S), 1794–1809
222 Peter Kirby, New York, 1736–88
223 Christoph Koehler, Stendal (DDR), c. 1713
224 Peter Young, New York and Albany (USA), 1775–95

225

226

227

228

229

225 Timothy Brigden, Albany (USA), 1816–19
226 Christoph Dietrich Geuthe, Salzwedel (DDR), 1700–65
227 Joseph Titschka, Prague/Old Town, 1st quarter of 19th century
228 Ludwig Poppe, Essen (D), 1807–52
229 Joseph Leddel, New York, 1712–53

230

231

232

233

234

230 Sven Ekström, Norrköping (S), 1824–52
231 François Ameline, Chalon-sur-Saône (F), c. 1710
232 Matthias (Martin) Dietrich, Stendal (DDR), 17th century
233 Frederik Basset, New York, 1761–80
234 Johann Georg Siegenitz, Stendal (DDR), 1799–1826

235

236

237

238

239

235 Johann Gottlieb Schrot, Pegau (DDR), before 1812
236 Niclas Adolph Falck, Skara (S), 1787–1828
237 Jakob Feyerabend, Chur (CH), 1538–1620
238 Sven Berglund, Malmö (S), 1811–44
239 Nicolas Lake, Vänersborg (S), 1751–81

240

241

242

243

244

240 Peter Öhlerg, Kristianstad (S), 1780–1812
241 Johan Lindblad, Turku (SF), c. 1827
242 Wilhelm Helleday, Stockholm, 1782–1830
243 Samuel Weigang, Stockholm, 1778–93
244 Johann Stark the Younger, Biberach/Riss (D), master 1716

245

246

247

248

249

245 Johan Petter Fagerström, Kalmar (S), 1789–1837
246 Jonas Sjöberg, Varberg (S), 1743–63
247 Carl Gottfried Matthaei, Eilenburg (DDR), 1800–74
248 Peter Larsson Holmin, Boras (S), 1777–93
249 P. Morane, Paris, c. 1875

250

251

252

253

254

250 Joseph Titschka, Prague/Old Town, 1st quarter of 19th century
251 Sven Bengtsson Roos, Göteborg (S), 1768–1802
252 Adolph Helleday, Jönköping (S), 1782–96
253 Johann Abraham Klingling, Frankfort on the Main (D), master 1669
254 Gabriel Syren, Frankfort on the Main (D), master 1727

255

256

257

258

259

255 Georg Friedrich Friesner, Weida (DDR), c. 1770
256 Bengt Christerson Stahlström, Turku (SF), c. 1698
257 Wolff Lange, Greiz (DDR), widow mark, 1st third of 18th century
258 M. Henkel, Spandau (West Berlin), c. 1640
259 Peer Henrik Lundén, Linköping (S), 1797–1834

260

261

260 Nicolaus Justelius, Eksjö (S), 1784–1819
261 Petter Samuelsson Norén, Hedemora (S), 1760–97

House marks and joined letters

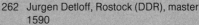

262

263

264

265

266

267

262 Jurgen Detloff, Rostock (DDR), master 1590
263 Jacob Richter, Cottbus (DDR), *c.* 1650
264 Jürge Beuch the Younger, Cottbus (DDR), *c.* 1650
265 Christoffel Hempel I, Chur (CH), 1592–1651
266 Jürgen Meyer III, Celle (D), died 1704
267 Johann Schünemann, Celle (D), 1665–92

268

269

270

271

272

273

268 Gregor Schwantes, Prenzlau (DDR), died 1661
269 Hans Georg Wolf, Prague/Malá Strana, master 1667
270 Heinrich Käsemacher, Frankenhausen (DDR), *c.* 1637
271 Adam Wallisch, Neusohl (Banská Bystrica/ČS), 1st half of 17th century
272 Petter Höijer, Örebro (S), 1796–1819
273 Carl W. Peters, Rosswein (DDR), from 1852

274

275

276

277

278

274 Gottfried Jacob Schröder, Celle (D), died 1880
275 Johann Jacob Basedow, Lüneburg (D), master 1822
276 Friedrich August Emmrich, Olbernhau (DDR), *c.* 1839–85
277 Henrik Philip Stickler, Hälsingborg (S), 1813–51
278 Brandt Brincken, Brunswick (D), 1682–86

279

280

281

282

283

284

279 Andreas Dahlin, Ystad (S), 1772–99
280 Johannes Georg Boehner, Prague/Malá Strana, *c.* 1650
281 Johann Christoph Fehrmann the Younger, Crossen (DDR), *c.* 1740
282 A. H. Grunge, Salzwedel (DDR), 1672–1742
283 Gottlob Friedrich Baumann, Olbernhau (DDR), *c.* 1776–1818
284 Ch. Baumann, Olbernhau (DDR), 1734–47

285

286

287

288

289

290

285 Christoph Geuthe, Salzwedel (DDR), 1658–1743
286 Johann George Lohs the Elder, Stollberg (Saxony) (DDR), died 1737
287 Johann George Lohs the Younger, Stollberg (Saxony) (DDR), 1705–58
288 Elias Weber, Eilenburg (DDR), died 1706
289 Johann Caspar Voigt, Crossen (DDR), 1688
290 G. W. August Meyer, Celle (D), master 1762

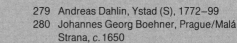

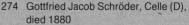

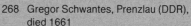

Human figures

291

292

293

294

295

291 Christian Teichmann, Berlin, *c.* 1710
292 Georg Phillip Briessnitz, Rudolstadt (DDR), *c.* 1673–*c.* 1713
293 Johann Gottlieb Günther, Altenburg (DDR), 2nd half of 18th century
294 Johann Friedrich Fischer, Gera (DDR), 1763–1823
295 Martin Dutzki, Erfurt (DDR), last third of 18th century

296

297

298

299

300

296 Johannes W. Pohmer, Jena (DDR), late 18th century
297 Christian Magnus Grosse I and II, Schleiz (DDR), 1746–1827
298 Johann Gottfried Hebenstreit, Zeitz (DDR), widow mark, 1st third of 19th century
299 Johann Jakob Arnold, Altenburg (DDR), *c.* 1735–80
300 Hans Popsen, Tonder (DK), master 1721

301

302

303

304

305

301 Christian Gotthilf Weiss, Lobenstein (DDR), 1767–96
302 Martin Theile, Weissenfels (DDR), master 1685
303 Christian Weber the Elder, Eilenburg (DDR), 1684–1758
304 I. W. Lange the Younger, Greiz (DDR), master 1754
305 Johann Daniel Schulz, Salzwedel (DDR), born 1774

306

307

308

309

310

306 Gottfried Schumann, Wurzen (DDR), master 1700
307 Johann Friedrich Bielang, Stendal (DDR), *c.* 1790
308 Bernhard Meise, Saalfeld (DDR), *c.* 1836
309 Gottfried Erdmann Seiffarth, Erfurt (DDR), *c.* 1779
310 Christian Koch, Weissenfels (DDR), master 1664

311

312

313

314

315

311 Andreas Jakob Köhler, Erfurt (DDR), *c.* 1778
312 Johann Conrad, Zeitz (DDR), *c.* 1730
313 Claudius Paulus Heim, Erfurt (DDR), 2nd half of 18th century
314 Melchior Fleck, Altenburg (DDR), mentioned 1725–53
315 Johannes Pfeiffhaus, Libau (Liepaja/SU), *c.* 1703

316

317

318

319

320

316 Andreas Jüngel, Torgau (DDR), 2nd half of 17th century
317 Christian Frommelt, Gera (DDR), *c.* 1722
318 Anton Zimmermann, Eilenburg (DDR), 1638–99
319 C. E. Kühne, Halberstadt (DDR), *c.* 1832
320 Matthias Niedhard, Zeitz (DDR), master 1614

321

322

323

324

325

321 Johann Heinrich Fischer, Gera (DDR), *c.* 1736
322 Joachim Hartmann, Kaschau (Košice/ČS), *c.* 1656
323 Christoph Friedrich Seiffarth, Erfurt (DDR), 18th century
324 Samuel Friedrich Schultz, Prague/Old Town, master 1738
325 Elias Schäfer, Jüterbog (DDR), *c.* 1700

326

327

328

329

330

326 Andreas Friedrich José, Cottbus (DDR), master 1819
327 Richard Bowler, London, after 1750
328 Joseph Johannes Diebel, Prague/New Town, master 1720
329 Johann Christoph Schmiet, Erfurt (DDR), *c.* 1737
330 Christian Fischer, Gera (DDR), 1691–1736

331

332

333

334

335

331 Johann Tobias Möhrling, Rudolstadt (DDR), 1712–35
332 Johann Wolfgang Günther, Altenburg (DDR), mentioned 1723–47
333 David Heinrich Teichmann, Pössneck (DDR), master 1788
334 Heinrich August Grosse, Schleiz (DDR), 1751–77
335 Heinrich Grosse, Schleiz (DDR), 1712–33

336

337

338

339

340

336 David Samuel Teichmann, Pössneck (DDR), master 1737
337 Andreas Valentin Heinrich Ahlant, Brunswick (D), 1748–1805
338 Christoph Gottfried Matthaei, Eilenburg (DDR), master 1793
339 Christian Richter, Cottbus (DDR), 1693–1772
340 Johann Friedrich Richter, Schleiz (DDR), 1778–1821

341

342

343

344

345

341 Johann Gottfried Giffein the Elder, Torgau (DDR), *c.* 1702
342 Gottfried Michael Schmidt, Lobenstein (DDR), *c.* 1755
343 Johann G. Huttig, Wurzen (DDR), master 1752
344 Johann Christian Dressler (Drechsler), Rudolstadt (DDR), 1712–53
345 Ernst Schuch, Schleiz (DDR), 1894–1931 (copier of old pewters)

346

347

348

349

350

346 Michael Richter, Eilenburg (DDR), *c.* 1660
347 Johann Benjamin Giese, Berlin, master 1699
348 Christian Stephan Meyerhan the Elder, Potsdam (DDR), 1726–53
349 Johann Gottfried Matthaei, Eilenburg (DDR), 1724–94
350 Karl Friedrich Andreas Enke, Pössneck (DDR), 1807–44

351

352

353

354

355

351 Karl Friedrich Andreas Enke, Pössneck (DDR), widow mark, 1844–*c.* 61
352 Peter Kruvelly, Kaschau (Košice/ČS), 1st half of 19th century
353 Adam Heinrich Fischer, Gera (DDR), 1708–44
354 Johann Andreas Keppel, Saalfeld (DDR), *c.* 1770
355 James Excell, London, 1st half of 18th century

356

357

358

359

360

356 Jacob Peseler, Grimma (DDR), *c.* 1611
357 Jacob Glander, Wolfenbüttel (D), died 1715
358 James Everett, London, 1st half of 18th century
359 August Friedrich Schulze (probably), Altenburg (DDR), *c.* 1710
360 Johann Hieronymus Werlin, Marburg (D), died before 1700

361

362

363

364

365

361 Wilhelm Daniel Schulz, Salzwedel (DDR), born 1802
362 Richard Alderwick, London, *c.* 1775
363 Johann Jonas Werlin, Marburg (D), 1705–90
364 Paul Fisher, London, died 1837
365 Richard Austin, Boston (USA), 1793–1817

Angels

366

367

368

369

370

366 Johann Christian Biertümpfel, Erfurt (DDR), *c.* 1819
367 Christian Grosse, Schleiz (DDR), *c.* 1823
368 Michael Jäger (probably), Frankfort on the Main (D), master 1718
369 Johann Joachim Mewes, Salzwedel (DDR), 1722–94
370 Michael Prignitz, Stendal (DDR), *c.* 1699

371

372

373

374

375

371 Johann Andreas Siegenitz, Stendal (DDR), *c.* 1741
372 Dietrich Christoph Bergmann, Brunswick (D), 1710–30
373 Christian Bitter-Thier, Dortmund (D), from 1763
374 Bartholomaei Cracco (probably), Marburg (D), 1st half of 18th century
375 Hans Rudolf Manz, Zurich (CH), 1771–1829

376

377

378

379

380

376 Johann Georg Rese, Brunswick (D), 1740–43
377 John King, London, 2nd half of 18th century
378 John Davis, London, 1st half of 18th century
379 P. Nootens, Brussels, *c.* 1838
380 Max Hediger, Zurich (CH), from 1851

381

382

383

384

385

381 Johann Henrich Hoffmann (probably), Marburg (D), died 1732
382 Wilhelm Henrich Thier, Dortmund (D), *c.* 1821
383 W. Hermsen, Soest (D), 1st half of 19th century
384 Christoffer Bonn, Hamm (D), 2nd half of 18th century
385 Andreas Normann, Brunswick (D), 1732–75

386

387

388

389

390

386 Friedrich Friderichsen, Copenhagen, *c.* 1747
387 Josef Anton Peretti, Summaprada (CH), 1815–91
388 L. Lessel (probably), Dortmund (D), *c.* 1848
389 Johann Christoph Voigt, Eberswalde (DDR), master 1767
390 Johann Martin Seiffarth the Younger, Erfurt (DDR), master 1799

391

392

393

394

395

391 Dietrich Jakob Trippe, Soest (D), *c.* 1775
392 Christian Köpke, Brunswick (D), 1729–60
393 Johann Baptista Bawier, Chur (CH), 1770–1842
394 Johann Dietrich Finck the Younger, Frankfort on the Main (D), master 1779
395 Johann Matthaeus Werlin, Marburg (D), 1709–77

396

397

398

399

400

396 Carl Reutlinger, Frankfort on the Main (D), master 1768
397 J. Georg Benedikt Jäger, Frankfort on the Main (D), master 1753
398 Gabriel Syren, Frankfort on the Main (D), master 1727
399 Erik Lodin, Lovisa (SF), *c.* 1792
400 Heinrich Elias Friedrich Bartels, Brunswick (D), 1767–1805

401

402

403

404

401 Johann Georg Denecke, Brunswick (D), 1780–1826
402 Carl Mitterbacher, Prague/Old Town, master 1823
403 Joseph Ernst, Prague/Old Town, master 1785
404 Andreas Johannes Diebel, Prague/Malá Strana, master 1687

405

406

405 Jean Louis Davied, Berlin, *c.* 1777
406 Hans Michelsen Sperling, Copenhagen, master 1782

Animals

407

408

409

410

411

407 Jonas Osterlamb, Eperies (Prešov/ČS), 2nd half of 17th century
408 Johann Fleischmann, Schleiz (DDR), 1739–63
409 Daniel Lehmann the Elder, Freiberg (DDR), died 1666
410 Johann Bruhn, Västervik (S), 1778–89
411 Peter Reuter, Gera (DDR), *c.* 1755

412

413

414

415

416

412 Benjamin Krause the Younger, Delitzsch (DDR), *c.* 1740
413 Christoph Heinrich Seerig, Rudolstadt (DDR), 1794–1824
414 Eric Björkman, Stockholm, 1741–61
415 Erasmus (Asmus) Lemme the Younger, Salzwedel (DDR), *c.* 1649
416 Johann Georg Fiedler, Schleiz (DDR), 1739–56

417

418

419

420

421

417 Johann G. Schäfer, Wurzen (DDR), master 1779
418 Johann Gottfried Geelhaar, Gera (DDR), 1722–1804
419 Johan Henrik Bodecker, Karlskrona (S), 1758–85
420 Johann Gottfried Fehrmann, Crossen (DDR), 1775
421 Johann Gottfried Fleck, Altenburg (DDR), *c.* 1770

422

423

424

425

426

422 Johann Gottlieb Hasert (probably), Rudolstadt (DDR), master *c.* 1757
423 Johann Christian Seerig, Rudolstadt (DDR), died 1800
424 Carl Friedrich Fischer, Gera (DDR), 1725–42
425 Johann Gotthard Ötterich-Rätz, Saalfeld (DDR), *c.* 1711–67
426 Johann Paul Geelhaar, Torgau (DDR), master 1718

427

428

429

430

431

427 Ezechiel F. Risspler, Prague/Old Town, master 1685
428 Ezechiel F. Risspler, Prague/Old Town, master 1685
429 Christian Friedrich Baumann, Olbernhau (DDR), *c.* 1760–1807
430 Johann Wolraht Horstmann, Brunswick (D), 1740–91
431 Johann Gottlieb Holberg, Potsdam (DDR), master 1781

432

433

434

435

436

432 Anton Ferdinand Fabricius, Saalfeld (DDR), master 1733
433 Johann Cuno Ferdinand Ötterich-Rätz, Saalfeld (DDR), master 1792
434 William J. Elsworth, New York, 1767–98
435 Charles Clarke, Waterford (IRL), 1790–1810
436 Martin Wolf, Prague/Malá Strana, master probably 1651

437

438

439

440

441

437 Georg Michael Ortfort, Neustadt/Orla (DDR), 1728–1801
438 C. D. Zausch, Gera (DDR), *c.* 1755
439 Eberhardt Vahle, Celle (D), died 1755
440 Jacob Christoph Vahle, Celle (D), master 1760
441 Rudolph Vahle, Celle (D), master 1765

442

443

444

445

446

442 Christian Kohl, Eilenburg (DDR), 1633–81
443 Heinrich Ernst Schröder, Celle (D), master 1776
444 Johann Peter Wilhelm Müller, Celle (D), died 1811
445 Georg Heinrich Müller, Celle (D), master 1767
446 Georg Wilhelm Struve, Salzwedel (DDR), 1687–1732

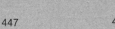

447

448

449

450

451

447 Andries Michel, New York, *c.* 1742–52
448 Martin Wolfmüller, Kaschau (Košice/ČS), 17th/18th century
449 Samuel Knauth, Weissenfels (DDR), *c.* 1744
450 A. Parqui, Bruges (B), *c.* 1780
451 George Noster, Eilenburg (DDR), 1645–88

452

453

454

455

456

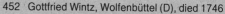

452 Gottfried Wintz, Wolfenbüttel (D), died 1746
453 Hans (Heinrich) Noel, Hall (A), 17th century
454 Johann Christoph Hohenner, Schleiz (DDR), 1763–1806
455 Claes Eric Heland, Norrköping (S), 1766–84
456 Carl Frederik Treyer, Uppsala (S), 1752–69

457

458

459

460

461

457 A. A. Vosmaer, Delft (NL), *c.* 1600
458 Joseph Anton Rissppler, Prague/Old Town, master 1713
459 Ignatz A. Rissler, Prague/Old Town, master *c.* 1740
460 Henry Wood, London, 2nd half of 18th century
461 John Kent, London, 1718–59

462

463

464

465

466

462 Anton Steinlechner the Elder and the Younger, Hall (A), 2nd third of 19th century
463 Heinrich Billot, Prenzlau (DDR), master 1728
464 Hans Schröter (probably), Prague/Old Town, *c.* 1664
465 M. Coustard, Angers (F), master 1640
466 Conrad Schröder, Prague/Old Town, *c.* 1700

467

468

469

470

471

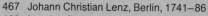

467 Johann Christian Lenz, Berlin, 1741–86
468 Henrich Christoffel Volckmar, Siegen (D), from *c.* 1731
469 Esaias Hirsch, Schleiz (DDR), 1665–1705
470 Christian August Lange, Altenburg (DDR), before 1821
471 Gregor Benjamin Auermann, Eilenburg (DDR), 1662–1700

472

473

474

475

476

472 Carl Christian Friedrich Junge, Stollberg (Saxony) (DDR), 1762–1835
473 Michael Rehfeld, Prenzlau (DDR), 1695–1776
474 Joseph Haase, Schleiz (DDR), 1706–45
475 Hans Christoph Häseler, Berlin, up to *c.* 1677
476 Carl Logren, Falun (S), 1750–75

477

478

479

480

481

477 Piter van Doorn, Utrecht (NL), 18th century
478 Martin Friedrich, Erfurt (DDR), probably 17th century
479 Georg Friedrich, Erfurt (DDR), probably 17th century
480 Georg Fröhlich, Kaschau (Košice/ČS), 1st half of 18th century
481 Johann Gottfried Rothe, Altenburg (DDR), *c.* 1736

482

483

484

485

486

482 Chr. Heinrich Wirth, Gera (DDR), 1757–1813
483 Peter Gillman, Stockholm, 1770–98
484 Johann Paul Stiegelitz, Erfurt (DDR), *c.* 1714
485 Georg Kiemel, Kaschau (Košice/ČS), 2nd half of 17th century
486 Johann Heinrich Ohrdorf, Celle (D), master 1727

487

488

489

490

491

487 Hans Taub, Prague/New Town, master 1653
488 Christian August Tausch, Erfurt (DDR), *c.* 1745
489 Burchhard Walter Wiehe, Stendal (DDR), *c.* 1700
490 Johann Christian Richter, Cottbus (DDR), master 1761
491 Wolff Lange, Greiz (DDR), *c.* 1700

492

493

494

495

496

492 Martin Gustaf Moberg, Jönköping (S), 1777–1815
493 Thomas Batteson, London, 2nd half of 17th century
494 Samuel Danforth, Hartford (USA), 1795–1816
495 Christian Krämer (probably), Marburg (D), *c.* 1772–1849
496 Jean Maizieres, Crossen (DDR), *c.* 1794

497

498

499

500

501

497 Gottfried Etzold, Altenburg (DDR), *c.* 1821
498 Johann Daniel Sonntag, Torgau (DDR), master 1737
499 Wolrad Badendieck, Prenzlau (DDR), *c.* 1695
500 Gottfried Hermann, Altenburg (DDR), *c.* 1730
501 M. H. Jüngel, Torgau (DDR), *c.* 1628

502

503

504

505

506

502 Johann Christoph Teutsch, Saalfeld (DDR), *c.* 1774
503 Johann Christoph Matthaei, Eilenburg (DDR), 1721–1804
504 Johann David Sayffarth, Altenburg (DDR), *c.* 1725
505 Jacob Büttner, Grimma (DDR), died 1668
506 Roger Pye, London, *c.* 1740

507

508

509

510

511

512

507 Richard Austin, Boston (USA), 1793–1817
508 August Ludwig Klingmüller, Cottbus (DDR), master 1797
509 Andreas Friedrich José, Cottbus (DDR), master 1819
510 Ralph Hull, London, *c.* 1790
511 Heinrich Andreas Brandes, Peine (D), 1787–1855
512 M. Rollet, Dijon (F), *c.* 1743

Plants

513

514

515

516

517

518

513 Jakob Schüler, Cottbus (DDR), *c.* 1630
514 Jakob Schüler, Cottbus (DDR), *c.* 1630
515 Johan Anjou, Gärle (S), 1763–1804
516 Abraham Friedrich Fischer, Prenzlau (DDR), 1712–1803
517 Martin Klave, Berlin, *c.* 1700
518 François Beaussier, Angers (F), *c.* 1732

519

520

521

522

523

524

519 Hans Stahr, Prague/Malá Strana, master 1657
520 Paul Stellmacher, Berlin, 1619–51
521 Gunder Pedersen Schmidt, Odense (DK), *c.* 1725
522 Johann Christoph Beer (Bär), Erfurt (DDR), 17th century
523 Ch. Bernstein, Saalfeld (DDR), master 1650
524 G. Krumpholz, Saalfeld (DDR), master 1702

525

526

527

528

529

530

525 Mathias Rundquist, Karlskrona (S), 1778–1820
526 Martin Friedrich Fischer, Gera (DDR), 1655
527 Louis Gabriel Samain, Montargis (F), 1766
528 Johann Joachim Schultze, Salzwedel (DDR), 1719–91
529 Petter Lagerwall, Jönköping (S), master 1739
530 Johann Benedict Kooke, Eutin (DK), *c.* 1805

531

532

533

534

535

536

531 Gottlob Schumann, Wurzen (DDR), *c.* 1738
532 William Charlesley, London, died 1770
533 Gottfried Erdmann Seiffarth, Erfurt (DDR), *c.* 1779
534 Georg Gebhardt, Altenburg (DDR), mentioned 1686–1707
535 Nathanael Simon, Berlin, *c.* 1710
536 C. Steinhart, Salzwedel (DDR), died 1667

537

538

539

540

541

537 Melchior Leffler, Visby (S), 1748–91
538 Gottlob Friedrich Baumann, Hudiksvall (S), 1789–1826
539 Autor Friedrich Siegmund Kraegelius, Brunswick (D), 1743–58
540 Johann Friedrich Blumentritt, Neustadt/Orla (DDR), 1764–1836
541 Ludwig Wilhelm Schrader, Celle (D), master 1849

542

543

544

545

546

542 Robert Matthew, London, *c.* 1730
543 Michael Witko, Kaschau (Košice/ČS), 2nd half of 17th century
544 Jacob Dürnreiter, Burghausen (D), 1622 up to before 1651
545 Hans Gesterding, Brunswick (D), 1690–1718
546 Martin Scholz, Crossen (DDR), *c.* 1676

547

548

549

550

551

552

547 Gottlieb Adam Becker, Saalfeld (DDR), 1781–1837
548 Georg Kosse, Salzwedel (DDR), 1635–1704
549 Jakob Christoph Kosse, Salzwedel (DDR), 1707–78
550 Tobias Fessel, Eilenburg (DDR), 1669–1740
551 Ch. Geuthe, Salzwedel (DDR), 1658–1743
552 Wilhelm Beyendorf, Salzwedel (DDR), 1735–92

553

554

555

556

557

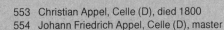

553 Christian Appel, Celle (D), died 1800
554 Johann Friedrich Appel, Celle (D), master 1790
555 Johannes Zetzsche, Altenburg (DDR), *c.* 1764
556 Christian Gottlob Osswald, Altenburg (DDR), master *c.* 1798
557 Christoffel Hempel III, Chur (CH), 1652–98

558

559

560

561

562

558 Johann Tobias Fessel, Eilenburg (DDR), 1725–75
559 August Ludwig Klingmüller, Cottbus (DDR), master 1797
560 Johann Christoph Grünewald, Luckau (DDR), 1730–68
561 Johann Christoph Beyer, Helmstedt (D), died 1836
562 Carl Wilhelm Böttger, Erfurt (DDR), 18th century

Roses

563

564

565

566

567

563 Jacob Glander, Wolfenbüttel (D), died 1715
564 Christoffer Bonn, Hamm (D), 2nd half of 18th century
565 Nicolas Deschamps, Liège (B), *c.* 1818
566 Daniel Rothe, Kaschau (Košice/ČS), 2nd half of 18th century
567 P. Nootens, Brussels, *c.* 1838

568

569

570

571

572

573

568 F. van den Bogaard, s'Hertogenbosch (NL), 19th century
569 H. van der Linde, Deventer (NL), 18th century
570 Piter van Doorn, Utrecht (NL), 18th century
571 D. Friedrich Keggemann, Soest (D), *c.* 1800
572 Johann Melchior Ortfort, Neustadt/Orla (DDR), master 1715
573 Wolfgang Micklas Dappert, Leutschau (Levoca/ČS), 1st half of 18th century

574

575

576

577

578

574 Johann Caspar Weber, Kaschau (Košice/ČS), 18th/19th century
575 Johann Andreas Meinhart, Kaschau (Košice/ČS), late 18th century
576 Johann Ludwig Rothe, Kaschau (Košice/ČS), late 18th century
577 Johann Samuel Steiner, Neusohl (Banská Bystrica/ČS), 18th/19th century
578 P. Marchionini, Ödenburg (Sopron/H), 19th century

579

580

581

582

579 Johann Anton Briscken, Soest (D), *c.* 1709
580 Georg Friedrich Braun, Kronstadt (Braşov/R), early 19th century
581 Johannes Caspar Diettel (Diebel), Prague/New Town, died 1720
582 Sebastian Heiling, Ofen (Buda/H), 1789–96

583

584

583 Markus Rosenberger, Schleiz (DDR), 1504–48
584 Samuel Hamlin, Providence (USA), 1771–1801

Jugs, anchors, hammers

585

586

587

588

589

590

585 Franz Weiss, Burghausen (D), 1688–1720
586 Elias Forster, Prague/Old Town, *c.* 1606
587 Christian Kägler, Gardelegen (DDR), before 1720
588 Joachim Böhm, Kaschau (Košice/ČS), 2nd half of 17th century
589 Ernst Kester, Ödenburg (Sopron/H), 2nd half of 17th century
590 Caspar Schadl, Prague/New Town, *c.* 1690

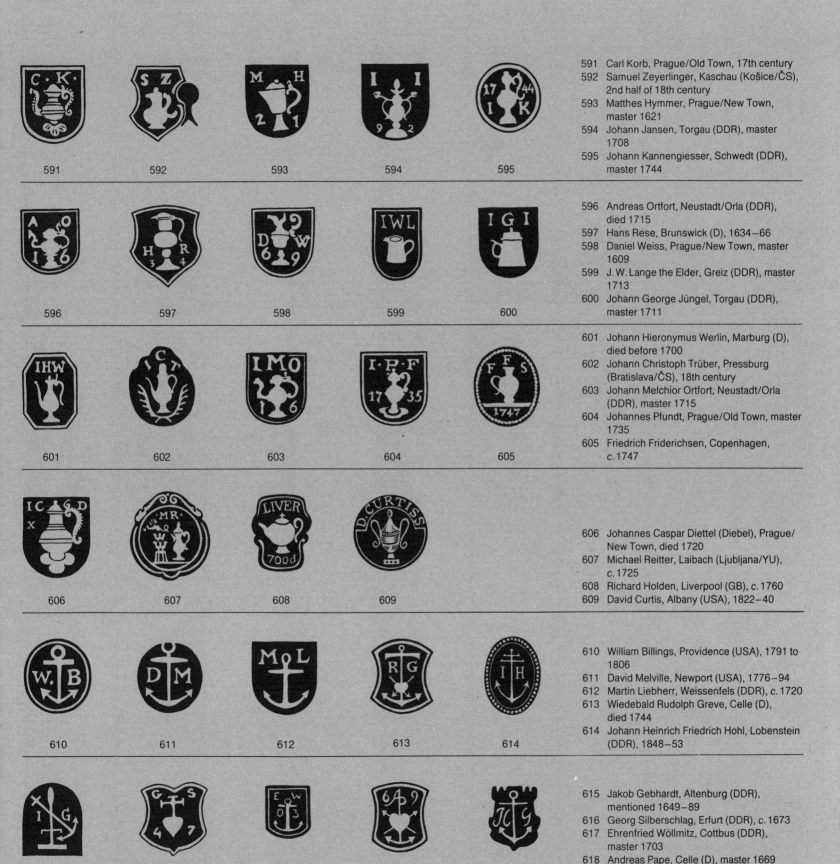

591

592

593

594

595

591 Carl Korb, Prague/Old Town, 17th century
592 Samuel Zeyerlinger, Kaschau (Košice/ČS), 2nd half of 18th century
593 Matthes Hymmer, Prague/New Town, master 1621
594 Johann Jansen, Torgau (DDR), master 1708
595 Johann Kannengiesser, Schwedt (DDR), master 1744

596

597

598

599

600

596 Andreas Ortfort, Neustadt/Orla (DDR), died 1715
597 Hans Rese, Brunswick (D), 1634–66
598 Daniel Weiss, Prague/New Town, master 1609
599 J. W. Lange the Elder, Greiz (DDR), master 1713
600 Johann George Jüngel, Torgau (DDR), master 1711

601

602

603

604

605

601 Johann Hieronymus Werlin, Marburg (D), died before 1700
602 Johann Christoph Trüber, Pressburg (Bratislava/ČS), 18th century
603 Johann Melchior Ortfort, Neustadt/Orla (DDR), master 1715
604 Johannes Pfundt, Prague/Old Town, master 1735
605 Friedrich Friderichsen, Copenhagen, *c.* 1747

606

607

608

609

606 Johannes Caspar Diettel (Diebel), Prague/New Town, died 1720
607 Michael Reitter, Laibach (Ljubljana/YU), *c.* 1725
608 Richard Holden, Liverpool (GB), *c.* 1760
609 David Curtis, Albany (USA), 1822–40

610

611

612

613

614

610 William Billings, Providence (USA), 1791 to 1806
611 David Melville, Newport (USA), 1776–94
612 Martin Liebherr, Weissenfels (DDR), *c.* 1720
613 Wiedebald Rudolph Greve, Celle (D), died 1744
614 Johann Heinrich Friedrich Hohl, Lobenstein (DDR), 1848–53

615

616

617

618

619

615 Jakob Gebhardt, Altenburg (DDR), mentioned 1649–89
616 Georg Silberschlag, Erfurt (DDR), *c.* 1673
617 Ehrenfried Wöllmitz, Cottbus (DDR), master 1703
618 Andreas Pape, Celle (D), master 1669
619 Johan Christoffer Georgi, Karlskrona (S), 1731–54

620

621

622

623

624

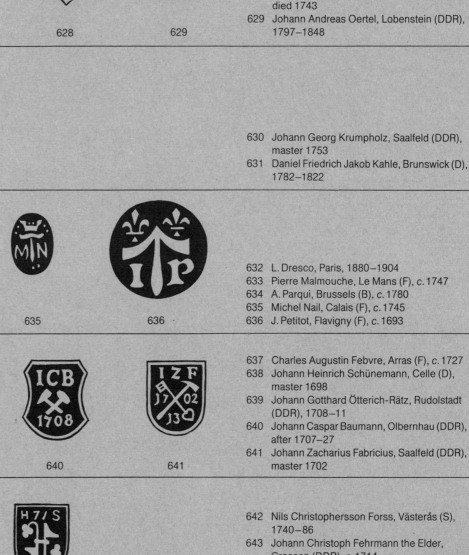

620 Johann Peter Hess, Gera (DDR), 1780 to 1844
621 Heinrich Severus Meyer, Pössneck (DDR), master 1714
622 Johann George Schröter, Wurzen (DDR), master 1719
623 Carl Christian Junge, Stollberg (Saxony) (DDR), 1721–81
624 Johann Gottlieb Richter, Luckau (DDR), 1768–*c.* 1815

625

626

627

628

629

625 Johan Heinrich Pape, Celle (D), 1674–1724
626 Johann Heinrich Misselwitz, Gera (DDR), *c.* 1746
627 Joachim Andreas Pape, Celle (D), master 1728
628 Jürgen Friedrich Reinhardt, Celle (D), died 1743
629 Johann Andreas Oertel, Lobenstein (DDR), 1797–1848

630

631

630 Johann Georg Krumpholz, Saalfeld (DDR), master 1753
631 Daniel Friedrich Jakob Kahle, Brunswick (D), 1782–1822

632

633

634

635

636

632 L. Dresco, Paris, 1880–1904
633 Pierre Malmouche, Le Mans (F), *c.* 1747
634 A. Parqui, Brussels (B), *c.* 1780
635 Michel Nail, Calais (F), *c.* 1745
636 J. Petitot, Flavigny (F), *c.* 1693

637

638

639

640

641

637 Charles Augustin Febvre, Arras (F), *c.* 1727
638 Johann Heinrich Schünemann, Celle (D), master 1698
639 Johann Gotthard Ötterich-Rätz, Rudolstadt (DDR), 1708–11
640 Johann Caspar Baumann, Olbernhau (DDR), after 1707–27
641 Johann Zacharius Fabricius, Saalfeld (DDR), master 1702

642

643

644

645

642 Nils Christophersson Forss, Västerås (S), 1740–86
643 Johann Christoph Fehrmann the Elder, Crossen (DDR), *c.* 1714
644 Johann Christoph Bühler, Altenburg (DDR), 2nd half of 17th century
645 Hermann Struve, Salzwedel (DDR), 1642–1716

Architecture, ships, celestial bodies, other

646

647

648

649

650

646 Johann Baptista Bawier, Chur (CH), 1770–1842
647 Andrew Kinnear, Edinburgh (GB), 2nd half of 18th century
648 John Schmidt, Koge (DK), *c.* 1674
649 J. J. Hoch, Bergen (NOR), *c.* 1756
650 Georg Martin Staudinger, Weissenburg (D), *c.* 1770

651

652

653

651 H. C. Byssing, Bergen (NOR), *c.* 1745
652 Christian Nicolajsen Lemberg, Aalborg (DK), *c.* 1746
653 Hans Christensen Hoy, Copenhagen, master 1843

654

655

656

657

658

654 August Sigmund Kauffmann, Gera (DDR), *c.* 1750
655 Ferdinand Gottlieb (Ötterich) Rätz, Saalfeld (DDR), master 1727
656 Johann Gottlieb Koch, Berlin, *c.* 1745
657 Carl Theodor Mezieres, Cottbus (DDR), master 1735
658 Nicolas Deschamps, Liège (B), *c.* 1818

659

660

661

662

663

659 Thomas Jacobszoon, Harlein (NL), *c.* 1619
660 Georg Döhren, Magdeburg (DDR), master probably 1669
661 J. Mouceau, Aix-en-Provence (F), *c.* 1696
662 Christian Beer (Bär), Erfurt (DDR), *c.* 1680
663 Christian Beer (Bär), Erfurt (DDR), *c.* 1680

664

665

664 Görgen Rokus, Stockholm, 1726–59
665 Georg Christoph Stampehl, Salzwedel (DDR), 1718–86

666

667

668

669

670

666 Johann Gabriel Wühlert, Tyrnau (Trnava/ČS), 2nd half of 18th century
667 Hans Birr, Mühlhausen (Mulhouse/F), 1631–75
668 John Carr, London, *c.* 1723
669 Jean Jacques Brucker, Mühlhausen (Mulhouse/F), 1738–95
670 Frédéric Dollfus, Mühlhausen (Mulhouse/F), 1754–68

671

672

673

674

675

671 J. Lusseau, Tours (F), *c.* 1759
672 Georges Gras, Angers (F), 1897–1925
673 Claude Adam, Chalon-sur-Saône (F), *c.* 1708
674 Eberhard Tremplau, Menden (D), *c.* 1810
675 Johann Christopher Heyne, Lancaster (USA), 1754–80

676

677

678

679

680

676 Daniel Martz, Eperies (Prešov/ČS), 1st half of 19th century
677 David Brocks, London, *c.* 1710
678 Thomas Simpkins, Boston (USA), 1727–66
679 Abraham Wiggin, London, 1st half of 18th century
680 Aper Zeegersz, Leyden (NL), *c.* 1596

681

682

683

684

685

681 Adolf Gottlob Christian Wilhelm Richter, Celle (D), master 1838
682 Johann Gottlob Richter, Celle (D), died 1830
683 John Wright, London, *c.* 1717
684 Nikolaus Fichtner, Brunswick (D), 1669–1706
685 Nathaniel Meakin the Younger, London, 2nd half of 18th century

686

687

688

689

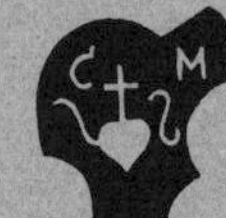
690

686 Christian Gottlieb Krause, Delitzsch (DDR), *c.* 1839
687 Carl Heinrich Klemm, Gera (DDR), 1782–1812
688 Christian Leiche, Halle (DDR), master probably 1763
689 Hans Luzi de Cadenath I, Chur (CH), 1655–1710
690 Caspar Möschlitzer, Schleiz (DDR), 1647–87

691

692

693

694

695

691 Georg Johann Christoph Olfermann, Salzwedel (DDR), 1738–1803
692 Johann Wilhelm Hildebrand, Salzwedel (DDR), 1707–65
693 Gregor Starcklauff the Elder, Pressburg (Bratislava/ČS), late 16th century
694 Jürgen Paul Piel, Brunswick (D), 1696–1733
695 Engelke Piel, Brunswick (D), 1634–65

Bibliography

The bibliography—which at the same time reflects the author's source material—includes the principal international writings since the beginning of this century. Publications devoted mainly to "noble" pewter have not been considered. For practical reasons arrangement of the literature to conform with the individual chapters of the book is not feasible.

The publications are alphabetically subdivided into books, periodicals and exposition catalagues.

Books

AICHELE, F.: *Zinn (Battenberg Antiquitäten-Kataloge)*, Munich, 1977.

BAER, I., H.-U. HAEDEKE et al.: *Zinn—Kopie, Imitation, Fälschung, Verfälschung*, Hanover, 1981.

BAUER, D.: *Kirchliches Zinngerät aus dem Kreise Marburg*, Marburg, 1970.

BELLONCLE, M.: *Les étains*, Paris, 1968.

BERGER, W.-L.: *Zinn*, Munich, 1974.

BERGER, W.-L.: *Schönes altes Zinn*, Bayreuth, 1980.

BERLING, K.: *Altes Zinn*, Berlin, 1920.

BERTRAM, F., and H. ZIMMERMANN: *Begegnungen mit Zinn*. Prague, 1967.

BOSCHIAN, N.: *Il petro*. Milan, 1966.

BOSSARD, G.: *Die Zinngiesser der Schweiz und ihr Werk*, Zug, 1920 (Vol. I), 1934 (Vol. II).

BOUCAUD, P., and C. FRÉGNAC: *Zinn—Die ganze Welt des Zinns von den Anfängen bis ins 19. Jahrhundert*, Berne/Munich, 1978.

BOUCAUD, P., and C. FRÉGNAC: *Les étains. Des origines au début du XIXe siècle*, Fribourg, 1978.

BOUCAUD, P.: *250 poinçons d'étains, faux, copies, imitations, trucages*, Paris, 1970.

BRETT, C.: *Phaidon Guide to Pewter*, Oxford, 1981.

BROWN, J. A.: *Das Zinngiesserhandwerk der Schweiz*, Solothurn, 1930.

BRUZELLI, B.: *Birger, Tenngjutare i Sverige under kontrolltiden 1774–1912*, Stockholm, 1967.

CALDER, C. A.: *Rhode Island Pewterers and their Work*, Providence, 1924.

COTTERELL, H. H.: *Old Pewter, its Makers and its Marks in England, Scotland and Ireland*, London, 1929.

COTTERELL, H. H.: *Pewter down the Ages*, London, 1932.

DELDEN, E. VON: *Norddeutsches Zinn*, Osnabrück, 1976.

DOLZ, R.: *Antiquitäten/Zinn*, Munich, 1970.

DOUROFF, B. A.: *Étains français du XVIIe siècle*, Paris, 1960.

DUBBE, B.: *Tin en Tinnegieters in Nederland*, Zeist, 1965.

GAHLNBÄCK, J.: *Russisches Zinn. Zinn und Zinngiesser in Moskau*, Leipzig, 1928.

GAHLNBÄCK, J.: *Zinn und Zinngiesser in Liv-, Est- und Kurland*, Lübeck, 1929.

GOULD, M. E.: *Antique Tin and Tole Ware*, Rutland, 1958.

HAEDEKE, H.-U.: *Metalwork*, London, 1969.

HAEDEKE, H.-U.: *Zinn*, Brunswick, 1973.

HAEDEKE, H.-U.: *Zinn (Zentren der Zinngiesserkunst von der Antike bis zum Jugendstil)*, Leipzig, 1973.

HAEDEKE, H.-U.: *Sächsisches Zinn*, Leipzig, 1975.

HAEDEKE, H.-U.: *Zinn sammeln*, Munich, 1980.

HARDOW, R.: *Stolper Zinngiesser und ihre nachweisbaren Arbeiten*, Stolp, 1931.

HATCHER, J.: *A History of British Pewter*, London, 1974.

HEDGES, E. S.: *Tin in Social and Economic History*, London, 1964.

HINTZE, E.: *Die deutschen Zinngiesser und ihre Marken*, Leipzig, 1921–1931.

HUBER, U., and G. OERTEL: *Siebenbürgisch-sächsisches und anderes Zinn*, Reichenberg, 1936.

JAKOBS, C.: *Guide to American Pewter*, Boston/New York, 1924.

KAUFMANN, H.: *Early American Copper, Tin and Brass*, New York, 1950.

KERFOOT, J. B.: *American Pewter*, Boston, 1924.

KITSON, E.: *Pewterwork*, London, 1953.

KLEIN, W.: *Gmünder Kunst*, Vol. II: *Das Zinngiesserhandwerk in Gmünd*, Stuttgart, 1922.

KOCH, H.: *Aus der Geschichte der Jenaer Zinngiesserei*, Mainz, 1974.

KOHLMANN, T.: *Zinngiesserhandwerk und Zinngerät in Oldenburg, Ostfriesland und Osnabrück*, Göttingen, 1972.

LAUGHLIN, L. I.: *Pewter in America. Its Makers and their Marks*, Barre, Mass., 1969.

LÖFGREN, A.: *Finländska tenngjutare och deras stämpling före 1809*, Helsingfors, 1927.

LÖFGREN, A.: *Det Svenska Tenngjutarehandverkets Historia*, Vols. I–III, Stockholm, 1925–1950.

MARKHAM, C. F.: *The New Pewter Marks and Old Pewter Ware*, New York, 1928.

MARTENSON, G.: *Vart Gamia Tenn*, Porvoo, 1967.

MASSÉ, H. J. L. J.: *Pewter Plates. A Historical Descriptive Handbook*, London, 1910.

MASSÉ, H. J. L. J.: *The Pewter Collector*, London, 1921.

MASSÉ, H. J. L. J.: *Chats on Old Pewter*, New York, 1971.

MICHAELIS, R. F.: *British Pewter*, London, 1969.

MICHAELIS, R. F.: *Antique Pewter of the British Isles*, New York, 1971.

MONTGOMERY, C. F.: *A History of American Pewter*, New York/Washington, 1974.

MORY, L.: *Schönes Zinn. Geschichte, Formen und Probleme*, Munich, 1972.

MORY, L., E. PICHELKASTNER and B. HÖFLER: *Bruckmanns Zinn-Lexikon*, Munich, 1977.

MÜLLER-STYGER, R.-J.: *Das Zinngiessergewerbe*. In: Creux, R.: *Volkskunst in der Schweiz*, Paudex, 1970.

MYERS, L. G.: *Some Notes on American Pewterers*, New York, 1926.

NAEF, E.: *L'étain et le livre des potiers d'étain genévois*, Geneva, 1920.

PEAL, C. A.: *More Pewter Marks*, Norwich, 1976.

PIEPER-LIPPE, M.: *Zinn im südlichen Westfalen*, Münster, 1974.

PIEPER-LIPPE, M.: *Zinn im nördlichen Westfalen*, Münster, 1980.

REINECKE, W.: *Lüneburger Zinn. Das Amt der Lüneburger Zinngiesser*, Lüneburg, 1947.

RIFF, A.: *L'orfèvrerie d'étain en France* (I/II), Strasbourg, 1925/26.

RIFF, A.: *Les étains strasbourgeois du XIVe au XIXe siècle*, Colmar, 1977.

SANTESSON, N. E.: *Tennets Historia*, Norrköping, 1906.

SANTESSON, B. O.: *Gammalt tenn*, Västerås, 1962.

SCHNEIDER, H.: *Schweizer Gebrauchszinn*, Berne, 1965.

SCHNITZLER, H., et al.: *Email, Goldschmiede- und Metallarbeiten*, Lucerne/Stuttgart, 1965.

SOMOGYI, A., and P. WEINER: *Fejér megye ötvösmüvészeti és ónmüvességi emlékei,* Budapest, 1969.
STARÁ, D.: *Markenzeichen auf Zinn,* Prague, 1977.
STARÁ, D.: *Konvářske značky pražkých mistrů,* Roztoky, 1974.
STEMPEL, C.: *Deutsche Zinngiesser im Wartheland,* Posen, 1943.
STERNER, G.: *Zinn. Vom Mittelalter bis zur Gegenwart,* Munich, 1979.

TARDY: *Les étains français,* Paris, 1959.
TARDY: *Les poinçons des étains français,* Paris, 1974.
TISCHER, F.: *Böhmisches Zinn und seine Marken,* Leipzig, 1928.
TOEPEL, C.: *Zur Geschichte der Geraer Zinngiessermarken.* In: Piana, T. R.: *Geraer Museum im Aufbau,* Gera, 1949.
TORANOVÁ, E.: *Cinárstvo na Slovensku,* Bratislava, 1980.

ULDALL, K.: *Gammelt tin,* Copenhagen, 1963.

VERSTER, A. J. G.: *Tin door de Eeuwen,* Amsterdam, 1954.
VERSTER, A. J. G.: *Old European Pewter,* London, 1957.
VERSTER, A. J. G.: *Das Buch vom Zinn,* Hanover, 1963.
VETTER, R. M., and H. H. COTTERELL: *European Continental Pewter,* London, 1927.
VETTER, R. M., and G. WACHA: *Linzer Zinngiesser,* Vienna/Munich, 1967.
VIEBAHN, E.: *Bergisches Zinn*, Wuppertal, 1978.
VITAL, D.: *Die Churer Zinngiesser,* Chur/Bottmingen/Basle, 1979.

WARNCKE, J.: *Die Zinngiesser zu Lübeck,* Lübeck, 1922.
WEDLAKE, W. J.: *Excavations at Camerton,* Somerset, 1958.
WEINER, P.: *La poterie d'étain: les plus beaux étains des collections hongroises,* Budapest, 1971.
WEINER, P.: *Zinngiessermarken in Ungarn (16.–19. Jh.),* Budapest, 1978.
WELCH, C.: *History of the Worshipful Company of Pewterers of the City of London,* London, 1902.
WITTICHEN, I.: *Celler Zinngiesser,* Celle, 1967.
WOLFBAUER, G.: *Die steirischen Zinngiesser und ihre Marken,* Graz, 1934.
WOOD, I.: *Scottish Pewter-ware and Pewterers,* Edinburgh, no date.
WÜHR, H.: *Altes Zinn,* Darmstadt, 1961.

ZELLER, R. VAN: *Estanhos portugueses,* Barcelona, 1969.

Periodicals

ACHILLES, W.: "Merkwürdiges um die Fleegel, eine Hildesheimer Zinngiesserfamilie," in: *Hildesheimer Heimat-Kalender,* Hildesheim, 1975, pp. 68–72.
ACHILLES, W.: "Strukturwandel im Hildesheimer Handwerk in vorindustrieller Zeit, dargestellt am Beispiel der Bauhandwerker und Zinngiesser," in: *Alt-Hildesheim,* Hildesheim, 1974, 45, pp. 7–13.
ARISTE, P.: "Kritische Bemerkungen zu J. Gahlnbäck: Zinn bei Esten und Finnen," in: *Sitzungsberichte d. gelehrten estn. Ges.,* Dorpat, 1927, pp. 66–77.
ARNOLD, H.: "Alte Eichgefässe aus Zinn," in: *Pfälzer Heimat,* Speyer, 17 (1966), 1, pp. 14–15.
ASCHE, S.: "Ein Apothekergefäss des Görlitzer Zinngiessers Hans Sachse," in: *Oberlausitzer Beiträge. Festschrift für Richard Jecht,* Görlitz, 1938, pp. 82–85.
ASCHL, A.: "Das Handwerk der Zinngiesser in Rosenheim," in: *Das bayerische Inn-Oberland,* Rosenheim, 36 (1970), pp. 5–78.
AUTENBOER, E. VAN: "Tin en tingieters te Turnhout," in: *Noordgouw. Culturell tijdschrift van de provincie Antwerpen,* Antwerp, 13 (1973), pp. 53–87.
AZYNMAN, K.: "De achttien oude wijnkannen der illustre Lieve Vrouwenbroederschap te 's Hertogenbosch," in: *Oude Kunst*, Hertogenbosch, 1918/19, Part IV, pp. 20ff.

BADER, K.: "Von den Würzburger Kandelgiessern," in: *Mainlande,* Würzburg, 1956, 7, pp. 27–28.
BALET, L.: "Das alte Zinngiesserhandwerk in Esslingen," in: *Württemb. Vierteljahreshefte f. Landesgesch.,* Stuttgart, N. F. 22 (1914), pp. 423–427.
BARTHEL, F.: "Von Zinngiessern und Zinnmarken," in: *Kulturspiegel f. d. Kreis Auerbach/Vogtl.*, Auerbach, 1965, pp. 64–66.
BAUERMANN, O.: "Das Zinngiesserhandwerk im Bergischen Land," in: *Installateur- u. Klempnerztg.,* Arnsberg, 4 (1951), 12, pp. 394–395.

Bengtsson, B.: "Rutger von Aschebergs 'fältservis'," in: *Kulturen,* Lund, 1971, pp. 33–38.

Berger, F.: "Rieder Zinngiesser," in: *Rieder Heimatkde.*, Ried, 1909, 1, p. 15.

Berling, K.: "Einiges über Zinnfälschungen," in: *Jb. f. Kunstsammler,* Frankfurt-on-the-Main, 4/5 (1925), pp. 45–50.

Bisset, J. S.: "Scottish Pewter Tankards," in: *Antique Collector,* London, 1937, 9.

Bohnstedt, F.: "Salzwedeler Zinngiesser," in: *Jahresber. d. Altmärk. Vereins f. vaterländ. Gesch. u. Industrie,* Salzwedel, 50 (1936), pp. 115–123.

Bondy, K.: "Das alte Zinngiesserhandwerk in Böhmisch-Leipa," in: *Mitt. d. Nordböhm. Vereins f. Heimatforschg. u. Wanderpflege in Böhmisch-Leipa,* Böhmisch-Leipa, 1938.

Bonhoff, F.: "Lüneburger Zinngiesser und ihre Marken," in: *Z.f. niedersächsische Familienkde,* Hamburg, 26 (1951), 1, pp. 7–10.

Bonness, A.: "Die Zinngiesser Meyerheine," in: *Mitt. d. Vereins f. d. Gesch. Potsdams,* Potsdam, 12 (1937), N. F. 7, pp. 360–362.

Borchers, W.: "Bäuerliches Zinn in Westfalen und im angrenzenden Niedersachsen," in: *Rheinisch-Westfälische Z. f. Volkskunde,* Bonn/Münster, 1958, 5, pp. 175–183.

Born, W.: "Der Egerländer Hochzeitskrug auf einem Zinnteller aus Schönfeld bei Schaggenwald," in: *75 Jahre Museum f. Volkskunde 1889–1964. Festschrift,* Berlin (West), 1964, pp. 177–190.

Bossard, G.: "Zinnplatten und -kannen als schweizerische Schützengaben des 16. bis 18. Jahrhunderts," in: *Z.f. schweizerische Archäologie u. Kunstgeschichte,* Basle, 1 (1939), 3, pp. 147–155.

Bossard, G.: "Die Zinngiesser der Stadt Zug," in: *Zuger Neujahrsblätter,* Zug, 1941, pp. 3–6.

Bourquin, W.: "Die Bieler Zinngiesser," in: *Blätter f. bernische Gesch., Kunst- u. Altertumskde,* Berne, 17 (1921), 3/4, pp. 277–292.

Brachmann, G.: "Das Zinngiesserhandwerk in Freystadt," in: *Der Heimatgau,* Linz, 1 (1938/39), 6, pp. 12–18.

Brandt, K.: "Zinngiessereien in Recklinghausen und Herne," in: *Vestisches Jahrbuch,* Recklinghausen, 62 (1960), pp. 149–151.

Braunerhielm, C.: "Tenngjutarna i Eskilstuna," in: *Eskilstuna stads museer, Årsbok,* Eskilstuna, 1966, pp. 52–54.

Brockpähler, R.: "Zinngeschirr und Zinngiesser in Coesfeld," in: *Westfälischer Heimatkalender,* Münster, 15 (1961), pp. 174–177.

Bruzelli, B.: "Tenngjutare i Örebro," in: *V (Från) bergslag och bonde-bygd,* Från 18 (1963), pp. 11–95.

Bruzelli, B.: "Tennkontroll och tennproduktion i Eskilstuna," in: *Eskilstuna stads museer. Årsbok,* Eskilstuna, 1966, pp. 17–44.

Bütikofer, H. R.: "Das Zinngiesserhandwerk in alter Zeit," in: *Der Hochwächter,* Berne, 7 (1951), pp. 129–133.

Bütikofer, H. R.: " Zinnkannen," in: *Der Hochwächter,* Berne, 7 (1951), pp. 133–141.

Bursian, K.: "Erzgebirgische Zinngiesser —weltbekannte Kunsthandwerker," in: *Sächsische Heimatblätter,* Dresden, 4 (1958), 3, pp. 172–181.

Bursian, K.: "Zinngiesser und Töpfer," in: *Kultur und Heimat,* Annaberg, 4 (1957), 4, pp. 47–50; 5, pp. 69–72.

Cazalet, L.: "Notes on Russian pewter," in: *The Connoisseur,* London, 1916, pp. 83–93.

Choisy, A.: "Les potiers d'étain genévois," in: *Bull. de la Société d'Histoire et d'Archéologie,* Geneva, 1907.

Clapperton, L.: "Some Scottish Pewter Measures," in: *Antiques,* Boston, 35 (1948), 2.

Cotterell, H. H.: "Old Pewter Plates and Chargers," in: *Bazaar, Exchange and Mart.,* 1923, 8/9.

Cotterell, H. H.: "National Types of Old Pewter," in: *Antiques,* Boston, 12 (1925), 3.

Cotterell, H. H.: "European Continental Pewter," in: *Antiques,* Boston, 15 (1928), 8.

Cotterell, H. H.: "Dating the Pewter Tankard," in: *The Connoisseur,* London, 1932, 4.

Cotterell, H. H.: "Early Pewter Baluster Measures," in: *Apollo,* London, 1933, 5.

Cotterell, H. H.: "Porringers, Caudle, Posset and Toasting Cups," in: *Apollo,* London, 1938, 8; 1939, 3; 1942, 10.

Cotterell, H. H., and R. M. Vetter: "Identifying Dutch Flagons," in: *Antiques,* Boston, 16 (1929), 12.

Csányi, K.: "Ónjeguek az Erdélyi Nemzeti Múzeum óntárgyain," in: *Dolgozatok az Erdélyi Nemzeti Múzeum Erem—és Régiségtárából,* Kolozsvár, 1919.

Dietz, H.: "Das Frankfurter Zinngiessergewerbe und seine Blütezeit im 18. Jahrhundert," in: *Festschrift zur Feier des 25-jährigen Bestehens d. Städt. Hist. Museums in Frankfurt/M.,* Frankfurt-on-the-Main, 1903, pp. 149–180.

Döring, E.: "Meine Zinnkannen," in: *Jahrb. d. Thüringer Vereinigung f. Heimatpflege,* Erfurt, 1914, pp. 128–131.

Drees, H.: "Oldenburger Zinngiesser," in: *Installateur- u. Klempnerztg.,* Arnsberg, 5 (1952), 15, p. 562.

Drees, H.: "Zinngiesser in Ostfriesland," in: *Installateur- u. Klempnerztg.,* Arnsberg, 5 (1952), 1, p. 23; 9, p. 292.

Drees, H.: "Kannemaker, Kannegeiter, Kannegiesser (Osnabrücker Zinngiesser)," in: *Installateur- u. Klempnerztg.,* Arnsberg, 5 (1952), 6, p. 191.

Drees, H.: "Die Kandelgiesser zu Bamberg," in: *Fränkische Blätter f. Geschichtsforschg. u. Heimatpflege,* 8 (1956), 14, pp. 53–56; 15, pp. 59–60.

Dreier, F. A.: "Eine Lübecker Zinngiesserwerkstatt des frühen 18. Jahrhunderts," in: *Z. d. Vereins für lüb. Geschichte u. Altertumskunde,* Lübeck, 1958, 38, pp. 142–156.

Dreier, F. A.: "Die mittelalterlichen Baluster-Zinnkannen Nordostdeutschlands," in: *Z. f. Kunstwissenschaft,* Berlin (West), 13 (1959), pp. 27–50.

Drescher, H.: "Zinnerne Sargbeschläge des 18. Jahrhunderts," in: *Harburger Jahrbuch,* Harburg, 9 (1959/60), pp. 36–68.

DRESCHER, H.: "Einige Arbeiten Harburger Zinngiesser im Helms-Museum und in Privatbesitz," in: *Harburger Jahrbuch,* Harburg, 12 (1965/67), pp. 53–64.

DUBBE, B.: "Het tinnegietersambacht te Deventer," in: *Verslagen en Mededelingen van de Vereeniging tot beofening van overijsselsch Regt en Geschiedenis,* Zwolle, 77 (1962), pp. 37–145.

DUBBE, B.: "De tinnen kamerpot en zijn voorgangers van aardewerk," in: *Antiek,* Lochem, 2 (1967), 4 pp. 162ff.

EBERLEIN, H.: "Early American Pewter," in: *Arts and Decoration,* 4 (1914), pp. 374–377.

ELMANN PEDERSEN, H.: "Kulturhistorie levendegores i tin," in: *Almanak,* Reykjavik, 1968/69, 1, pp. 2–7.

ENKELMANN, H.-W.: "Die Pössnecker und Neustädter Zinngiesser," in: *Rudolstädter Heimathefte,* Rudolstadt, 19 (1973), 7/8, pp. 166–169.

ENKELMANN, H.-W.: "Die Rudolstädter Zinngiesser," in: *Rudolstädter Heimathefte,* Rudolstadt, 19 (1973), 1/2, pp. 20–24.

ENKELMANN, H.-W.: "Die Saalfelder Zinngiesser," in: *Rudolstädter Heimathefte,* Rudolstadt, 19 (1973), 3/4, pp. 63–66.

FAHRINGER, F.: "Der Seelenwäger Michael in Zinn- und Meistermarken," in: *Blätter f. Heimatkunde,* Graz, 44 (1970), 2, pp. 92–96.

FALKE, O.: "Schweizer Zinn," in: *Pantheon,* Munich, 1936, 2, pp. 64–68.

FIESEL, L.: "Mecklenburgische Zinngiesser," in: *Mecklenburgische Monatshefte,* Ludwigslust, 6 (1930), pp. 536–539.

FLUE, J. VON: "Einheimische Zinngiesser in Unterwalden," in: *Bruderklausen-Kalender,* Sarnen, 1922, pp. 58ff.

FREI, K.: "Zwei gotische Zinnkannen aus dem Wallis," in: *39. Jahresbericht 1930. Schweizerisches Landesmuseum in Zürich,* Winterthur, 1931, pp. 50–66.

FRITZ, R.: "Dortmunder Zinngiesser der Barockzeit," in: *Beitr. z. Geschichte Dortmunds u. der Grafschaft Mark,* Dortmund 62 (1965), pp. 61–78.

GAHLNBÄCK, J.: "Zinn bei den Esten und Finnen," in: *Sitzungsberichte d. gelehrten esthnischen Gesellschaft,* Dorpat, 24 (1925/26), pp. 25–43.

GAHLNBÄCK, J.: "Das Amt der 'Estnischen Fuhrleute' in Dorpat und ihre Zinnkannen," in: *Sitzungsberichte d. gelehrten esthnischen Gesellschaft,* Dorpat, 26 (1927), pp. 48–65.

GASK, N.: "Mediaeval Pewter Spoons," in: *Apollo,* London, 1949, 12.

GEUENICH, J.: "Zwei alte Dürener Kannengiesser-Meistermarken," in: *Dürener Geschichtsblätter,* Düren, 1963, 32, pp. 685–700.

GRÄNICHER, T. G.: "Das Zinngiesserhandwerk in Zofingen," in: *Anz. f. schweizer. Altertumskunde,* Zurich, 19 (1917), pp. 26–42, pp. 99–121.

GROTEFEND, H.: "Die Schweriner Zinngiesser bis 1800," in: *Jahrbücher d. Vereins f. mecklenburgische Geschichte u. Altertumskunde,* Schwerin, 77 (1912), pp. 109–126.

GÜTTINGER, M.: "Brugger Zinngiesser und Zinngegenstände im Heimatmuseum Brugg," in: *Brugger Neujahrsblätter,* Brugg, 88 (1978), pp. 75–104.

HAEDEKE, H.-U.: "Die sogenannten 'Lichtenhainer' Bierkrüge," in: *Jahrbuch 1976 d. Ges. f. d. Geschichte u. Bibliographie des Brauwesens e.V.,* Berlin (West), 1975, pp. 91–106.

HAEDEKE, H.-U.: "Stope aus Zinn," in: *Kunst u. Antiquitäten,* Hanover, 1980, pp. 41ff.

HÄNSEL, R.: "Die Zinngiesser in Schleiz und ihre Marken," in: *Das Thüringer Fähnlein,* Jena, 11/12 (1942/43), pp. 103–109.

HANSEN, O. W.: "Lidt om Randers tin og tinstøbere," in: *Randers Årb.,* Randers, 1957, pp. 5–20, 110.

HELFER, E.: "Les fondeurs d'étain du passé," in: *Folklore Suisse,* Basle, 45 (1955), pp. 26–29.

HINTZE, E.: "Formengeschichte des schlesischen Zinns," in: *Schlesiens Vorzeit,* Breslau, N. F. 8 (1924).

HOCHENEGG, H.: "Die Kreuzgruppen am Grunde alter Zinnkrüge," in: *Tiroler Heimatblätter,* Innsbruck, 35 (1960), 7, 9, pp. 93–96.

HRÁSKÝ, J.: "O pražských konvářich," in: *Kniha o Praze 1960,* Prague, 1960, pp. 115–131.

HUEBNER, P.-H.: "La peste de l'étain," in: *Mouseion,* 27/28 (1934), pp. 237–241.

HUGHES, G. B.: "Old pewter spoons," in: *Country Life,* London, 111 (1953), pp. 1728–1729.

HUGHES, G. B.: "Ancient Craft of the Pewterer," in: *Country Life,* London, 108 (1950), pp. 290–291.

HYCKEL, R.: "Die Zinngiesser von Ratibor," in: *Ratiborer Heimatbote (Volkskalender f. Stadt u. Land),* Ratibor, 4 (1929), p. 68.

IVEN, G.: "Zinnarbeiten der Sammlung Clemens im Kölner Kunstgewerbe-Museum," in: *Pantheon,* Munich, 21 (1938), 6, pp. 182–187.

JESSE, W.: "Eine alte Braunschweiger Zinngiesserwerkstatt im Städtischen Museum," in: *Niederdeutsche Z. f. Volkskunde,* Bremen, 20 (1942), pp. 55–68.

KARAFIAT, K.: "Die Teplitzer Zinngiesser," in: *Mitt. d. Erzherzog Rainer-Museums f. Kunst u. Gewerbe,* Brünn, 34 (1916), 8, pp. 95–98; 9, pp. 109–112.

KARLSON, W.: "Tenn i Kulturen," in: *Kulturen,* Lund, 1937, pp. 17–69.

KIERDORF-TRAUT, G.: "Südtiroler Zinngiesser," in: *Der Schlern,* Bozen, 39 (1965), 8, pp. 313–316.

KIERDORF-TRAUT, G.: "Schraubflaschen und Schraubkannen aus Zinn," in: *Der Schlern,* Bozen, 43 (1969), pp. 305–307.

KINDT, H.: "Die Zinngiesskunst im alten Braunschweig," in: *Braunschweiger Kalender,* Brunswick, 1959, pp. 33–36.

KLAMROTH, A.: "Alte Zinngiesser—merkwürdige Schicksale ihrer Formen," in: *Antiquitäten-Rundschau,* Eisenach, 26 (1928), 8, pp. 113–114.

KLEINEBURG, G.: "Eine private Zinnsammlung," in: *Westfalen (Hefte f. Gesch., Kunst u. Volkskunde),* Münster, 29 (1951), pp. 97–99.

KOCH, A.: "Haller Zinngiesser," in: *Tiroler Heimatblätter,* Innsbruck, 40 (1965), 4/6, pp. 40–44.

KOCH, H.: "Von den Zinngiessern in Jena," in: *Altes und Neues aus der Heimat,* Jena, 1934/36, pp. 25–26.

KOCK, B. DE: "Stille getuigen van de overwintering op Nova Zembla," in: *Oud Nederland,* Rotterdam, 4 (1950), pp. 127ff.

KOROŠEC, B.: "Kositrarji baročne Ljubljane," in: *Kronika,* Ljubljana, 13 (1965), pp. 182–196.

KOROŠEC, B.: "Kositrarska obrt na Slovenskem Štajerskem," in: *Kronika,* Ljubljana, 14 (1966), pp. 155–164.

KRAHN, K.: "Die Zinnbestände des Regenwalder Kreisheimatmuseums," in: *Heimatkalender f. d. Kreis Regenwalde,* Regenwalde, 18 (1940), pp. 64–66.

KRÁL, A. B.: "O Brnenském Cinařstvi," in: *Umeni,* 18 (1970), pp. 395–402.

KRATZENBERGER, K.: "Altes norddeutsches Zinngerät und seine Marken," in: *Brandenburgisches Jahrbuch,* Berlin, 6 (1931), pp. 99–112.

KRATZENBERGER, K.: "Etwas über ältere Zinnkannen mit Giesstüllen," in: *Die Weltkunst,* Munich, 30 (1960), 20, pp. 32–33.

KRATZENBERGER, K.: "Die älteste deutsche Hansekanne und ihr Meister," in: *Die Weltkunst,* Munich, 32 (1962), 3, p. 9.

KRATZENBERGER, K.: "Ein Beitrag zum Markenwesen alter Zinngefässe," in: *Die Weltkunst,* Munich, 32 (1962), 24, p. 18.

KRATZENBERGER, K.: "Etwas über Glockenkannen," in: *Die Weltkunst,* Munich, 33 (1963), 7, pp. 18–19.

KRINS, F.: "Die Zinngiesserfamilie Maranca in Minden," in: *Mindener Heimatblätter,* Minden, 26 (1954), 1/2.

KRINS, F.: "Der Versuch zur Bildung eines Zinngiessergewerks in Minden-Ravensberg im 18. Jahrhundert," in: *Ravensberger Blätter,* Ravensberg, 13 (1956), pp. 164ff.

KRINS, F.: "Ein Dortmunder Schützenbecher aus dem Jahre 1848," in: *Der Märker,* Altena, 13 (1964), 1, p. 9.

KYRLE, E.: "Schärdinger Zinn," in: *Innviertler Heimatkunde auf das Jahr 1917,* Braunau/Inn, 1917, pp. 40ff.

LAMY-LASALLE, C.: "Enseignes de pèlerinage," in: *Bulletin de la Société Nationale des Antiquaires de France. Sitzungsbericht vom 25. März 1964,* pp. 64–69.

LAMY-LASALLE, C.: "Quelques enseignes de pèlerinage," in: *Bulletin de la Société Nationale des Antiquaires de France. Sitzungsbericht vom 6. Dezember 1967,* pp. 283–285.

LAMY-LASALLE, C: "Recherches sur un ensemble de plombs trouvés dans la Seine," in: *Revue des Sociétés Savantes de Haute-Normandie,* No. 49, 1er trim, 1968, pp. 5–24.

LANGER, P.: "Die Zinngiesser unserer Heimat," in: *Frankenstein-Münsterberger Heimatblatt,* Lengerich, 3 (1961), 11, pp. 14–15.

LAUFFER, O.: "Spätmittelalterliche Zinnfunde aus Hamburg und einige niederdeutsche Vergleichsstücke," in: *Mitteilungen aus dem Museum für Hamburgische Geschichte,* Hamburg, 1913, Supplement 7.

LAUGHLIN, L. I.: "The American Pewter Porringer," in: *Antiques,* Boston, 17 (1930), pp. 437–440.

LEOPOLD, H. M. R.: "De rol van het tin in de geschiedenis van de oud—Grieksche beschaving," in: *Mededelingen van het Nederl. Hist. Instituut,* Rome, 1927.

LIEDTKE, V.: "Burghausener Goldschmiede und Zinngiesser vom 14. bis Ende des 18. Jahrhunderts," in: *Ars Bavarica,* Munich, 3 (1975), 4, pp. 66–78.

LIEDTKE, V.: "Goldschmiede und Zinngiesser des 17. und 18. Jahrhunderts in den Bürgerbüchern von Salzburg," in: *Ars Bavarica,* Munich, 7 (1977), 8, pp. 86–87.

LÖFGREN, A.: "Den semmedeltida bukiga tennkannan," in: *Fornvännen,* Stockholm, 28 (1933), pp. 280–305.

LUGAUER, X.: "Zinngiessen—eine alte Handwerkskunst," in: *Die Oberpfalz,* Kallmünz, 1958, 8, pp. 188–191.

LUHNITZ, E.: "Schlesisches Zinngerät," in: *Schlesische Rundschau,* Wangen/Allgäu, 10 (1958), 4, p. 8.

LUNSING-SCHEURLEER, D.: "Tin op Schilderijen uit de 15e en 16e eeuw.," in: *Oud Nederland,* Rotterdam, 1950, pp. 113ff.

MAIS, A.: "Die 'Katzelmacher'," in: *Mitt. d. Anthropologischen Gesellschaft in Wien,* Horn-Vienna, 87 (1957), pp. 37–52.

MAIS, A.: "Die Zinngiesser Wiens," in: *Jahrbuch d. Vereins f. Gesch. d. Stadt Wien,* Vienna, 14 (1958), pp. 7–46.

MALOTKI, VON: "Der Zartner Zinnkrug von 1624," in: *Unser Pommerland,* Stettin, 13 (1928), 5/6, pp. 250–251.

MARCEL, L. F., and L. E. MARCEL: "Artistes et ouvriers d'art à Langres avant la Révolution," in: *Bulletin de la Société Historique et Archéologique de Langres,* 10 (1933/34), pp. 229–309.

MARTERER, R.: "Zinnmarken aus dem Egerland," in: *Der Egerländer,* Geislingen, 7 (1956), 11, pp. 197–198.

MATTOS, A. DE: "Um estanho marcado," in: *Douro-Litoral,* Porto, 4 (1950), 1/2, pp. 146–148.

MELZER, K.: "Die Formen der Thüringer Gebrauchszinne als Ausdruck der Land- und Stammeseigenart," in: *Sächsische Heimat,* Dresden, 4 (1920), 5, pp. 110–112.

MELZER, K.: "Das Weihnachtszinn wird hergerichtet," in: *Bunte Bilder aus dem Sachsenland,* Dresden, 3 (1926), pp. 104–108.

METZNER, K.: "Schleswig-holsteinische Metallgefässe aus drei Jahrhunderten. Zinn, Messing, Kupfer," in: *Schleswig-Holstein, Monatshefte f. Heimat u. Volkstum,* Flensburg, 1956, pp. 203ff.

MEYER-EICHEL, E.: "Die bremischen Zinngiesser," in: *Veröffentlichungen aus dem Stadtarchiv d. freien Hansestadt Bremen,* Bremen, 1931, 7, pp. 61ff.

MICHAELIS, R. F.: "English Pewter Porringers," in: *Apollo,* London, 1942, pp. 7–9.

MICHAELIS, R. F.: "Collecting Old Pewter Snuffboxes," in: *Apollo,* London, 1947, 1.

MICHAELIS, R. F.: "Old Pewter Wine Measures," in: *Antique Collector,* London, 1953, 2 and 8.

MICHAELIS, R. F.: "Capacity Marks on Old English Pewter Measures," in: *Antique Collector,* London, 1954, 10.

MICHAELIS, R. F.: "English Commemorative Porringers in Pewter," in: *Antique Collector,* London, 1956, 10.

MICHAELIS, R. F.: "More about English Commemorative Porringers," in: *Antiques,* Boston, 47 (1960), 7.

MICHAELIS, R. F.: "Pear-shaped Flagons in Pewter," in: *Antique Collector,* London, 1961, 10.

MINCHIN, C. C.: "Flagons and Tankards in Pewter," in: *Antique Collector,* London, 1952, 2.

MIROW, G.: "Berliner Zinngiesser," in: *Mitt. d. Vereins f. d. Geschichte Berlins,* Berlin, 35 (1918), pp. 31–32.

MIROW, G.: "Stadtmarken brandenburgischer Zinngiesser," in: *Mitt. d. Vereinigung brandenburg. Museen,* Müncheberg, 1918, 4.

MIROW, G.: "Der Zinnschatz der Crossener Amtsfischer und etwas von den Crossener Zinngiessern," in: *Crossener Kreiskalender,* Crossen, 23 (1935), pp. 137–143.

MIROW, G.: "Brandenburgische Zinngiesser," in: *Brandenburg. Jahrbuch,* Brandenburg, 2 (1927), pp. 83–94.

MIROW, G.: "Eine Zinnschüssel im Senftenberger Heimatmuseum," in: *Brandenburgische Museumsblätter,* Brandenburg, N. F. 6 (1927), pp. 41–42.

MIROW, G.: "Arbeiten des brandenburgischen Zinngiessers Wilhelm Altmann um 1649," in: *Brandenburgische Museumsblätter,* Brandenburg, N. F. 8 (1928), pp. 59–61.

MIROW, G.: "Luckauer Zinngiesser," in: *Mitt.-Blatt d. Vereins der Luckauer in Gross-Berlin,* Berlin, 5 (1936), pp. 38–39.

MIROW, G.: "Ein Königsberger Schatzfund und die Zinngiesser von Königsberg (Neumark)," in: *Königsberger Kalender,* Königsberg, 1937.

MIROW, G.: "Altes Zinngerät im Kreise Teltow," in: *Teltower Kreiskalender,* Teltow, 1939, pp. 57–62.

MIROW, G.: "Pommersche Zinngiesser," in: *Monatsblätter d. Ges. f. Pommersche Geschichte u. Altertumskunde,* Stettin, 55 (1941), p. 33.

MIROW, G.: "Die Prenzlauer Zinngiesser," in: *Heimatkalender Kreis Prenzlau,* Prenzlau, 1942, pp. 97–102.

MOESER, K.: "Die Zinngiesser in Imst," in: *Beiträge zur Heimatkunde von Imst u. Umgebung,* Innsbruck, 1954.

MÖTEFINDT, H.: "Zur Geschichte der Brandenburger Zinngiesser," in: *Geschichtsblätter f. Technik, Industrie u. Gewerbe,* Berlin, 6 (1920), pp. 210ff.

MORREN, R.: "Tingieter—Koperslager," in: *Ons Heem,* Genk, 19 (1965), pp. 198–203.

MORRIS, W. H.: "Kidwelly tinplate works: 18th century leases," in: *Carmarthen Antiquary,* Carmarthen (Wales), 5 (1964/69), pp. 21–24.

MÜLLER, P.: "Olbernhauer Zinngiesser," in: *Sächsische Heimatblätter,* Dresden, 9 (1963), 5, pp. 159–163.

MÜLLER, R.: "Geschichte der Zittauer Zinngiesserinnung," in: *Zittauer Heimatblätter,* Zittau, 1925, 8.

MURRAM, W. G. D.: "De Rotterdamsche Tinnegieters," in: *Rotterdamsch Jaarboek,* Rotterdam, 1938, pp. 1–32.

MYRTHE, J. H.: "18th Century Baluster Measures," in: *Antique Collector,* London, 1954, 2.

NADOLSKI, D.: "Eilenburger Zinngiesser und ihre Marken," in: *Sächsische Heimatblätter,* Dresden 23 (1977), 6, pp. 284–285.

NADOLSKI, D.: "Über Wurzener Zinngiesser," in: *Sächsische Heimatblätter,* Dresden, 26 (1980), p. 206.

NAGEL, A.: "Zinn im Hause," in: *Die christliche Frau,* Cologne, 25 (1927), pp. 250–253.

OBERWALDER, O.: "Altes Zinn," in: *Heimatgaue,* Linz, 1 (1919/20), pp. 247–261.

PEAL, C.: "Pewter Salts, Candlesticks and some Plates," in: *Apollo,* London, 1949, 5.

PEAL, C.: "Tankards and 'Housemarks' on early Measures," in: *Apollo,* London, 1949, 6.

PEAL, C.: "Notes on Pewter Baluster Measures and their Capacities," in: *Apollo,* London, 1950, 1.

PICHELKASTNER, E.: "Kurioses Trinkgerät aus Zinn," in: *Dresdner Kunstblätter,* Dresden, 8 (1964), 8, pp. 123–126.

PICHELKASTNER, E.: "Altes Zinngerät," in: *Bildende Kunst,* Dresden, 1965, 4, pp. 204–207.

PIEPER-LIPPE, M.: "Altes münsterisches Zinn," in: *Z. Westfalen (Hefte f. Geschichte, Kunst u. Volkskunde),* Münster, 36 (1958), 3, pp. 234–254.

PIEPER-LIPPE, M.: "Altes Dülmener Zinn," in: *Z. Westfalen (Hefte f. Geschichte, Kunst und Volkskunde),* Münster, 45 (1967), 2/3, pp. 154–164.

PNIOWER, O.: "Mittelalterliche Zinnkannen aus der Mark Brandenburg," in: *Brandenburgia,* Berlin, 25 (1917).

POOLE, J. W.: "The Care of Pewter," in: *Antiques,* Boston, 34 (1947), pp. 248–249.

QUERNER, H.: "Die Zinngiesserfamilie Querner," in: *Braunschweigische Heimat,* Brunswick, 53 (1967), 2, pp. 52–58.

RENAUD, J. G. N.: "Iets over tinmerken," in: *Oudheidkundig Jaarboek,* September 1944, p. 7.

RIISMØLLER, P.: "En lübsk tinkande i Ålborg," in: *Arv o Eje,* Odense, 1959, pp. 19–25.

ROCH, W.: "Die Annaberger Zinngiesser," in: *Mitteldeutsche Familienkunde,* Neustadt/Aisch, 11 (1970), 3, pp. 68–79.

RUSCH-HÄLG, C.: "Die Appenzeller Zinngiesser, ihre Marken und ihre Erzeugnisse," in: *Innerrhoder Geschichtsfreund,* Appenzell, 14, (1968), pp. 3–32.

RYDBECK, M.: "Trå slutna fynd av medeltida tennkannor och bronsgrytor från nordöstra Skåne," in: *Meddelanden från Lunds univ. hist. mus.,* Lund, 1945, pp. 84–97.

SAGEBIEL, F.: "Aus der Geschichte der bergischen Zinngiesser," in: *Rheinisch-Westfälische Z. f. Volkskunde,* Bonn/Münster, 3 (1956), 3/4, pp. 196–216.

SAGEBIEL, F.: "Zinngiesser und Zinngiesserei im Bergischen Land," in: *Romerike Berge Zeituhr f. Heimatpflege im Bergischen Land,* Opladen, 2 (1951/52), pp. 100–110.

SAGEBIEL, F.: "Zinngerät und Zinngiesserei," in: *Heimatblätter f. Hohenlimburg u. Umgebung,* Hohenlimburg, 14 (1953), pp. 97–103.

SÁNDOR, M.: "Pest-budai ónmüves emlékek," in: *Tanulmányok Budapest múltjából,* Budapest, 7 (1939).

SCHAEFFER, K.: "Zinnkannen und Dröppelminna," in: *Bergische Heimat,* Ronsdorf, 13 (1939), 11, pp. 281–283.

SCHEURLEER, D. F. L.: "De tinnen stadskannen in Nederland," in: *Oudheidkundig Jaarboek,* September 1940, pp. 15ff.

SCHEURLEER, D. F. L.: "Tin op Schilderijen," in: *Oud Nederland,* Rotterdam, 1950, pp. 1ff.

SCHEURLEER, D. F. L.: "Iets over de gebieden waar tin wordt gewonnen, de handel en de oudste tinnen voorwerpen," in: *Oud Nederland,* Rotterdam, 1950, pp. 132ff.

SCHIEMER, R. H.: "Altes und neues Zinn aus Schweden," in: *Schwabenland. III. Heimatz. f. d. Gau Württemberg-Hohenzollern,* Stuttgart, 16 (1940), 3, pp. 24–27.

SCHIREK, C.: "Das Zinngiesserhandwerk in Mähren," in: *Mitt. d. Erzherzog Rainer-Museums in Brünn,* Brünn, 1904, pp. 162ff.

SCHLECHTRIEM, G.: "Menso Hoyer, Zinngiesser zu Amsterdam," in: *Jahrbuch der Männer vom Morgenstern,* Bremerhaven, 42 (1961), pp. 209–214.

SCHMIDT, W. M.: "Alt-Passauer Zünfte IV," in: *Niederbayerische Monatsschrift,* Passau, 9 (1920), 1–3, pp. 25–33.

SCHMIDT, E. E.: "Vaihinger Zinngiesser, ihre Marken und ihre Erzeugnisse," in: *Mitteilungsblatt des Württembergischen Museumsverbandes e. V.,* Stuttgart, 1970/71.

SCHNEIDER, H.: "Schweizer Gebrauchszinn und sein Formenschatz," in: *Die Weltkunst,* Munich, 47 (1977), 16, pp. 1544–45; 17, p. 1627.

SCHRÖDER, A.: "Mitteilungen über Eilenburger Zinngiesser," in: *Bilder aus der Heimat,* Eilenburg, 1932, 18, p. 4.

SCHRÖDER, A.: "Die Zinngiesserfamilie Lichtenhain aus Schneeberg," in: *Glückauf,* Schwarzenberg, 56 (1936), 9. pp. 129–132.

SCHRÖDER, A.: "Grimmaer Zinngiesser," in: *Die Grimmaer Pflege,* Grimma, 16 (1937), 7.

SCHRÖDER, A.: "Beiträge zur Geschichte der Weissenfelser Zinngiesser-Innung," in: *Die Heimat*, Weissenfels, 3 (1939), 16, pp. 121–124.

SCHRÖDER, A.: "Zinngiesser zu Fürstenau," in: *Heimatkalender f. d. Kreis Bersenbrück,* Bersenbrück, 1967, p. 43.

SCHUBERT, A.: "Kölner Zinn der Spätgotik und Renaissance," in: *Rheinische Blätter,* Cologne, 13 (1936), 12, pp. 849–852.

SEELIG, L.: "Süddeutsches Zinn im Bayerischen Nationalmuseum," in: *Die Weltkunst,* Munich, 46 (1976), 12, pp. 1236–1237.

SEIFFERT, G.: "Zinngiesserei und Zinngeschirr in Schleswig-Holstein," in: *Schleswig-Holstein,* Flensburg, 26 (1974), pp. 123–124.

SMOLA, G.: "Zinngefässe von Stadt- und Landmeistern der Linzer Lade in Graz und Rottenmann," in: *Kunstjahrbuch der Stadt Linz,* Linz, 1974/75, pp. 25–32.

SMOLA, G.: "Altes Zinn," in: *Die Weltkunst,* Munich, 45 (1975), 18, pp. 1490–1491.

SOMMERFELDT, G., and F. WEISS: "Schneeberger Zinngiesser," in: *Ekkehard, Mitteilungsblatt d. deutschen genealog. Abende,* Halle/Saale, 16 (1940), 1, pp. 103–104.

SPANKA, E.: "Zinnforschung, Kannengiesseramt Lüneburg," in: *Der Niedersachse,* Soltau, 111 (1975), pp. 32–35, 40–41.

SPEIGHT, H. W.: "Verification Marks on Old Pewter Measures," in: *Antique Collector,* London, 1938, 12.

SPIES, G.: "Braunschweiger Zinngiesser," in: *Kunst u. Antiquitäten,* Hanover, 1978, pp. 24–31.

STUART, S.: "Old Scottish Pewter," in: *Scottish Field,* Glasgow, 112 (1965), 7, p. 28.

SUPKA, G.: "The colours of pewter," in: *The Connoisseur,* London, 1915, pp. 71–80.

SUTHERLAND GRAEME, A. V.: "Old Pewter Snuffboxes," in: *Bazaar, Exchange and Mart.,* 2nd November, 1937.

SUTHERLAND GRAEME, A. V.: "Pewter of the Channel Islands," in: *Antique Collector,* London, 1938, 5.

SUTHERLAND GRAEME, A. V.: "Some Pewter Plates," in: *The Connoisseur,* London, 1941, 12.

SUTHERLAND GRAEME, A. V.: "Pewter Spoons," in: *The Connoisseur,* London, 1947, 12.

SUTHERLAND GRAEME, A. V.: "Some Uncommon Pewter Inkstands," in: *Country Life,* London, 106 (1948), 10.

SUTHERLAND GRAEME, A. V.: "Pewter Tavern Pots," in: *Country Life,* London, 112 (1954), 10.

TINGVALL, S.: "Tenngjutarna i Boras," in: *V. (Fran) Boras och de sjn häraderna,* 24 (1969), pp. 45–52.

TISCHER, F.: "Das Zinngiesserhandwerk in Böhmen," in: *Kunst u. Handwerk,* Vienna, 20 (1917), pp. 231ff.

TITZ, H.: "Die schlesischen Zinngiesser," in: *Sagan-Sprottauer Heimatbriefe,* Detmold, 17 (1966), 5, pp. 143–145.

TOEPEL, C.: "Meister- und Stadtzeichen auf Geraer Zinngeräten," in: *Heimatblätter,* Gera (1936), leaf 2, pp. 6–7.

TOEPEL, C.: "Ein Streifzug durch das Greizer Zinngiesserwesen," in: *Mitt. d. Freunde des Kreismuseums Hohenleuben,* Hohenleuben, 1947, pp. 15–18.

UTRILLO, M.: "Bacines de leanto de colecciones publiques i particulars," in: *Buttleti dels museus d'Art de Barcelona,* Barcelona, 4 (1934), pp. 65–73.

VETTER, R. M.: "Tableguards and cake plates of pewter," in: *Antiques,* Boston, 58 (1971), 5, pp. 712ff.

VISSER, M. A. DE: "Drie Groningsche Hanzetin-kannen," in: *Oud Nederland,* Rotterdam, 1950, pp. 123ff.

WACHA, G.: "Zinn und Zinngiesser in Österreich," in: *Alte und moderne Kunst,* Vienna, 23 (1978), 157, pp. 20–29.

WACHA, G.: "Italienische Zinngiesser nördlich der Alpen," in: *Mitt. d. Österreichischen Staatsarchivs,* Vienna, 31 (1978), pp. 106–120.

WAIDACHER, F.: "Die Zinngiesserfamilie Zamponi," in: *Alte und moderne Kunst,* Vienna, 12 (1967), 95, pp. 28–31.

WALCHER VON MOLTHEIM, A.: "Das Zinngiesserhandwerk der Stadt Salzburg," in: *Kunst u. Kunsthandwerk,* Vienna, 12 (1909), pp. 520–542.

WALCHER VON MOLTHEIM, A.: "Tiroler Zinngiesser," in: *Altes Kunsthandwerk,* Vienna, 1927, 5, pp. 222–228.

WALTER, H.: "Aussiger Zinngiesser," in: *Beitr. z. Heimatkunde des Elbetales,* Aussig, 4 (1942), pp. 108–113.
WARNCKE, J.: "Die Zahl 79 in den älteren Lübecker Zinngiessermarken," in: *Z. d. Vereins f. Lübeckische Geschichte u. Altertumskunde,* Lübeck, 29 (1938), 2, pp. 345–347.
WAWRA, W.: "Beiträge zur Geschichte der Komotauer Zinngiesser," in: *Erzgebirgs-zeitung,* Teplitz-Schönau, 62/63 (1942), pp. 34–36.
WEINER, P.: "Zinngiesser, Zinngefässe und Zinnmarken in Ungarn," in: *Acta Historiae Artium, Academia Scientiarum Hungarica,* Budapest, 15 (1969), pp. 139ff.
WENHAM, E.: "Salt Cellars," in: *Antique Collector,* London, 1948, 4.
WERNER, O. H.: "Ein Gifhorner Zinnteller," in: *Kreiskalender Gifhorn-Isernhagen,* Gifhorn, 1973, p. 43.
WIDEEN, H.: "Tre medeltidskannor funna i mossar," in: *Falbygden,* Falköping, 17 (1962), pp. 6–13.
WIDEEN, H.: "En kanna från Abild," in: *Varbergs museum. Årsbok,* Varberg, 14 (1963), pp. 131–136.
WIEDNER, J.: "Schlesische Birnkrüge aus Zinn," in: *Schlesien, eine Vierteljahres-schrift f. Kunst, Wissensch. u. Volkstum,* Würzburg, 11 (1966), 3, pp. 155–157.
WILSTADIUS, G.: "Tenngjutare i Karlskrona och Karlshamn," in: *Blekingeboken,* Karlskrona, 43 (1965), pp. 21–37.

ZIMMERMANN, H.: "Die hannoversche Zinngiesserfamilie Lohmann," in: *Hannoversche Geschichtsblätter,* Hanover, 12 (1959), pp. 345–348.
ZUKAL, J.: "Troppauer Zinngiesser bis zum Beginn des 19. Jahrhunderts," in: *Z. f. Gesch. u. Kulturgeschichte Österreichisch-Schlesiens,* Troppau, 8 (1913), 1/2,
pp. 42–43.

Museum and exposition catalogues

Altenberg/Erzgebirge

QUELLMALZ, W., H. WILSDORF and G. SCHLEGEL: *Das erzgebirgische Zinn in Natur, Geschichte u. Technik. (Führer durch d. Ausstellung in d. techn. Schauanlage Pochwerk u. Zinnwäsche Altenberg),* Altenberg, 1976.

Amsterdam, Antwerp, Rotterdam

Keur van tin nit de havensteden Amsterdam, Antwerpen en Rotterdam. (Georganiseerd in het kader van het Belgisch-Nederlands cultureel verdrag), Amsterdam, 1979.

Angers

GUILBERT-GUIEN, M., and J. BRETON: *Les étains. Trésors des Musées d'Angers,* Angers, 1973.

Antwerp

Antwerpen Tin. Katalog des Museums Vleeshuis, Antwerp 1959.

Berlin

REINHECKEL, G.: "Zinn," in: *Metall im Kunsthandwerk,* Berlin: Kunstgewerbemuseum Schloss Köpenick, 1967, pp. 167–177.

Bratislava

WAGNEROVÁ, O., and A. MAYEROVÁ: *Katalóg mesta Bratislavy,* Bratislava, 1933.
KRESÁNKOVÁ, L.: *Z dejin bratislavských cinárov. Spisy Mestského múzea v Bratislave,*
Bratislava, 1965.

Brno

FLODROVÁ, M., and B. SAMEK: *Cin ve sbirkách muzea města Brna,* Brno, 1970.
Český a moravský cin 18. a 19. stoleti. Holičská fajáns a kamenina. Moravské galerie, Brno, 1973.

Brooklyn

GRAHAM, J. M.: *American Pewter.* Brooklyn, The Brooklyn Museum, 1949.

Brunswick

WISWE, M.: *Historische Zinngiesserei im südöstlichen Niedersachsen,* Brunswick, Braunschweigisches Landesmuseum, 1981.

Cloppenburg

Altes Zinn aus dem westlichen Niedersachsen. Ausstellungskatalog des Museumsdorfes Cloppenburg, Löningen: Schmücker, 1972.

Cologne

HAEDEKE, H.-U.: *Zinn. Katalog des Kunstgewerbemuseums der Stadt Köln.* Cologne, 1968.

Copenhagen

KRISTENSEN, P. H.: *Hans Tobiesens Tinsamling,* Copenhagen, 1944.

Cracow

Cyna w dawnych wiekach, Cracow, 1973.

Dresden

REINHECKEL, G.: *Zinnsammlung im Zwinger,* Dresden: Staatliche Kunstsammlungen, 1966.
REINHECKEL, G.: *Nürnberger Zinn,* Dresden: Staatliche Kunstsammlungen, 1971.
Deutsches Zinn aus dem Museum für Kunsthandwerk Dresden—Schloss Pillnitz, Exhibition, 1980.

Delft

Tentoonstelling museum "Prinsenhof". Delft, 1950.

Demmin

THIELSCHER, P.: *Die Zinngeräte und ihre Meister,* Demmin: Kreisheimatmuseum, 1937.

Dresden

REINHECKEL, G.: *Zinnsammlung im Zwinger,* Dresden: Staatliche Kunstsammlungen, 1966.
REINHECKEL, G.: *Nürnberger Zinn,* Dresden: Staatliche Kunstsammlungen, 1971.
Deutsches Zinn aus dem Museum für Kunsthandwerk Dresden—Schloss Pillnitz, Exhibition, 1980.

Flensburg

Gebrauchsgut des 14. bis 19. Jahrhunderts in Zinn und Bronze aus den Sammlungen C. J. v. Negelein, Kiel, Flensburg: Städtisches Museum, 1963.

Frankfurt-on-the-Main
OHM, A., and M. BAUER: *Steinzeug und Zinn,* Frankfurt/M.: Museum für Kunsthandwerk, 1977.

Fribourg
LEHNHERR, Y.: *Étains fribourgeois (Contribution à l'histoire des potiers d'étain fribourgeois),* Château de Gruyères, 1972.

Gdańsk
WŁODARSKA, B.: *Cyna. Katalog zbiorów Muzeum narodowego w Gdańsku,* Gdańsk, 1975.

Geel
Oud tin van het Sint-Dimpnagasthuis te Geel, Tentoonstelling, Geel, 31. 5.–30. 9. 1973, Leuven, 1973.

Graz
Die Zinngiesserfamilie Zamponi. Museum f. Kulturgeschichte u. Kunstgewerbe am Landesmuseum Joanneum, Graz: Sonderausstellung, 1967.
WAIDACHER, F.: *Zinngiesser der Steiermark. Katalog der 5. Landesausstellung 1970,* Graz, 1970.
Altes Zinn. Aus der Sammlung f. Kunstgewerbe am Steiermärkischen Landesmuseum Joanneum mit Leihgaben der Stadt Rottenmann, Graz, 1975.

Herne
SEYER, D.: *Zinn aus vier Jahrhunderten. Ausstellung in der Städtischen Galerie im Schlosspark Strümkede vom 17. 7.–6. 9. 1981, Emschertal-Museum Herne,* Recklingshausen: Bitter (no date).

Iglau
LEISCHING, J.: *Die Zinnsammlung des Iglauer Museums,* Brünn: Erzherzog Rainer-Museum f. Kunst und Gewerbe, 1916.

Leiden
Tentoonstelling museum "de Lakenhal", Leyden, 1927.

Leipzig
HANISCH, A.: *Zinn. Schriftenreihe des Museums des Kunsthandwerks Leipzig,* No. 17, Leipzig, 1972.

Neuchâtel
REUTTER, L.: *Les potiers d'étain neuchâtelois. Muséum Neuchâtel,* Neuchâtel, 1919 and 1920.

Olomouc
KAPUSTA, J.: "Značkovaný cin olomoucké provenience ve sbirkách v Olomouci," in: *Sbornik Vlastivédneho muzea v Olomouci,* 6 (1960/62), pp. 133–169.

Prague
Cin z dějin českeho konvářstvi. Národni muzeum, Prague, 1972.

Rotterdam
Tin. Rotterdam: Museum Boymans-van Beuningen, 1954; Verzameling A. J. G. Verster.

Saarbrücken
PURBS, B.: *Silber und Zinn aus der Friedrich-Sicks-Stiftung. Katalog zur Ausstellung vom 10.–30. 1. 1981,* Saarbrücken, 1981.

Sibiu
HALDNER, A.: *Colectia de cositrare. Muzeul Brukenthal,* Sibiu, 1972.

Stollberg/Erzgebirge
WOLF, A.: *Ausstellung schöner Zinngegenstände.* Stollberg: Heimatmuseum, 1957.

Teplice
STARÁ, D.: *Krušnohorské konvářstvi. Oblastnyz muzeum,* Teplice, 1966.

Warsaw
MYSLINSKA, J.: *Konwisarstwo toruńskie XVII–XVIII w.,* Warsaw, 1968.

Wrocław
SIEDLECKA, W.: *Cyna Śląska. Muzeum Śląskie,* Wrocław, 1969.

Zurich
SCHNEIDER, H.: *Katalog der Sammlung des Schweizerischen Landesmuseums Zürich,* Olten/Freiburg (Breisgau), 1970.

Zutphen
Tentoonstelling. Museum Zutphen, Zutphen, 1938.

Index

The index of masters' names comprises all those masters mentioned in the table of marks. The numbers correspond with those in the tables.

In the subject index unitalicized numbers refer to text pages, numbers in italics to illustrations.

Masters' names

Subject index

Sources of illustrations

Antikvarisk-Topografiska Arkivet, Stockholm 113
Bergisches Museum Schloss Burg a. d. Wupper/Soechting, Solingen 366
British Museum, London 44, 45
Brooklyn Museum, Brooklyn/New York 277
Elswing, Niels, Copenhagen 57, 81
Foto Eschenburg, Warnemünde 349, 352, 353
Gewerbemuseum der Landesgewerbeanstalt Bayern, Nuremberg 92
Göteborgs Historiska Museet 180, 181
Historisches Museum Basel 135, 279
Historisches Museum Schloss Lenzburg 107, 108
Institut für Denkmalspflege, Berlin 211
Kriloff, Georges, Lyons 11
Kulturgeschichtliches Museum/Strenger, Osnabrück 80
Kunstindustrimuseet/Teigens, Oslo 56
Larsen, Lennart, Copenhagen 165
Musée communal, Huy 30
Musée gruérien, Bulle 123
Musées royaux d'Art et d'Histoire, Brussels 99
Musées royaux des Beaux Arts de Belgique, Brussels 16
Museum Boymans-van Beuningen, Rotterdam 25, 48, 82, 116, 196, 266, 312
National Board of Antiquities and Historical Monuments, Helsinki 62, 109, 112
Nordiska museet, Stockholm 49, 66, 321, 371
Norsk Folkemuseum, Oslo 58
Oberösterreichisches Museum/Franz Hangl, Linz 171
Österreichisches Landesmuseum für angewandte Kunst/Ingrid Schindler, Vienna 71, 114
Platteeuw, M., Bruges 284
Rätisches Museum/D. Vital, Chur 373
Rheinisches Bildarchiv, Cologne 356, 382
Schweizerisches Landesmuseum/Peter Grünert, Zurich 129, 195, 306, 307, 309, 354, 365, 398
Service de documentation photographique de la Réunion des musées nationaux 21
Staatliche Museen Preussischer Kulturbesitz, Museum für Deutsche Volkskunde, Berlin (West) 75
Stad Turnhout 367
Städtisches Museum Schwäbisch Gmünd 226–229
Stedelijk Museum/Uipko Berghuis, Alkmaar 24, 27, 84
Stedelijk Museum "De Lakenhal", Leyden 289, 305, 358
Tiroler Volkskunstmuseum, Innsbruck 130
Victoria & Albert Museum, London 163, 355, 396
Virginia Museum of Fine Arts, Richmond/Virginia 59, 170
Winterthur Museum, Winterthur/Delaware 102, 121, 141, 260
Woldbye, Ole, Copenhagen 311

All other photos were supplied by Ulrich Piekara, Leipzig.

For apothecaries and barbers they make boxes, measures, syringes, spatulae, probes and the tooth-drawer's chairs still customary of old. For shop-keepers, oil-flagons, funnels, etc. And who would wish to name all their work without omitting something? They know how to finish these in the most attractive, beautiful and skilful way, each in his own style or according to a customer's wishes, decorating them with floral designs, cords, stippling, borders, bright or matt and, as is popular, in the style of silver.

Christoph Weigel

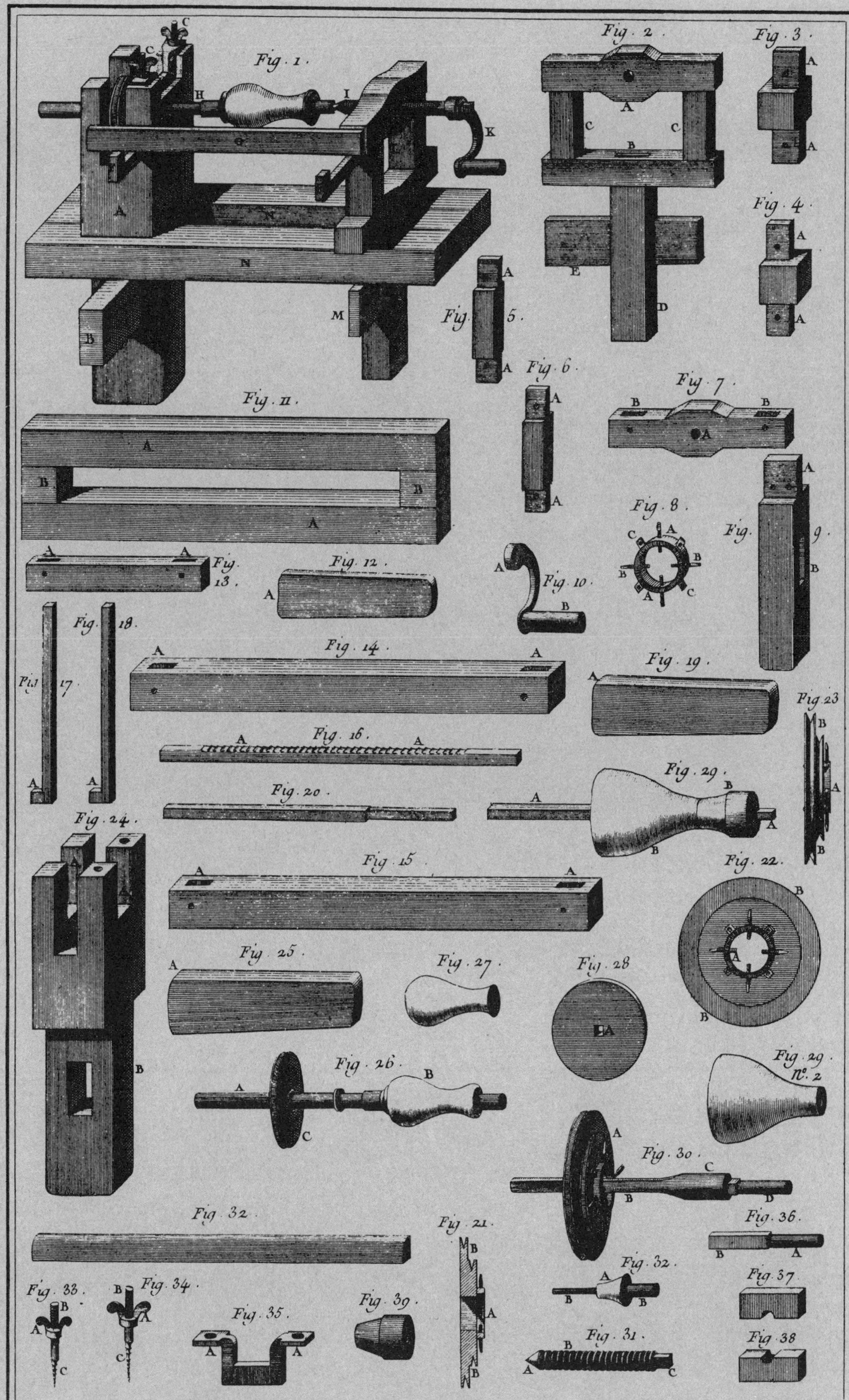

Once it has been expertly cast, it is brought to the lathe, finish turned and made bright and of good appearance. This lathe is not treadled with the foot as with turners but is driven by a wheel or, as in the Spazisch workshop in Nuremberg, to my knowledge almost alone and otherwise not easy to find in Germany, by a horse.

Christoph Weigel